Birdlike and Barnless

Birdlike and Barnless

Meditations, Prayers and Songs
for Progressive Christians

Jim Burklo

St. Johann Press
Haworth, New Jersey

ST. JOHANN PRESS

Published in the United States of America
by St. Johann Press
P.O. Box 241
Haworth, NJ 07641

Library of Congress Cataloguing in Publication Data pending

The paper used in this publication meets the minimum requirements of the American National Standard for Information Sciences—Permanence of Paper for Printed Library Materials, ANSI/NISO Z39/48-1992

Manufactured in the United States of America

To Elizabeth D. Burklo,
my spiritual teacher and daughter

Contents

Dedication v
Preface ix

Meditations I
Heartwork, *1*
Faithful Living, *20*
Transformation, *52*
The Soul's Journey, *81*

Meditations and Celebrations for the Sacred Seasons 141
All Saints' Day, *141*
Election Day, *143*
Thanksgiving, *144*
Advent, *145*
Christmas, *148*
Epiphany, *159*
Lent, *162*
Palm Sunday, *172*
Good Friday, *176*
Easter, *184*
Tax Day, *191*
Pentecost, *193*
Mother's Day, *197*
St. Buddha's Day, *199*

Rites and Sacraments 201
Communion, *201*
Baptism, *208*
Marriage, *212*
Blessing of the Driver's License, *218*
Death, *219*

Prayers 220

Psalms 227

Words for Worship 232

Index 235

Preface

A Credo for Progressive Christians

I worship and adore God,

source, essence, and aim of all things,

spirit that enlivens all beings.

I follow the way of Jesus, who found God in himself

and shared a way for others to find God in themselves.

He was born through love,

He lived for love,

He suffered for love,

He died for love,

But love never dies.

I submit myself to the leadings of the love that is God,

that I may be compassionate to all beings,

that I may live and serve in community with others,

that I may ask for and offer forgiveness,

that I may praise and enjoy God forever. Amen!

Meditations

With questions for personal reflection and group conversation

HEARTWORK

An Introduction

From my home in northern California, I drove south to go camping alone in the Desert Mountains around the Coachella Valley. I hiked up to the hidden clefts of palms and sand from which cool water bubbles up. The day after I returned home, I found a heart drawn on the dusty window of my car. It must have been Liz, my daughter, who was four years old at the time. Her hearts drawn on paper were scattered all over the house. They were as distinctive as her handwriting and as profligate as her love. At least some of Liz's "heartwork" made it into the scrapbook. Otherwise she would have left no hard copy from that precious period of her life.

At least once a year, I feel compelled to go to the desert for a while, to refresh my familiarity with God's hard copy: the naked mountains glowing in the sunrise, cactus and mesquite scattered across the landscape. In solitude I need to witness the testament of the Almighty in the banded rock of the canyon walls. I need to taste the sacrament of the sage-scented air. I return with a dusty vehicle, ready to engage again with family and community.

Ministry has been my heartwork. For years I did it with homeless and other very low-income people. They know the desperate loneliness of the asphalt wasteland that passes for so much of what we call civilization. Cast into the remotest parts of our cultural desert, they are left to listen to voices howling from within; voices heard only when people are terribly alone. At the same time, there is beauty in the desert of the homeless. It has its verdant oases, places where love springs. Some of the most profound acts of compassion I witnessed in those years were among homeless people who comforted and cared for each other in their toughest times.

Much of my heartwork has been serving as the pastor of churches, where people gather to quench an overwhelming thirst. Most of my parishioners have been materially comfortable. But that can't mask the spiritual drought suffered by so many of them in their work and in their relationships. Sometimes our souls seem lost in the desert. In church we paw at the sand, hoping that the Spirit will bubble up.

"I am thirsty," said Jesus on the cross (John 19:28). And so do the rest of us, inside and outside of the church. The oasis of Christianity has been obscured by dunes of dead dogma. It has been hidden by backward, literalistic interpretations of the Bible, by chauvinism against other religions, by a muddled morality that presumes that what happens in the bedroom is more important than what happens in the boardroom or the war-room. So much heartwork is needed to open the faith to all whose souls are parched!

A good story opens an oasis in the desert. My heartwork often consists of listening to people talk about their lives until the water begins to spring. Tears of joy or grief give life to otherwise forgettable incidents and isolated thoughts that seemed dull and dusty. Meaning, purpose, and redemption are found in events that seemed their antithesis. These stories aren't necessarily good because all goes well in them, but rather because they reveal so much more than the sum of their parts.

Today, the primary medium of my ministry is writing. It is my privilege to witness and record the discovery of the good news, otherwise known as the gospel, as it wells up from the lives of the people I have served. Through these meditations, prayers, poems, and songs, I join them in reaching down for this living water.

What is your heartwork?

Carrying Baggage

Before dawn, fueled with the adrenaline of joy, I climbed the pediments of the Mesa de Yeso below a sheer cliff facing the valley of the Chama River. The glow on the heights to the east yielded to the sun, and as I moved up the mesa my shadow, cast hundreds of feet below, raced along the edge of the day. The sun blasted into brilliant shards through the translucent spines of cholla cactus.

It overwhelmed me with holiness. Each pounding footstep sang a psalm of hallelujah, of glory and praise to God.

Ghost Ranch, New Mexico. The retreat compound was still bathed in cool shadow below, an inlet of night in the sea of day above on the mesa. I found a spot and sat cross-legged facing the sun to let divine wonderment overwhelm me. Through my nose I breathed in the resiny scent of the dew evaporating from the chaparral.

I settled into a meditation, finding a pose of relaxation and alertness. And there, in my awareness, were my same old life issues. The glory of Ghost Ranch at dawn didn't change anything within. Instead of getting away from it all, I brought all my baggage with me to this holy of holies in the wilderness. By the grace of God, I was able to prayerfully observe this irony, and laugh out loud about it.

When he was preaching in Galilee, Jesus withdrew before dawn to a lonely place (Matthew 14:13). He didn't get much peace and quiet. Not long after dawn, his disciples and followers found him and clamored for his healing and preaching power. So he got up and went back to work. And the rest of us have a similar difficulty. When we find a quiet place and time, let ourselves be who we really are, and accept the reality of our feelings, we'll find that we take this clamor with us wherever we go. I take my metropolis of relationships and entanglements with me. I'm the spiritual equivalent of the businesswoman carrying her laptop computer in one hand and her Blackberry in the other. I'm wired all the time, connected to countless projects and ongoing interactions, and so accustomed to the clamor that I deny it exists. It's a background noise that I tune out of my awareness in spite of the fact that it is running most of my life.

Jesus couldn't escape his fate, couldn't avoid the clamor altogether, but by going to a desert place he could get a different perspective on it. A divine point of view. Within himself, God observed Jesus' thoughts and actions with unconditional love.

That divine observer within Jesus was the same One within me as I sat on the rim of the mesa that morning. God is the experience of watching my thoughts, urges, intentions, and sensations while filled with profound compassion. God doesn't solve my problems or take away my burdens. But God radically changes my relationship to them, liberating me from unhealthy attachments and unrealistic expectations. In prayer, I recognize that God is the true center of my being. In prayer, the divine capital "S" Self lovingly observes my small "s" self. This inner relationship of prayer enables me to discern what matters more from what matters less, to sort out what is good from what is not so good, to see which thoughts and urges are worth pursuing, and which are less worthy. I don't pray to some kind of celestial deity beyond me. I pray with the One who is closer to me than my own skin.

It wasn't long before the stones began to bake that skin with radiant heat, so down to the cooler canyon floor I descended. The baggage of my life was still on my back, but prayer had lightened the load.

What baggage do you carry with you wherever you go?
How can you lighten that load?

Ghost Ranch Meditation

Each tuft of desert grass
God gives a separate place
Profligate with space
That pilgrim feet may pass.

In each confluence below
The canyon's colored bands
Each sinew of the sands
God draws with water's flow.

Each layer of the past
On cliffs God raised in view
So we'll confess it's true
Our age won't be the last.

Each cloud that God displays
Defined in desert light
We honor with our sight
And let it lift our praise.

Testament of Dust

It's a story we almost missed.

Some Bibles leave out the memorable account of Jesus' encounter with the woman caught in the act of adultery. In some Bibles, the eighth chapter of the gospel of John starts, oddly, with verse 13. In other Bibles, it is in parentheses, and in yet others, it can be found in italics at the bottom of the page. While it appeared in the old Latin Vulgate Bible and in the King James English version, more recent scholarship has found that this passage is not to be found in the most reliable ancient Greek biblical manuscripts. Does it belong in the Bible, or not?

Confusion about the adulterated status of this story cuts across theological divisions of the church. John 7:53 through 8:1-12 is a testament to the ephemeral nature of things that humans wish were incorruptible. It's a proof-text against taking the Bible literally, even as it inspires us to take it very seriously. This story is a myth with a life of its own, one that can sink into the soul, take root, and grow.

Jesus was confronted with a group of scribes and Pharisees who tried to stump him. Should this woman before him, caught in the capital crime of adultery, be stoned to death? If he said yes, his hands would be as bloody as theirs, and his ministry of forgiveness and reconciliation would be over. If he said no, he would contradict blatantly the Law of Moses, and perhaps no Jew would take him seriously again.

While they presented the situation to him, he "wrote with his finger on the ground." He seemed to be preoccupied with whatever he was writing. The scribes and Pharisees wouldn't let him ignore the question, so finally he looked up and said, "Let anyone who is without sin among you be the first to throw a stone at her." He then resumed writing his testament of dust.

Now, this one-liner has become such excellent sermon fodder, such a classic comeback for so many everyday situations in our time, that it is only at their peril that biblical scholars excise it completely from the text. What the historical Jesus really said and did is interesting to explore, but it isn't essential. The gospel that is invisibly engraved on our hearts: that's the one that matters most. The gospel really does live in our souls more than it exists between the covers of a canonized book.

Jesus was so intent on his writing project that he didn't even notice as the men walked away, embarrassed. His finger just kept moving in the sand. I can understand how this would happen. There are times when nuclear war could not distract me from my writing sessions in front of the computer. Whatever he wrote in the dust must have been good stuff. No writer's block for him that day, if he could not be interrupted by a situation as interesting as this one.

For all we know, some of the scribes and Pharisees had once had sex with the woman. The sight of those men whose bodies had sweated against hers, now glaring at her with stones lifted in their hands, must have been terrifying. Perhaps she was too shaken to tell him that they were gone.

Finally, he looked up. "Woman, where are they? Has no one condemned you?"

"No one, sir."

"Neither do I condemn you. Go your way, and from now on do not sin again."

Now, some biblical scholars suspect that this passage was inserted long ago to refute a suggestion made in John 7: 15 that Jesus did not know how to read or write. Perhaps the people who laboriously copied the Bible from older manuscripts could not conceive that Jesus was less educated than they were. Perhaps they could not let stand the accusation that he was illiterate. So this story, which apparently came from an ancient text called the "Gospel of the Hebrews," not included in the New Testament canon, was inserted to let the world know that Jesus was not a rabbinical-school dropout.

What would the church do if we knew his only written words, the words he wrote on the ground that day? We'd probably repeat those words every Sunday in worship. Those words would be woven into countless hymns and prayers. They would be copied in gold leaf onto the walls of chapels and cathedrals around the globe. The world would not just know those words: the world would not be able to forget them.

But we have no idea what Jesus wrote. In the only recorded incident of his writing, we are left with no hard copy. Perhaps he wrote things that the scribes and Pharisees, who certainly could have read them, wanted to forget. Maybe the woman was the only one who remembered that he had scribbled in the dust, and since she was not likely to have been afforded the privilege of literacy, she couldn't relate the content.

Would the words Jesus wrote, if they had been remembered, belong in the New Testament, given the questionable provenance of this story? We will never know.

I want to leave a tangible legacy. It matters much to me that when I die, my daughter will live on, carrying my genetic legacy into a new generation, keeping a bit of myself alive. I want to write books that people will still read after I'm reduced to dust. I want to leave a legacy, a clear imprint of change on society and the church.

But Jesus wasn't like this, and I don't understand this part of his personality. He didn't copy his earthy writings on paper. He didn't take up with the woman caught in adultery. She owed him her life, and might have given him progeny, as well. He did not set up a church organization to outlive himself. The loose community of disciples disintegrated even before his death on the cross, and it was Paul, whom he never knew nor could have anticipated, who built the institutional church that lives today. Jesus seemed disinterested in what might or might not become canonical about his life. His was but a gospel of dust, and yet that good news lives and breathes in me and others to this day.

Am I ready to reconcile my own testament with the dust in which it is being written?

What do you think Jesus wrote in the dust?

What do you need to write in the dust?

Gospel Song

earthsized waves ring gospel truth
in measures long as swells of surf
wide as air among redwood trees
a word or a tune will catch the beat
long enough to make us yearn
for the rest of the song of the universe

the space to the sun is a guitar string
struck to make our emptiness sing
of beginnings and ends and folds of time
layers of worlds we pass through blind

a fractal chord suggests the song
and even the earless sing along

we're shown more truth than we can say
but we each have an instrument to play

noise of day adds up to a hum
night is the skin of a beaten drum
so deep we barely hear its din
keeping time for the gospel hymn

Good News, As Is

Her name was Debbie. She had epilepsy which may have resulted from drug abuse. She lived in a car in front of the apartment house where her daughter, alcoholic mother, and aged grandmother lived. Because the landlord wouldn't let four people live in a one-bedroom unit, Debbie, being the least vulnerable of the family, used the car as her bedroom and took her showers in the apartment during the day.

Debbie was a tall, spare woman with wild blonde hair that was thinning in spots. Her medical problems made her hair fall out and her gums recede, giving her a cadaverous but still bright smile. She was a fun, funny character despite all her challenges, and I loved spending time with her at our center for homeless people on the Peninsula south of San Francisco.

One day she came to me and asked "Can I get some phone numbers from you?" She wanted some information about clinics for her 14-year old daughter, Julie, who was 7 months pregnant. Julie had come to my office a month earlier with her boyfriend, asking about adoption. "Hey, I won't get busted, will I?" asked the boyfriend, age 18 and guilty of statutory rape. "Don't worry about that. Let's worry about the child," I replied. He was a skinny fellow with tattoos (one of which had another girl's name in it) and a dangling silver cross earring. His mother, whom I also knew, had been on welfare when he was born. Julie was a pale, pimply, very lively young woman who told me she had no business raising a baby at her age and in her circumstances. She had found she was pregnant after abortion was no longer an option: "I just thought I was getting a little fat, that's all." I put her on the phone to get her started on the process of adoption.

"Isn't she still planning to have the baby adopted?" I asked Debbie.

"No," said Debbie. She shrugged her shoulders, as she often did. "Julie changed her mind."

I was appalled. "Well, Debbie, it sounds like you changed your mind, too. You could make it pretty hard for your daughter to keep the baby if you wanted it to be adopted instead." I went on to explain all her options, urging on her my strong opinion that Julie should not keep the child.

Debbie's face went vacant, glazed in front of her thoughts, as my lecture continued.

Only after I finished did I awaken to what I had done. I had ignored her story. Instead, I told her the story I wanted to hear. Debbie already knew her options. She had made up her mind to take care of the baby with and for her daughter. She knew that there would not be enough welfare money to make any real difference in the household income, and that the housing situation would get tighter, and that it would lock her daughter into the poverty cycle. Her decision was motivated by something quite apart from my reasoning. All that my forceful oratory had achieved was to deny the value of her life.

Julie's baby would be born into the same sort of circumstances into which Julie was born, which was the way her mother Debbie came into the world, and which was the way Debbie's mother was raised, as well. This was the fourth, and maybe the fifth, sixth, or seventh generation of birth into poverty and family instability. If it was wrong for Julie to keep the baby, then it had been wrong for Debbie's mom to have kept Julie. Or even to have conceived Julie in the first place. And the same would be true for Debbie and her mom. My speech had the effect of telling Debbie that her life was a mistake.

According to my ideal version of her life, Debbie herself should have been adopted away to a nice, middle-class suburban family. She should have been married to somebody with a solid, middle-class job and Julie should have been living in one of four bedrooms in a house with a two-car garage. Julie should have been doing well in school and had plenty for which to live besides getting pregnant at age 14.

But Debbie's life had infinite value just the way it was. Debbie had the right family already. The infant would be born to the right mother, the right grandmother, great-grandmother, and great-great grandmother. Sure, life was hard and messy. But there was love and joy in their family. And this child coming was full of promise, bringing new meaning and purpose to them. If I could have had ears to hear it, I could have found the gospel in her story, without my attempt to edit it.

So obvious, yet so easy to forget. I was not Debbie. It was good that she knew my values; that she knew of people who made different kinds of choices than she made. It was good that she knew that if they had made the choice for adoption, there would have been more support for it. Information was good to share, but not the lecture I had given her.

And so I apologized. "Debbie, forgive me. Let me know whatever I can do to help when the baby comes. And now, let's get those phone numbers."

A few months later, a baby girl was born. Things got even harder for the family, as I had predicted. But her mother, grandmother, and great-grandmother loved her.

So often, my ability to be compassionate awakens later than I wish it did. By the time I've figured out what kind of love is required, the magic moment to offer it might have passed. I pray, over and over, that my compassion will be received even when it is tardy.

Compassion begins when I let others into my heart and my imagination. Compassion means "co – passion." Feeling with. Not feeling at. Not preaching at.

Perhaps I'm slow at the art of compassion because I don't ask for enough of it myself. I fancy myself to be a strong, self-reliant, unneedy guy. Why would I need any compassion from anybody else? But if I opened myself to receive more of it, it might be more natural for me to offer it to others.

And this may explain why the sacred myth of the gospel is such a powerful inspiration for empathetic love. Jesus suffered. He was laid low. The early Christians thought of him when they remembered these words from the prophet Isaiah, chapter 53, verse 5: "But he was wounded for our transgressions, crushed for our iniquities; upon him was the punishment that made us whole, and by his bruises we are healed. "In Jesus we have a teacher of compassion who needed compassion himself. He had times when he was weary and hungry, and people shared with him and comforted him. People criticized him for being so willing to accept care from others. But his ability to receive it made his teaching of compassion all the more believable.

Can I set aside my preoccupation with my own story long enough to receive the good in the story of another, just as it is?

When have you heard the gospel in the story of another?
When have you failed to hear it?

Wayfaring Stranger

Every morning at our drop-in center for the homeless, he helped serve breakfast. He hardly ever said a word. To my knowledge, he had no job and no income. After many weeks of being there every day, I began to notice that he talked to himself when he thought nobody was looking. I wondered if he might be suffering from schizophrenia. But he was polite and caring, and that was all that mattered for the task at hand. While I was the director of the Urban Ministry of Palo Alto, we encouraged home-less and home-full people to work together, side-by-side, as volunteers.

One day he took me aside and handed me a manila folder and asked me to read and to comment on its contents. I took it back to my office. Inside the folder was a 50 page, perfectly typed, legally-numbered court brief which he had written and prepared. It was an elaborate argument for why he did not need to have a driver's license to drive a car.

This man took the Bible literally. St. Paul's statement that a Christian is an ambassador for Christ (2 Corinthians 5: 20) was, for him, no figure of speech. He took at face value the biblical metaphor that a Christian is an alien who is passing through this world on the way back home to the kingdom of heaven. Jesus said that we are in this world, but not of it. And that's an apt description of schizophrenia. This man felt deeply estranged from the people and the society around him.

He was living outdoors as a social outcast, suffering from a mental illness that isolated him profoundly. I deduced that he found resonance in these biblical ideas and seized upon them as a way of making sense of his predicament. He drove his car without getting a license, and when the police busted him for it, he declared that he had diplomatic immunity from needing a license, since he was an ambassador for Christ. It is true that an ambassador does not need a California driver's license. But obviously things don't work that way for Christ's ambassadors. So this man spent a lot of time in jail for driving without a license. He became what we called a "jailhouse lawyer," an inmate who took advantage of his right to use the legal library and research his case on his own. His legal case was completely spurious, but elegantly crafted. Though useless in court, it expressed a special kind of gospel.

A gospel this man shared with Jesus and Paul. If you are in touch with your spiritual dimension, you belong to another country: the land of the soul. You discover that you may be in the world as it is, but you are put here to pursue a transformed world that is yet to be.

As the old-time hymn puts it:

I am a poor wayfaring stranger,
While traveling through this world of woe.
Yet there's no sickness, toil nor danger
In that bright world to which I go.
I'm going there to see my Father;
I'm going there no more to roam.

We may not hold a physical passport issued by the Heavenly Department of State. We may not have the consular papers needed to exempt us from getting a driver's license. But we are indeed citizens of that bright world within and beyond this one. We really are just passing through this land, on our way to see our Father and Mother God, on our way to create a new country of peace, justice, and compassion. The more we are in touch with our true citizenship, the more gracefully we can travel through this world, our heads high, as dignified as ambassadors.

To whom, or to what, have you been sent as an ambassador?

We're All Mojados

Among the diverse contents of the Bible are detailed building plans. You'll find them in the first book of Kings, in the book of Ezekiel, and in the prophecies of Isaiah. The book of Revelation, in chapters 21 and 22, offers the dimensions and materials used to build the New Jerusalem, a heavenly city descending to earth. It's a city with open doors, lit all the time by the light of God at its center. It's planned for pluralism and multi-ethnicity. Revelation says that by the light of God the nations shall walk, and the kings of the earth shall bring their glory into it. There's no religion except the simple, continuous praise of God in many languages. The city has no "migra," no border patrol. It has no "illegal aliens" who have to hire "coyotes" to get them into it. Everybody in the city is a "mojado," a wetback, because a bright river runs through it, flowing out of the divine throne at its center:

We are all mojados in the promised land
We'll cross that bright river today
All our backs will be wet when we finally stand
At the throne of God someday
Nobody's thirsty in the promised land
Coyote can't steal your soul
Buzzards don't glide over desert sands
There is no border patrol
There are no migra at the pearly gates
No fake ID's to buy
They don't take your money and leave you to fate
You can't get caught in a lie
You won't get deported from the promised land
You cross over there, you are home
It's our place to build and our place to stand
Heaven to earth, kingdom come

"Mojados in the Promised Land": words by Jim Burklo and Lisa Atkinson, music by Lisa Atkinson and George Kincheloe, on "Connie's Songbird", CD by Lisa Atkinson, www.atkinsonkincheloe.com, reprinted with permission.

Jim Corbett was a Quaker and a cattle rancher in southern Arizona. He smuggled Central American civil war refugees from Mexico into the United States in the 1980's, and co-founded the Sanctuary Movement which sheltered them in churches and synagogues around the country. I learned much from this wise and gentle man. After he died in 2001, my wife and I attended his memorial service, which was held at Southside Presbyterian Church in Tucson, a congregation with a long history of work and witness on border justice issues. The church was constructed in the form of an Anasazi Indian kiva, a circular adobe ritual structure. For a few hours, the kiva manifested the biblical vision of the heavenly city. Guatemalans, Salvadorans, Native Americans, African-Americans, Mexican-Americans, European-Americans, Jews, Christians, and others faced each other in that round room. One by one, they stood to share memories of a man who lived as if boundaries did not exist, a man who did his part to bring heaven closer to earth.

I've gazed at the metal border fence that slices the desert like a rusty knife, and have been haunted by Corbett's example. Why not create a society where the whole concept of undocumented aliens is an anachronism? Why not create a society with open doors, with deep religious and cultural pluralism? Why not create a society that is transparent, where the light of truth shines all the time, revealing the deeds of its leaders and inspiring them to do and be their best? Why not create a place that is truly beautiful, designed for conviviality, where lovely trees grow, where pure water flows naturally through its center, where there is great delight in public virtues, art, and architecture? Where the best things in the society are available to everyone?

Easier said than done, of course. But it must be done.

We're all mojados. Wet on the back, wet behind the ears, just born, so to speak. If not from the physical womb, at least born again every time we cross that river and wash away our self-righteousness, our hubris, our sense of privilege and entitlement and superiority. We're all 'illegals'. We've broken the laws of Moses, the laws of nature, the unwritten laws of social and political correctness, and we've broken the law of love.

Christians in America are all wet, but, unfortunately, not enough of us know it. The dominant paradigm of the faith claims to be superior to all other religions, claiming to be the only path to God, the only way to salvation, claiming to know in detail who God is and what God wants. But it is time that we confessed our spiritual sogginess and let the world know that no, we Christians don't claim to have a religion superior to all others. There are many doors into the holy city.

It's time to work alongside everybody who wants to build the New Jerusalem. What we say we believe isn't the real mark of our religion. Rather, our striving for the common good is the ultimate expression of our faith.

Right now, a lot of Christians are giving up on tasting the pie in the sky that they have been promised by their preachers. Instead of waiting to be transported magically to a city in the air, they are looking at the grim condition of the city on the ground, and are resolved to do something about it. They're ready to build the New Jerusalem here and now. They're ready for a humble, hard-working Christian religion that is progressive, pro-justice, and pro-peace. And profoundly aware that, before the throne of God, we're all wet. We're all mojados in the kingdom of heaven that we are challenged to build together.

What is your special task, right now, in bringing the kingdom of heaven down to earth?

Progressive Christian Elevator Speeches

For years I've been writing and collecting "tag lines", short phrases that we can share with others about the kind of Christianity we represent. Lots of folks are embarrassed to call themselves Christians, because of all the bad things that have been done in the name of our faith, and particularly by the traditional Christian claim that Christianity is the only true faith. Our progressive Christian movement is about re-imagining and re-defining our religion, boldly reclaiming our identity, and finding succinct ways to express it. Here is a list of "elevator speeches" that can be used to express the kind of Christianity by which I seek to live:

I'm a progressive Christian who:

☆ keeps the faith and drops the dogma
☆ experiences God more than I believe in any definition of God
☆ thinks that my faith is about deeds, not creeds
☆ takes the Bible seriously because I don't take it literally
☆ thinks spiritual questions are more important than religious answers
☆ cares more about what happens in the war-room and the board-room than about what happens in the bedroom
☆ thinks that other religions can be as good for others as my religion is good for me

- ☆ goes to a church that doesn't require you to park your brain outside before you come inside
- ☆ thinks that God is bigger than anybody's idea about God
- ☆ thinks that God evolves

What is your progressive Christian elevator speech?

The River

I learned something that impressed me when I visited Wichita recently. As a passenger in a car driving over the river that bisects the city, I said, "Oh, there's the Arkansas (ARkansaw)!" It brought back memories of a cross-country road trip I took many years ago, following the river down from the foothills of the Rockies. At Cañon City, Colorado, the river tumbled through a gorge lined with mica-laden rock that shimmered in the sunlight. Then it flowed placidly across the endless plain of Kansas. It's one of America's longest and most important waterways.

The driver of the car corrected me immediately in my pronunciation. "No. Here we call it the Arkansas (OurKANsas) River!"

I was enchanted by the idea that this river could be the Arkansas (ARkansaw) in Colorado, the Arkansas (OurKANsas) in Kansas, and once again the Arkansas (ARkansaw) in Oklahoma and Arkansas (ARkansaw).

It's a linguistic misunderstanding, I suppose. The best-known version of the river's name came from an Indian word transliterated by the French, who aren't in the habit of pronouncing the last "s". But not all Americans bought everything that came with the Louisiana Purchase.

The pronunciation of the river's name says much more. Not just about the French. Not just about Kansas. Not just about America. It says something about the human and divine condition.

What, or whom, I call God is a river that flows through many, many souls. Some call the river Watanka. Others call it Allah. Others name it Brahman. Others pray it Yahweh. Some sing it Nature. Others refuse, on grounds of religious principle, to name it at all. Meanwhile, the water is the same. The river flows on, without apparent concern for what it is called or how it is defined. Fish happily swim up and down its current, oblivious to theological attempts to constrain it. Some people stand by its banks and declaim its intentions and directions, without bothering to follow it. Without taking the trouble to jump into it and go with its flow. Without honoring how others might experience it, elsewhere along its path. Some people have adamant opinions about it, instead of just enjoying it and letting it exist on its own terms. Some people call the river "Our God," as if they could control or own it, or as if it had chosen them to be its exclusive spokespersons.

Meanwhile, the river runs its long and steady course through every heart and soul, bringing life to all, regardless of what any might think of it, regardless of the names we give it.

Perhaps the highest praise we can give to God is to appreciate how very many ways we describe and name the transcendent dimension. Honoring the fact that there is no one way to say God's name is itself a profound act of worship.

So, more power to the people of Kansas for their special way of saying the name of the great river that defines their landscape. Thanks to them for their addition to the cacophonic poetry of America's language about itself. With a wink and a chuckle, let us thank them for reminding us of the infinite possibilities for naming the river that flows through us all.

Matthew 13 Revisited

(A readers' theater in four voices.)

Matthew:	*The kingdom of heaven is like a mustard seed.*
Martha:	*That a woman mixed in with three measures of flour.*
Mark:	*What was that?*
Mary:	*It was a pearl of great value.*
Matthew:	*Which, when it was leavened,*
Martha:	*Turned into the greatest of shrubs.*
Mark:	*What did she hide?*
Mary:	*It becomes a tree, so that the birds of the air come and make nests in its branches.*
Matthew:	*When the man found it, he sold everything he had and bought the field where he had found it.*
Martha:	*Until all of it was all leavened.*
Mark:	*What is the kingdom of heaven like?*
Mary:	*It's like a merchant in search of fine pearls.*

Matthew: *It's like a woman.*
Martha: *It's like yeast.*
Mark: *It's like who?*
Mary: *It's like a net which was thrown into the sea.*
Matthew: *It's the smallest of all seeds.*
Martha: *When it was full, they drew it ashore, sat down, and put the good into baskets but threw out the bad.*
Mark: *What was full?*
Mary: *What is the kingdom of heaven like?*
Matthew: *The kingdom of heaven is like a mustard seed.*

What else is the kingdom of heaven like?

Hubris and Humility

> "Let the same mind be in you that was in Christ Jesus, who, though he was in the form of God, did not regard equality with God as something to be exploited, but emptied himself, taking the form of a slave, being born in human likeness. (Philippians 2: 5-7)

Christianity is one of many expressions of the direct, mystical encounter of human beings with God. This encounter is beyond our comprehension, and humbles us with awe, no matter how much we know of the Divine. The One in the burning bush, who answers with "I AM" when we ask the source of the flame (Exodus 3: 14), transfixes us with wonder. "I AM" invites us into a theology of humility: questioning, exploring, and doubting any assumptions we may develop about God.

But the theology of hubris declares on a bumper sticker that "God said it, I believe it, that settles it." The theology of hubris provides both the questions and the answers. Its preachers and politicians declare that God is on their side. Some Christians revel in their spiritual superiority, strutting it pridefully for all to see. Others are genuinely embarrassed that they just so happen to have the only true religion. They sincerely wish they didn't sound so chauvinistic, but they still make a claim that violates common sense and insults the followers of other great faiths.

Christianity follows the humble faith of an empty man. So how did we Christians become so full of ourselves?

It's time to empty ourselves of the belief that our religion is better than others. Other spiritual or secular paths to the Divine may be as right for other people as ours appears to be for us. Humble religion doesn't focus on its walls, but rather on its openings. It's time to keep the church's doors and windows open to inspirations that enter from beyond our communities of faith. Mystical spirituality leads to progressive revelation, which strains our eyes to see, our ears to hear, and our hands to serve.

It's time to embrace the humbling challenge of following a path that leads us to love not only our neighbors, not only strangers, but even our enemies. The theology of humility is embodied in Jesus' statement that "the greatest among you shall be your servant." (Matthew 23:11) It's hard to be faithful when you put your trust in a mystery, when questions matter more than answers. It's a tough choice to become a servant. But then, is faith supposed to be easy?

What's the true test of Christian faith? Is it to accept that all, or even most, of the stories of the Bible are literally, factually true? The enormous success of the gambling industry proves that it's easy for people to believe the unbelievable. There's nothing wrong with reading the miracles of Jesus as literal facts. Implausible things do happen sometimes. But why should such credulity, so facile for so many, be the price of admission to the Christian faith? What if the true test is to love and serve the unlovable? That's a very steep price for everyone to pay. It's a challenge vastly more worthwhile than simply believing in the fantastic. At its best, the church is a movement of people practicing a faith that asks hard things of us.

Which unlovable people are you called to love, and how?

We Praise You, God of All

Tune: "All Hail the Power of Jesus' Name," Coronation C.M.

We praise you, God, with rousing song, we answer at your call
Your Word creates the universe, We praise you, God of all
Your Word creates the universe, We praise you, God of all

Your Christ appears among us now and gathers one and all
In one community of love, We praise you, God of all
In one community of love, We praise you, God of all
In birth and death, in joy and grief, you hear us as we call
In every language, every faith, We praise you, God of all
In every language, every faith, We praise you, God of all
With all our breath and strength we sing around this earthen ball
To be at one with you again, We praise you, God of all
To be at one with you again, We praise you, God of all

FAITHFUL LIVING

Raw Faith

Dan, one of my parishioners, suffered a big health setback. He already had plenty of physical challenges before he went into kidney failure. But when I went to see him in the hospital, he said, with a smile on his face, "Jim, I'm in a medical decathlon. I'm entered in all the events! And I've decided to enthusiastically embrace the inevitable." He looked forward to reading good books while on dialysis for hours on end, three times a week. He was sorely tested, but he still had faith, inspiring all who visited him.

Dan has raw faith. It's not faith in a set of beliefs so much as it is a faithful approach to living. I think Jesus had raw faith, too. Jesus didn't base it on some delicate structure of dogma or belief in the historical factuality of certain events. His faith was a trust in his relationship with God, which led him to love and serve courageously.

I take the Bible seriously because I don't have to take it literally. The faith of Jesus doesn't depend on whether or not the resurrection was an historical fact. The story of the resurrection of Jesus is a powerful, life-changing myth that resonates with my faith and inspires it.

What has more truth? The front page of the newspaper, which lists facts, or the story of the gospel, which consists largely of myth and poetry? I am convinced that you will find more truth in the gospel than in the newspaper. The gospel myth says that despite all the awful facts revealed in the headlines, despite the awful fact of the crosses on which human beings dangle in pain every day, life is very much worth living, and love is very much worth sharing. That is life-giving truth. Facts are important, but there is a truth that matters more than facts.

There is plenty of room in Christianity for those who read the gospels as fully historical accounts. And there also is plenty of room for those who don't think Jesus factually rose from the dead, and find their faith strengthened because it has been liberated from literalism.

"*For we walk by faith, not by sight,*" said St. Paul (2 Corinthians 5: 7). Some suggest that this means that while we can't see any historical or scientific support for the miracles in the Bible or the doctrines of the church, we should believe them to be factual and true anyway. I suggest that it doesn't much matter whether or not we have faith that the Bible is factual. What matters is a faithful, positive approach to life, a willingness to love and serve even when we can't see any reason for hope. That's the kind of faith that remains, even when angels don't swoop down to rescue us when we are in trouble. It's the raw faith that remains when the hard knocks of life break holes in our cherished assumptions and beliefs. It's the kind that gets us through the spiritual, financial, and medical decathlons into which we are entered. Raw faith is tougher than faith in doctrine and dogma. Raw faith enabled Dan to endure his health crises, and it enabled Jesus to face the otherwise frightful facts before him on the cross.

What are the scary facts in your life?
What gives you the faith to face them?

Mere Mountains

> "If you have faith the size of a mustard seed, you will say to this mountain, 'Move from here to there', and it will move; and nothing will be impossible to you." — Jesus (Matthew 17: 21)

I once stood at the rim of an open-pit copper mine in the Southwest, and looked down at the dump trucks that carried the ore up from the bottom of the pit. These were trucks so big that they'd barely fit in two lanes of a highway. They were so far down in the pit that they looked like matchbox toys. That alone was an impressive sight, but then I learned that at one time, this vast, deep pit had been a mountain. The spot where I was standing would have been at the base of that mountain, and I'd have been looking up, instead of down.

The ore was dug, the mountain was flattened, and the miners kept digging until they inverted it into a hole, and the remains of the mountain and the hole were piled up into a long, flat-topped mountain of tailings about a mile away. Somebody said to the mountain: "Move from here to there," and it moved.

People had faith that they could make small machines that in turn could make larger machines that could make even larger factories to make even larger machines. And they had faith that these really large machines could dig and haul away huge rocks and move them someplace else. Humble faith on the scale of mustard seeds can move things on the scale of mountains.

But why stop with mountains? Why not start with the faith we have now, however weak, and take up challenges harder than copper mining, such as forgiving those who hurt us most? Hard as it was to carve that hole in the ground, and the pile of tailings near it, it is even more difficult to extend appropriate compassion and protection to the most vulnerable people in our midst. Why stop with mountains, when we have before us the challenge of creating a new world community based on trust and respect rather than on selfish interest and brute force? Why stop with mountains, when we could move to end poverty in America, a shame inexcusable in this richest land on earth? Why stop with mountains, when tens of millions of Americans have no health insurance? It is a marvel to move a mountain by faith, and even more of a marvel when we faithfully and bravely dig into the depths of our souls to face the demons we find there, and work to heal ourselves and the world.

We can leverage the little faith we have today, so that we can move more than mere mountains tomorrow.

What mountains do you want your faith to move?
In your own life, and in the wider world?

Waterskiing the Gospels

Billy Collins was the Poet Laureate of the United States from 2001-2003. Like other Poet Laureates, he spent a good deal of his life trying to teach people to appreciate the medium. But often he found it difficult, especially in his role as a college English professor. Many people want to know the one, exact, unequivocal meaning of a poem, when even the Poet Laureate is only dimly aware of the many potential interpretations that his own good work may hold. He experienced many instances of this frustration, and so he responded as good poets often do. He wrote a poem about it.

And it is one in which I find resonance with my own profession. Very often, people in churches want to know the one, exact, unequivocal meaning of a passage in the Bible. But the Bible consists largely of a sort of poetry. Jesus understood this. He quoted the Hebrew scripture all the time. But he used it creatively, showing clearly that its passages had many potential meanings. He had no problem with freely, artfully applying scriptural images and stories to situations that had nothing to do with the contexts in which they appeared in the Torah and the prophets. He'd mix passages together, blending them freely, to get his points across. He did things with the scriptures that would get him turned down for ordination in a lot of Christian denominations today.

What would happen if we interpreted the New Testament as creatively and freely as Jesus interpreted the Hebrew scripture? First of all, we'd have some fun, and secondly, we'd discover that the Bible is a resource for us to use creatively to express our own spiritual experience, rather than being a rule-book full of clear-cut answers.

Billy Collins' poem, "Introduction to Poetry", included these lines:

I want them to water ski
across the surface of a poem
waving at the author's name on the shore.
But all they want to do
is tie the poem to a chair with rope
and torture a confession out of it.

Here's what happens when we replace the word "poem" with "the Bible":

I want them to water ski
across the surface of the Bible
waving at its many authors' names on the shore.
But all they want to do

is tie the Bible to a chair with rope
and torture a confession out of it.

With the inspiration of Billy Collins as our motorboat, let us water ski across the gospels, waving happily at Matthew, Mark, Luke, and John as they stand, cheering us, along Galilee's shore!

What would it be like to water ski across the story of your own life?

No Name God

My wife Roberta and I took a stroll down the main street of Sausalito , California, and heard live music coming from the No Name Bar. We leaned on its open windowsill and listened for a while. Al, the bar's owner, came out to the sidewalk to puff on a cigar, and we made his acquaintance. After a lot of friendly and funny banter, it came out that I was the minister of the church up the stairs. This surprised him.

"Sorry," he said, "but I don't believe in God!"

"Neither do I," I answered. "I don't believe in God, I just experience God."

This was enough to inspire Al to make us his guests for drinks on the back patio where we sat with a group of strangers and carried on a lively conversation about religion and lots else, late into the night.

Al and I had a lot in common in our understanding of God. The God he didn't believe in is the same God I don't believe in, either. He thought that made him an atheist, while I thought that made me a progressive Christian. Neither of us believed in a supernatural God who lives outside the universe and meddles in its affairs, showing favor to some and not to others. Neither of us believed in a God who expects us to believe unbelievable things or expects us to think one particular religion is right, to the exclusion of all others. Neither of us believed in a divine being who set up humans to "fall" and thus needed a bloody sacrifice to get right with him.

When I feel unconditional love from or for others, I experience God. When I am full of compassion for others and for the universe itself, when I feel deep kindness that comes from a Source beyond any one person or thing, then I experience God. When I am filled with awe and wonder as I encounter the natural world around me, I experience God. When I experience the kind of joyful hospitality that Al offered us that night, I experience God.

This experience is beyond any name I can give it. This is why the great religions of the world have always handled the name of God with great delicacy. All religions have poetic, mythical ways of saying that the experience of God cannot be contained or limited by the words we give to (him/her/it?). Each religion, in its own way, worships a God beyond naming.

At the No Name Bar, Al and I had a chat about the No Name God. The No Name God can be experienced in a saloon as well as in a sanctuary, on a sidewalk as well as in a pew, and by an "atheist" as well as a "believer." If Al could graciously offer a place for me at his table, the least I and other progressive Christians can do is to offer him, and others who disbelieve or question traditional religion, a place at our communion table.

What kind of God don't you believe in?

What does that say about your experience of God?

Love Now Ascending

("Holy, Holy, Holy"—tune: Nicaea)

Holy, holy, holy, love now ascending
Early in the morning our song shall rise to you
Holy, holy, holy, joy that has no ending
Giving, forgiving, breathing life anew.

Holy, holy, holy, love without a limit
Care that binds creation in sacred unity
Holy, holy, holy, birthing every minute,
Christ, Love's revealer, sets our spirits free.

Holy, holy, holy, infinite compassion,
Makes a place for every soul in God's eternal reign

Holy, holy, holy, truth beyond religion,
Love that endures should nothing else remain.

Holy, holy, holy, raise your voice in singing,
Join the cosmic chorus in praise of Love divine,
Holy, holy, holy, God beyond all naming,
Echoes our song in harmony sublime.

Talking Trees

As I walked up a sidewalk in Berkeley, I heard a tree talk. A soft, high-pitched, plaintive voice came from its mouth. I stood and listened.

After a while, a little finch poked its beak out of the hole in the trunk of the sycamore and then flew out. Its babies were still inside, blending their sounds into one sweet supplication.

I was taught in English class to avoid "pathetic fallacy," the temptation to write human characteristics into non-human things. But really, the tree did talk. I was there, and I heard it.

As I stood there, listening, I mused that while the tree's voice was that of birds inside a hole in its trunk, that didn't mean the tree didn't have a voice. There had once been a branch at that spot on the trunk: it fell or was cut off, and the wound festered with rot until a hole formed—an ideal habitat for finches to make a nest of little strands of grass and twigs. How different was my voice, really? My body is an ecosystem of diverse cells with very different shapes and functions. One set of cells found my voice-box to be an ideal habitat. Those cells formed a perfect nest of strands in my larynx, from which they issue a voice. They are as at home in my throat as the finches are in that sycamore trunk.

What I call my "self" is a congregation of billions of living beings, not one of which has any idea that they are part of me. Each cell is "nesting" among the others, relating symbiotically.

I serve the church, and see myself clearly as part of its ecology of interdependence. Together our sounds blend into voices that float out of the doors of countless sanctuaries on Sunday mornings. Because these buildings are our habitats for worship, they further examples of trees that talk.

I am only barely aware that I'm a constituent of another vastly larger entity called the human race. I add a tiny tone to a much larger voice, and I hardly know what it speaks, little more than those tiny baby finches could have known how their sounds would be synthesized into the voice of a tree.

But perhaps by listening to a talking sycamore, I might be trained to hear the voice of the human mega-being of which I am a micro-member. What are we saying? And is it what we really want to be saying?

But better yet, listening at the mouth of a tree, I might for a fleeting moment hear from it the voice of the One in whose throat all humanity is but one miniscule vibration, hardly louder than the peeping of baby finches in a sycamore.

How do you hear the voice of God? What is that voice saying?

Word Jazz
(to be recited with the accompaniment of a saxophone)

In the beginning is the Word

W-O-R-D
And the Word is with God
And the Word is God
And the Word is the bird
That Jesus talked about
When he pointed at the bird
In his Sermon on the Mount.
The birds of the air
Don't store in the barn,
The birds, they never worry
So don't you ever fret
Except against the strings
Of a guitar's fretted neck
Or you're gonna be a wreck
Wracked with anxiety

That you just don't need
In heaven's reality
That you are going to see
When you listen for the Word
In the singing of the bird
That the Almighty feeds
Day by day, while you pray
And say hey, Dear God
In your beginning is the Word
And like a winging bird
I'm feeling free
In the awesome presence
Of your eternity
That's beyond theology
Defying explanation.
But we groan in expectation
Oppressed with the cogitation
That it's cool to suffer from alienation
Drifting apart in inebriation
When we ought to be claiming your liberation
From fear and greed and discrimination.
Oh! the misery of comparing one to another
The wrongful judgment of sisters against brothers
Husband against wife
All that family strife
The religious hypocrisy
That claims superiority
To all of that the Word is No!
All that jive has got to go
Over the cliff where Jesus sent the hogs
Out of the eyes where he took out the logs
Out of the ears where he pulled out the mud
Off the cross where he shed all the blood.
The Word, the Word, the Word is YES
To all that for hearts and souls is best
Trust and faith and hope and grace
Belief in the future of the human race

The artistic, mystic
Pluralistic, humanistic
W-O-R-D
Whispered again to you and me
Can you hear it? Can you feel it?
Can you start to catch the beat?
Can you stand to feel the heat?
Can you sense the buzz about it
That is spreading on the street?
Are you hip to the Word
The still small silent Word?
The Word insinuated in the coolness of a cat
Who shows a brother kindness
Even when he plays the brat?
The Word that changes spelling
The Word that keeps on telling
The Word that's still upwelling
From the depths of this and that
From the hearts of you and me
When we finally start to see
That the package that we bought
Was completely full of rot
That the only way to get it is to give up all we thought
That the way to find abundance is to share all that we've got
That the way to change the System is to blow 'em all away
With the love in our intentions and the truth in what we say.
The Word, the Word, W-O-R-D
The ultimate cosmic graffiti
The Alpha, Omega, beginning and the stop
I'm prayin' and I'm preachin' till I finally gotta drop.
The Word, W-O-R-D
The Word is the sound of the tables Jesus turned
Dumping all the money for the sacrifices burned
Dumping all the lies of the powers that be
They say that freedom's precious but they head toward tyranny.
Is the Word really heard when they tap our telephones
Can they hear the wails and moans

Of the mothers in the war
And the inner city poor
And the millions uninsured
To whose plight we're so inured?
Are we listening
To the W-O-R-D?
That's the ultimate verbal authority
Structuring our moral integrity
Giving us the spine
To stand for what's divine
And do the thing that's kind
Kind, kind.
Let's just be kind.
And patient.
And humble.
And sweet.
And bold!
And free!
And Whee!
The serendipity!
Of knowing you and me
Express divinity!
Oh yeah! W-O-R-D –
I hear you in the forest
Behind a redwood tree
I hear you in the waves
That are crashing in the sea
I hear you in the desert
Speaking soft to me:
Peace
Truth
Forgiveness
Acceptance
Courage
Is there more, more, more, more
More you have to say?
Can I bear to really hear

That I'm nowhere nearly clear?
My ears burn, my feet are sore
My eyes sting, my fingers ache
Can I type another Word?
W-O-R-D
It seems absurd
That more could be in store.
Resonations, conflagrations,
Inhalations, excitations,
Inspirations, exclamations
I'm ready.
I'm birdlike.
I'm barnless.
I'm as hollow as a swallow
I'm as pinched as a finch
I'm as slow as a crow
Eager as an eagle
Un-uptight as a goose in flight
I'm a bird, God,
I'm your bird, Word,
I'm ready, Lord,
W-O-R-D
O let me be
All yours.
Amen.

What helps you to listen to the WORD?

Ebb Tide

I walked along the San Francisco Bay shoreline on a beautiful afternoon. Out in the marsh, flotsam of boards and rusty iron was visible, coated in greenish-brown muck. The tide was so low that the secrets of the deep were revealed—an interesting sight, though not necessarily a pretty one! Shreds of broken dream boats, splintered planks from shattered harbors, anchors aweigh-ed no more.

Life at ebb tide reveals all that, and more. When contrary currents drain away your soul, you get a view of what lies at its bottom. You are confronted with memories and feelings that once you hoped would sink out of sight forever.

I have never suffered from anything close to a debilitating depression—knock on wood. I did, and I do, nothing to deserve my generally temperate disposition. I have my tides, but they are nothing like those in the Bay of Fundy in Canada, where the sea level rises and falls up to fifty feet. But every now and again, I wake up at 3:00 in the morning, when my tide is at its very lowest, and I get a taste of what depression might be like. At that hour, the ebbing tide of endorphins in my brain reveals a worry. And then a grudge. And then a bad memory. And then an unresolved conflict. And then a resentment. All are covered in greenish-brown muck. The best I can do is take deep breaths, observe my sad state as calmly and compassionately as I can, and try to remember that the tide will turn. Eventually I fall asleep again, positive brain chemistry quietly and imperceptibly flows back in, and I wake up, usually with a good attitude.

The same ebb and flow comes with the passages of my life. A few years ago I went through a family crisis that was, quite literally, a draining experience. And again, in my most drained moments, I noticed that I obsessed not only about the immediate causes of the crisis, but also about everything else that was wrong. When I'm drained by one thing, everything else lying at the bottom seems to come to the surface. But those are times when I'm least capable of dealing with them. When times are really good, I am too busy enjoying life to want to clean up the bottom-dwelling problems that I see when I'm drained!

The best I can do is to take the role of the observer, looking with calm and care at the broken jetsam that emerges when the water level sinks. Prayer is like a hike along the shore of the soul, whether it's full of dancing waves, or drained to reveal the mud and the junk. The observer within me, and within us all, is God, the unbreakable pier, the boat that stays afloat, divinely attuned to the ebb and the flow of the heart.

When have you been able to take on the role of the loving, accepting observer, for yourself or for others? When have others served you this way?

Speechless at Stanford

I served as the ecumenical Protestant campus minister at Stanford University. I got a wonderful education there, just by being on campus and listening to people. For nine years I was surrounded by faculty and students who often had brilliant things to say.

But I was also a witness to the silence that followed sudden and infrequent encounters with evil on campus. They were moments that reminded me of the final words of Job: "Therefore I have uttered what I did not understand, things too wonderful for me, which I did not know. I had heard of you by the hearing of the ear, but now my eye sees you: therefore I despise myself, and repent in dust and ashes." (Job 42: 3-6)

Stanford was and is an idyllic place. It's beautiful and rich in culture, knowledge, and all that money can buy. At Stanford, as was the case for Job until his sufferings started, evil was something we mostly knew only "by the hearing of the ear." The palm fronds fluttered above the red-tiled buildings around the Quad, the sun shone on students skateboarding to classes taught by professors who were always cracking tougher nuts, building better widgets, plumbing deeper depths. Nothing seemed too wonderful to comprehend or discover.

Until there was a suicide. Or a terrible accident. Three students who were dear to me died in one year. One rode her bike up into the hills above campus and hung herself on a tree. Another bought a pistol and shot herself. And another accidentally fell off a trail while hiking in the wilderness, cracked open his skull, and died instantly. These events left me saddened and speechless, unable to understand or explain them. These were brilliant, positive, friendly, caring people whose life-fires were snuffed out suddenly. Their friends were left slack-jawed, vacant-eyed. I spent much time with the dozens of students who were affected by these deaths. They became most visibly un-Stanford-like in their shock and grief. Stanford was a place where all problems seem tractable, if not today, then in the near future. The campus was marinated in a can-do, will-do culture. After the memorial service for the student who fell off the cliff, a student said to me, "The hardest thing when George died was knowing there was nothing I could do about it." Indeed. Young people get into Stanford because they appear to be able to do something about virtually everything.

But what could anyone have done to prevent a beautiful, energetic, multi-talented young woman from throwing a rope over a tree branch in the woods and hanging herself? Yes, she had a history of bipolar mental illness. But she was very conscious of her condition and got the very best possible treatment for it. Her family was caring and attentive. Her friends showered her with the same affection that she lavished on them. She was a superb communicator, at every level. My conversations with her ranged freely from the personal to the political, the philosophical to the spiritual. But when the stark force of depression overwhelmed her on that perfect California summer's day, she succumbed, out of reach of the help that seemed so available to her. The contradiction was so intense: the light of her life and the darkness of the death that claimed her.

To accept the inexplicability of such events might be easier if they were more visibly a part of the landscape at a place like Stanford. But even the leaves on the oak tree where her body hung, decomposing for weeks until it was found, remain green year-round in that privileged pocket of the world. Silence of the kind that followed Job's last words is all the more shocking because of the cheerful, up-beat chatter that precedes it at Stanford.

I was blessed to be surrounded by students who exhibited the most positive imaginable traits on a daily basis. But every so often I met one who appeared to be in the grip of an evil force. A few were driven by rapacious ambitions made more frightful by the competence and commitment with which they were pursued. I used to work with homeless people, some of whom were thieves, some of whom were violent. They mostly engaged in what I came to recognize as "disorganized crime." But on campus I met a few students who seemed just as badly motivated, but were highly skilled in following through on their motivations. These were rare encounters, but in them the presence of evil was palpable. My body registered its presence when it brushed near. I don't understand how this force works. I don't know how volitional it is. Are people in its thrall, or is it just a force that they freely manipulate? I sense that my effort to explain evil only feeds it. It is a reality that is a mystery, apparently out of reach of my ability to understand. Evil leaves me speechless.

But it is in these speechless moments that the still, small divine voice can be heard. God may or may not be to blame for suffering, grief, or evil. I do not think it is for me or for us to know. But through these experiences, awful though they may be, we reach the limits of our understanding, the dam past which our speech cannot flow, and there we come to a space where God can be met. It is in these moments with students that I shared profound spiritual communion, a soulful intimacy that revealed the love that I know as God.

Gently guiding students through their encounters with the unacceptable, the indescribable, and the insoluble was a special calling for me as a campus minister who did not presume to have a solution for the problem of evil. I had a steady stream of students coming to my door after being frustrated by other campus religious groups that did claim to have the answer. My job was to stay close and say little. Because faith is the affirmation of life and love in spite of, and sometimes because of, our inability to figure out why bad things happen to good people. Faith makes a sacred place in the soul for these moments of silence, without neatly resolving them into the trite theologies of Eliphaz, Bildad, and Zophar, Job's so-called friends who claimed to know why he suffered, and their present-day successors. "Such knowledge is too wonderful for me; it is so high that I cannot attain it." (Psalm 139: 6). It is wisdom to be aware of the depths of our ignorance. This was the hardest lesson to learn at that bastion of knowledge called Stanford.

What leaves you speechless?

Anchored Out

Every Wednesday, the church hosted a free lunch for those in the community of Sausalito who needed it. It was prepared and served by a team of volunteers from neighboring congregations. I refrained from calling it a "soup kitchen," because the food was better than that term might suggest. And I refrained from calling it lunch for the "homeless," because almost all of those who came to the meal had some kind of home, even if it might not have met standard cultural expectations. In Sausalito, that standard was already stretched, because so many people lived on boats tied to the docks along the water. These boats had electrical, water and sewer hookups to the docks.

But there was another group of boat dwellers, the "anchor-outs," many of whom were regulars at our Wednesday meal. Their boats floated away from the docks, anchored out in Richardson Bay (in some cases, tethered to buoys chained to old car engines sunk at the bottom). Eighty-odd of these boats dotted the water, and from them their dwellers ventured to land on rubber rafts or rowboats to get food, water, and fuel. It was the last frontier of freedom in America, one of the last places a person could live on "the commons" without paying rent of any kind.

But even the freest of the free must be tied down somehow, tethered to an anchor so that their boats can stay afloat in the wild weather of winter, and held close enough to land to get supplies. Some of these boat dwellers had very little income, and as a result, our Wednesday meal was a welcome source both of physical and social nutrition.

In the early days of the Christian church, "anchorites" were people who withdrew from society and lived in seclusion to practice spiritual disciplines. Many of them subsisted on very sparse and simple fare, and lived in caves in the wilderness. They were free from the cares and trials of community life, but they were still "anchored," tethered tightly to God through their prayerful meditations. Julian of Norwich was a 14th-century English "anchorite," a lay woman who retreated from the world to pray and compose classic essays on Christian spirituality. "I can never have full rest nor true bliss," she wrote, "till I am so fastened to Him that there is no created thing between my God and me." (Revelations of Divine Love, chapter 5)

How can we stay anchored in the ancient faith of Jesus, yet sail out of the oppressive doldrums of tradition? So often religion itself gets in the way of our relationship with God. We need freedom from many of the stifling, obsolete doctrines of the past. But without some anchor in spiritual tradition, we lose the common language, shared wisdom, and sacred rituals we need to express our souls' experience. The anchor can be public worship. It can be private prayer. It can be soul-centered journaling, writing, or artistry. It can be physical exercise that is focused on making our bodies into fine temples where the Spirit can reside. It can be works of service that make us channels for the compassion that is God. Lest we get carried away with freedom, and go adrift and sink against life's rocky shoals, we can drop anchor into God through the kind of spiritual practice that Julian described, a practice that "fastens" us to our Source and our Goal.

How much freedom does your soul need?

What practices help you stay "anchored"?

Spiritual and Religious

I had a roommate in college who was majoring in biology. His nose was always in the books. Academics didn't come easy to him, so he had to work very hard to get good grades. Each night, he would proudly announce to me the number of hours he had studied that day, as if somehow that would ensure that he'd do well in his classes. There was something slavish and tortured about his manner of studying. I was taking a class in logic and told him that hours of study time were necessary but not sufficient for academic success. Just because studying five hours for an exam one day resulted in a good grade, studying exactly that amount of time for the next test didn't logically assure the same result. But he would have nothing of my reasoned pleadings. He behaved as if there was some kind of bank into which he could deposit hours of studying, from which he could then withdraw good grades.

It takes discipline to experience God. It takes time to worship, pray, study, and serve. We do need to put in the hours to do these things, in order to maintain awareness of the presence of the divine. But religion and spiritual practice can slip into becoming mechanical processes that yield no result, without our active inner effort to seek God. We easily can forget the goal and get bogged down in the details if we assume that rituals and prayers will automatically deliver enlightenment.

I once was the minister of a church in perhaps the least formally religious place in America: Marin County, California. In Marin, most folks say they are "spiritual but not religious." It's fair to ask just what they mean. The word "religion" is from the Latin words for "bind together." How can a person be "spiritual" unless they bind themselves to at least a minimal amount of discipline? It takes an organized, intentional effort to activate the divine dimension of our lives.

People disavow being "religious" because they identify it with dull adherence to disciplines. But it hardly has to be that way. There is a way to use religion without being used by it. To employ it just enough to keep us on the path, just enough to keep us honest and focused, supported and challenged, but not so much that it wastes our time and energy, not so much that we get mired in minutia or overwhelmed with organizational details.

To use the language of logic, being religious is necessary for being spiritual. I don't think you can be spiritual without it. But it's not sufficient. Just going through the motions of standing up, sitting down, singing, and listening in church on Sunday isn't all there is to knowing God. You can easily get lost in the details and forget the aim of worship, which is to set aside time to become aware of God and energized to serve others as a result. Sometimes I have the God-experience for just a minute out of an hour's worship service. (Even I don't get inspired by every sermon I preach!) But that minute makes it worth the while. Would I have had that particular minute of basking in divine compassion, had I not put in the time to seek it in that structured manner? Probably not.

Religion doesn't have to be a dirty word, not even in Marin! It can be spirituality's partner, if we keep it in its place as a means to come closer to the love that is God.

What balance of religion and spirituality is right for you?

Where Are You?

Dear God, where are you?

Did you wander off like a small child who, not getting enough attention from his or her distracted parents, gives up on them and seeks out someone more interested or interesting?

Did you stop emailing me when I failed to return your messages in a timely fashion, because my in-box was so full?

Did you give up after repeatedly getting a busy signal when dialing my number?

Did you stop showing up because I kept missing my dates with you?

But maybe it would be more appropriate to ask: where am I?

Lost in my plans, schemes, demands, desires, duties, urges, schedules, responsibilities, relationships, expectations?

So self-absorbed that I forgot that your Self exists?

So focused on my mole-hill that I forgot it is just a little bump on the side of your mountain?

So bent on exercising my own will that I forgot about yours?

So sure that my activities and thoughts are what matters that I am unable to be awestruck by your omnipresent glory which surrounds me all the time?

Dear God, help me see you, even though your presence could not be more obvious.

Dear God, help me out of myself so that I can find my place in you.

Make room in my heart for you.

Wake me up from the sleep I call wakefulness, so that I can enjoy your wondrous company!

Amen.

Sorting Things Out

I was walking along Tomales Point on the ocean side of Point Reyes. I came upon a long wavy line, parallel to the incoming surf. It consisted of Frisbees, plastic paint can lids, and other objects of about the same size, shape, and weight, which had been washed high on the sand. Further up the beach I came upon another line, this one made up of driftwood sticks, all about the same size, shape, and weight. And then another long line, this one made up of plastic cigar tips and other similar objects. The wonder of it! All that garbage carelessly dumped all over the Pacific. Waves, varying in size, naturally separated and organized the junk. Mother Nature displayed the results of the process on the sand, transforming trash into a work of art.

If I let her, she'll do the same thing with the flotsam and jetsam that litters my mind. I have wasted so much of my life with fretting. I try to sort out my challenges with brute mental force and it never works. If it's a real problem, one that is refractory to an obvious fix, then there's no way to worry it to resolution. If I can stop flailing in a sea of frustration, then the elements of the problem and its solution can naturally float up to the surface. If I do my part, by asking good questions and staying alert, then waves of wisdom, swelling from the deep, will sort things out on the beach of my consciousness, in their own good time. I know it works; why don't I trust it more often?

"What sort of man is this, that even the winds and the sea obey him? Jesus' disciples asked after a storm threatened to sink their boat and he calmed the water (Matthew 8). The gospel myth tells us that Jesus was the master of the waves. He could sleep on the boat even when they threatened to capsize it. He could walk on the waves and order them to subside. "Why are you afraid?" Jesus asked his disciples on the boat. Just as he asked in his Sermon on the Mount: "Can any of you by worrying add a single hour to your span of life?"(Matthew 6:27) The waves rise and fall in the service of the divine, sorting things out for us if only we will allow them.

Walking along Sausalito's downtown waterfront, I found a coconut lying on the rocks. This clearly was not the kind of coconut one would find at the grocery store. It had spent a long time in the elements judging by the worn condition of its exterior. I stood by the shore, holding it up in my hand, and with a bit of a thrill I imagined that this coconut had fallen on a Hawaiian beach. I imagined that it had been swept out to sea, bobbing in the waves, carried by currents all the way to Alaska and down the coasts of Canada and the Northwest, and then sucked by the tide into the San Francisco Bay. I took it home and opened it, and its milk was still tasty.

If I can let the waves do their work, if I can stay patient, there is hope that the answers to my questions will bob up and be swept to my shore. What serendipities, what unexpected solutions, await me if only I can abandon my anxiety and stay close to the water's edge?

Have you ever experienced a "sorting-out" that happened without your conscious effort?

Eddy

On a rainy day I walked up Cascade Canyon in Mill Valley. Though houses surrounded me, I was surrounded by pristine natural beauty, stunning even on a wet, dark winter day. The creek roared, tumbling with rivulets pouring into it from the flanks of Mount Tamalpais. I looked down and saw a whirlpool of water spinning in an indentation in the bank of the creek. Bobbing on its surface, circling around and around, was a colorful beach ball. Water was rushing downhill next to it, but the ball was caught in the eddy current. The colorful, spinning ball was a brilliant sight in the dim grey light.

I stared for a while and mused that I, too, was something of a beach ball trapped in an eddy current. I was reminded of the charts that depict the biochemical pathways of the human body. Each of the metabolic processes that regulate the body is a whirlpool of interactions. Together, these processes keep us intact. Biochemical eddy currents whirling within me enabled me to stand in one spot and watch an eddy current in a swiftly moving creek.

And I mused further that, for good or ill, the mind works much the same way. The torrent of ideas and images that blasts through my consciousness must be channeled into hollow spots in my mind, where some of this overwhelming flow can spin in place long enough for me to contemplate it. Long enough to sort out its contents and make creative use of it. Long enough to become meaningful, so that I am not swept away and drowned by the sheer volume of what passes through my mind.

If the eddy current can last long enough before wearing away the indentation in the bank that holds it in place, and if I can pay close enough attention to it, perhaps something wonderful will happen. Perhaps something remarkable, a colorful plastic beach ball, for example, will find its way onto the surface of the whirlpool. So many times, when I have been able to keep focused in meditation or contemplation, some idea or sensation will appear, unbidden, and grace me with an unexpected insight or solution. The eddy current - the steady state created by focused contemplation - makes a place for that insight to be observed and appreciated, instead of being swept downstream and out of mindfulness.

The next time I walked up the creek, the clouds had blown away and the creek's level had subsided, and the whirlpool was gone. The ball re-entered the still-powerful current and was swept out of my sight. What other wonderful flotsam might I find, what other colorful, joyful surprises might delight me, if I carved out more detours in my life where eddy currents could form?

What is floating in the eddy current of your soul, right now?

Song on the Mount

Every hair on your head is counted
Every bird on the wing
Is fed by the hand of the one who loves us
And gives us voice to sing

Grass in the field
Lilies will yield
Birds needn't store any seed
Trust in the One whose word moves mountains
And answers every need

Love enemies
Answer their pleas
Justice will only be done
When judgment is left to the One who made us
And leads us to be One

Fortunes on earth
What are they worth?
When thieves can break in and steal?
Put your stock in the One with treasure
That every heart can feel

Unseen Crosses

In the 60's and 70's, many long-haired, free-spirited young people were starting to wonder if being stoned all the time, living in microbuses, not taking showers, and selling tofu burritos at Grateful Dead concerts was all there was to life. Might there be something more? A subset of this subculture tuned in and turned on to Jesus. After all, Jesus wore natural fiber clothes and had a beard and long hair, too. The Jesus People were a fusion of evangelical Christianity and hippie beach culture. One of the fads that came out of this movement was wearing a big, heavy cross around the neck. A lot of the Christian people I knew wore these chunky crosses, including many of the folks at a church convention I attended during that era.

I had long hair and a beard. I loved the Grateful Dead and Jesus, too. But I couldn't deal with the chunky cross. I was never one for jewelry of any kind, for that matter. So at the meeting a guy came up to me and said, "Why don't you wear a cross? Everybody else here seems to wear one." I found myself answering: "I don't wear a cross. The cross wears me." My response left him speechless. Just because he couldn't see it on my back, that didn't mean the cross wasn't there.

My cross was, and is, a lightweight one compared to others. I know people who are worn by heavy crosses that aren't plain to see. Depression, family burdens, weighty responsibilities, hard jobs, painful relationships. With eyes trained through the faithful practice of compassion, we can begin to see these crosses, and offer comfort to those who suffer upon them.

The good news about religion is that it helps us to see things that are invisible. And the bad news about religion is that it helps us to see things that are invisible. One challenge for us as faith-seeking people is just this: to sort out the difference between the unseen things that are worth seeing, and the unseen things that aren't. To sort out subtle, profound spiritual realities from hallucinations and unhelpful speculations. To sort out real crosses from the ones that are nothing more than jewelry.

What is the shape of your cross right now?

Sight Unseen

Because the earth is all around
The earth I cannot see
Because I use my eyes to look
My eyes are lost to me
Because my God is everywhere
And warms my heart with awe
The face of the One I love the most
Is the hardest one to draw

Tailings from the Mind

Below Zabriskie Point, a promontory of eroded sediment above Death Valley, is a nearly lifeless badland of multicolored spines and drywashes. Following a wash from the top to the valley floor, I came upon the mines in the painfully bright white walls of the wash. The mines could have been dug yesterday; the only force affecting them after many decades of abandonment had been the flash floods that undercut the walls into which they had been dug. I entered one of them. The inside of the mine gleamed with masses of white crystals of pure trona. Farther back, as the light began to fade, I found a newspaper lying on the floor of the mine. It was dated from the 1920's. It was cracked and yellowed, but kept intact by the nearly perfect aridity and sterility of the Death Valley air. It was a piece of trash cast on the floor of a mine at the very end of the earth. I doubt that the miner who left it had any idea that, many decades later, a person such as me might consider it a treasure. After all, the miner bought the paper to escape the drudgery of laboring in a place forsaken of whatever god lived in the city where the newspaper was published.

Reduced to fundamentals, cooked down to the white of the bone, a truth emerges from the dross of my life, and it is this: my life matters. My life is valuable. Its events add up to something important. It is not God-forsaken.

So much of the world around me denies this truth. The newspaper and the television tell me of the odds of being randomly shot, the odds of dying of cancer from this carcinogen or that, the odds of my life being completely different than it was or is or will be.

But the newspaper and the television are wrong. They preach from a false metaphysical text. I know: I am a refined person.

Not refined by birth or education, mind you.

Refined by fire.

I have been burnt by a first marriage that ended painfully. By family conflicts that seemed interminable. By threats of death from psychotic people on the streets when I was a chaplain with homeless people. By contentious internal politics in the church.

But for better or worse, no corner of my life seems God-forsaken. If it was devoid of divine meaning, then I wouldn't have to face the truth about myself. I wouldn't know that I need to grow. But, I am a refined person. Ignorance is not a real option for me anymore.

Down the drywash I hiked to the floor of Death Valley, the bottom of the world, where the sun distills the alluvium into its constituent salts and borates. So it is that God refines even the tailings from the mind of my soul.

How have you been refined by fire?
What else in your life needs refining?

Divine Friendship

She came to my church office seeking my counsel. She poured out her story and filled a quarter of a box of Kleenex with her tears. She was lonely in her middle age. Her kids were getting older and didn't need her as much as they once did. She thought she was too unattractive to present herself as a possible date to a man. She was berating herself up for feeling miserable, blaming herself for her troubles. She said she felt like she was a failure.

She was a lovely, warm, caring woman, kind and forgiving toward others. So I asked her: "If you encountered a friend who was feeling down, would you blame your friend for feeling that way? Would you accuse your friend of having caused his or her own problems? Would you be critical of your friend in a time of need for care and acceptance? Would you judge the person or suggest the person was a failure?"

"Of course not," she said.

"Then what would it be like if you treated yourself like you would treat one of your friends?" I asked. She stopped weeping and pondered the question.

Which is one I do well to ask myself. I fall into the same pattern, sometimes treating others better than I treat myself. Often I am much better at listening to other people than I am at listening to me. I have made a profession of tuning in to the emotional and spiritual states of other people. But very often I miss my own inner cues, the kinds of cues that friends give to each other, that could guide me through life in more positive ways.

I try hard not to ignore the requests of my friends, and I try to give them useful feedback, but I ignore my own body's request for a different diet. I try hard to attend to the spiritual needs of my parishioners, but I try less hard to attend to my soul's desire for a more conscious relationship with its Source.

And my Source is the divine presence that treats me kindly, without blame, without shame, without embarrassment, without revulsion. This Friend is paying kindly attention, whether I do so or not.

How would you treat yourself if you were your own friend? Because if you are truly a friend to yourself, you'll be kind to your soul and body. You'll pay attention to what your inner feelings are telling you. You'll give yourself what you most truly need and refrain from imposing on yourself what is harmful. In so doing you will discover that this inner Friend is divine. To be a real friend to you, listening and responding with love, is to be God's friend.

And from this compassionate relationship within, you will be moved to serve others more beautifully.

"I have called you friends, for all that I have heard from my Father I have made known to you."—Jesus (John 14:15)

How do you, and how do you not, treat yourself like a friend?

Source and Center

Source and Center, Goal and Way
Friend and Lover, hear us pray
Keep our minds and bodies still
Let your Holy Spirit fill
The sacred silent empty place
Where we meet you face to face

The Alabaster Jar

The secret is cheap cooking oil. I discovered it when I was working on my car engine one day and didn't have any hand cleaner. I found that cooking oil did a better job at a fraction of the price. When you are greasy from working on an engine, you just pour it on your hands, rub them together, wipe them on a rag, and then wash with soap and water. Your hands are not only cleaned, but nicely softened.

Wouldn't it be great if you could remove your anger and resentment with oil? And wash away any lingering resentments with water? Why is it that cleaning grease off your hands is easy, but forgiveness, cleansing your soul from the ongoing hurts you have suffered from others, is so difficult?

In November 1989, about 200,000 people thronged Wenceslas Square in Prague in the Czech Republic. The communist system in that country was collapsing, and people were joyful, but also very angry at the police who had enforced it so oppressively for so many decades. Some members of the police apologized publicly for their actions in stifling the democracy movement. But emotions in the crowd were running strong. And then a democracy activist named Vaclav Maly took to the stage in front of the huge crowd in the capital city and spoke these words:

"We have to be proud of these members of the security police who came forward to apologize. They could be risking jail for their actions, and we have to protect them. Thank you for your understanding. Whenever there's political change, there's always the danger of the powerless seeking retribution against the powerful. Now, I'm not asking you to forget what those in power have done. But I am asking you to show forgiveness. Forgiveness is more than a word. There's power in forgiveness. There's hope in forgiveness. Now, will you accept their apology?"

Two hundred thousand people, in unison, said "We forgive."

It changed them. It sealed their commitment to nonviolence, it enabled the communists to retreat with some kind of dignity, it enabled the secret police to come forward and confess their complicity. Two hundred thousand voices cleared the air so that a new system of democracy and freedom could emerge. "Forgiveness is more than a word. There's power in forgiveness. There's hope in forgiveness." The Czech people saw the results.

At a dinner party, Jesus was approached by a woman who washed his feet with her tears and wiped them with her hair, and then poured oil over his head as a sign of love and honor toward him (Luke 7). Jesus' host, a Pharisee, was appalled that this woman was showering affection on him. The Pharisees identified her as a sinner, which probably meant they disapproved of her sex life. Her effusive kindness to Jesus seemed outrageous, but it was yet more outrageous when Jesus told the woman that her sins were forgiven. Who was Jesus, to make such a statement? Words, yes, but more than words.

The woman's kindness took the form of cleaning Jesus. In Israel in those days, people wore sandals and walked to get anywhere they wanted to go, so their feet got really dusty and dirty. Washing the feet was an act of hospitality. And in those days, there was no shampoo, nor were there showers, so people used oil to clean and groom their hair. She emptied an alabaster jar with expensive oil over his head to the amazement of all who watched.

It's worth noting that John the Baptist was popular in Jesus' time as someone who performed a ritual of bathing in the Jordan River as an act of repentance, of changing ways, experiencing forgiveness. The soul was cleansed with the body in the water of the Jordan.

Jesus had been invited to have dinner at the home of a Pharisee. He was reclining at the table when forgiveness showed up, uninvited, unannounced. The woman walked right in the door, surprising everyone. She had an alabaster jar of expensive oil, and eyes full of wet tears, and with them she bathed Jesus. She cleaned Jesus' body, and Jesus cleaned the woman's soul. Whatever stain of guilt she wore, he wiped it from her in one short heartfelt sentence. "Forgiveness is more than a word. There's power in forgiveness. There's hope in forgiveness."

Will you forgive? the person who betrayed your love? the person who cheated you, or cheated on you? the person who completely disappointed you? the person who didn't even try? the person who should have known better? the person who talked the talk, but didn't walk the walk? the person who treated your heart like a doormat? the person who lied with a smile? the person who made such disastrous choices?

And what would forgiveness mean to you? Telling the people who hurt you that you aren't angry at them any more? Maybe so, but maybe not. Perhaps it is healthiest to cut off contact, but prayerfully release your attachment to your anger about those incidents. Sometimes you need to forgive yourself for not being able to forgive others in the way you wish you could. Does forgiveness mean that you need to like the people who have harmed you, or be their good friend? Perhaps not. Perhaps the healthiest thing is to embrace the Friend within you who can liberate you from your resentments. Forgiveness is mostly for you, not so much for those who have wronged you. You can hope that they will experience forgiveness for themselves, but you may not be the right messenger for the message.

I am fascinated by the gospel story of Jesus' baptism in the Jordan River by his kinsman, John the Baptist (Matthew 3). John's baptism was one of repentance, of cleansing people from their sins. So why did Jesus ask to be baptized? It flies in the face of the outdated Christian idea that Jesus was a perfect person who never sinned. But the story can be interpreted differently. The divine Self within Jesus, and within us all, needs repentance, redemption, and forgiveness. Through Jesus, God confessed that God's creation was full of terrible suffering. The structure God gave the universe results in dreadful violence. As was John the Baptist, all of us are asked to receive God's confession of failure to make the world a perfect place for us. No wonder, then, that it was so hard for John to baptize Jesus! At first, he refused to do it, until Jesus insisted on it. Can you forgive God for giving you an imperfect body, for surrounding you with difficult people, for subjecting you to so many dangers and trials? This is the supreme act of forgiveness for us all: to release our existential resentment about the cosmos' failure to be "HTOTB": "How Things Ought To Be."

A fight broke out one morning at the Urban Ministry drop-in center for the homeless in Palo Alto. A couple of men got into a tussle over who was first in line to use our telephone. One of them grabbed a bread knife from the food table and went after the other guy, who then threw a cup of hot coffee back at him, giving him second degree burns on his torso. I put him into our van and drove him straight to the hospital. He was writhing in pain as we drove, and the whole time he was cursing the other guy. I had an intuition to ask him, "Who are you really angry at? Surely not that other guy, just because he somehow got ahead of you in line. So who is it?"

He was stunned by my question. And after a pause he blurted out an answer. "My father!" And he proceeded to tell me the story of his life, and of how his father had abused him and abandoned him as a child, and how he was so angry at him that he wanted to kill him. And he was crying like a child as he spoke. And I asked him, "Do you need to forgive your father?" And as we pulled up to the emergency room he said, "Yes," sobbing.

I don't know what happened. I don't know if he ever forgave his father. I prayed that he did, before his anger ate him up even more, destroying himself and others around him. But I could not help thinking that moment was a powerful opening for his soul, a moment of healing. It could have been the soothing oil and the cleansing water to relieve him of overwhelming frustration. "Forgiveness is more than a word. There's power in forgiveness. There's hope in forgiveness." Why wait any longer? The woman with the alabaster jar is ready to cleanse us, body and soul, of the resentments toward others that stain our souls. The Christ invites you to join in saying the word that is more than a word. The Christ invites you to forgive, right now.

What forgiveness do you need, and what forgiveness do you need to offer?
Do you need to forgive God for anything?

Power in the Love
(Adapted from the old gospel song, *Power in the Blood*)

Would you be free from the burden of sin?
There's power in the love, power in the love
Would you o'er evil a victory win?
There's wonderful power in the love

chorus: There is power, (there is) power, wonder working
power in the love (in the love) that is God (that is God)
There is power, (there is) power, wonder working
power in the precious love that is God

Would you be freed from your greed and your pride?
There's power in the love, power in the love
Get started walking at Jesus' side,
There's wonderful power in the love (ch)

Would you let grudges and bitterness go?
There's power in the love, power in the love
Hate is erased by its life-giving flow,
There's wonderful power in the love (ch)

Would you serve others with everything?
There's power in the love, power in the love
Do you want daily God's praises to sing?
There's wonderful power in the love (ch)

The FeAST

The Swedes and the Hawaiians have something in common besides enjoying fish. They both have a deep understanding of the idea of "enough."

The Swedish word that roughly translates as "enough" is lagom. Lagom means exactly in balance, "just right," and the Swedes say it all the time, much more than we say the word "enough." Their culture ennobles the search for lagom. There's a minimalist quality, after all, to Swedish design. And while it's a very prosperous country with a lively capitalist economy, there is much less imbalance in it between the rich and the non-so-rich. A young Swedish couple at Stanford, with whom my wife Roberta and I became close, explained this to us. I asked Jenny and Peter to teach us one word in Swedish that was most important to know, and lagom was the one they didn't want us to forget.

And if you ever go to Hawaii, you'll quickly learn the word pau. If you've had enough to eat, you say, "I'm pau." When you've worked enough, or partied enough, you say, "Pau hana" which roughly means, "I've had enough of this activity and now I'm going home." Native Hawaiians and white haoles alike use the word "pau" constantly. Maybe it gets used so much because there is so much to be satisfied with in Hawaii. It's a reflection of that culture, too—one that focuses on simple pleasures, one that accepts all shapes, sizes, cultures, and styles of people. A friend of ours in Hawaii used to snitch a few avocados from his neighbor's tree now and again. She was an old Japanese-Hawaiian lady. One day he came home and there was a big sack of fresh avocados on his doorstep. On it was a note from the neighbor lady that said, "No need steal!" There's pau for everybody.

The Bible itself contains a powerful meditation on the idea of "enough":

"Is such the fast that I choose,
a day to humble oneself?
Is it to bow down the head like a bulrush,
and to lie in sackcloth and ashes?
Will you call this a fast,
a day acceptable to the Lord?
Is not this the fast that I choose:
to loose the bonds of injustice,
to undo the thongs of the yoke,
to let the oppressed go free,
and to break every yoke? (Isaiah 58: 5-6)

The prophet Isaiah is asking for balance here. For a day acceptable to the Lord, a day "lagom" for God, when, after it's over, God can look at human beings living in harmony with themselves, with each other, and with the earth. And then God happily can say, "Pau hana" and roll over and sleep sweetly on Cloud 9.

So let us feast on simple pleasures, and fast from all that gets our bodies and souls out of balance.

Let us feast on kindness, and fast from sarcasm.

Let us feast on compassion, and fast from holding grudges.
Let us feast on patience, and fast from anxiety.
Let us feast on peace, and fast from stirring up needless conflict.
Let us feast on acceptance, and fast from judgment.
Let us feast on joy, and fast from jealousy.
Let us feast on faith, and fast from fear.
Let us feast on creativity, and fast from all that deadens our souls.
Let us feast on social justice, and let us fast from negligence of
 the most vulnerable.
Let us feast on service to others, and fast from selfishness.
Let us feast on delight, and fast from despair.
Let us feast on bread and wine in spiritual communion, and fast
 from all that keeps us from communing deeply with each
 other and with God.
So that our lives might be sufficient, fulfilled, complete, whole,
 enough.
So that we might have no less than lagom and no more than pau.
Amen!

On what do you need to feast?
And from what do you need to fast?

TRANSFORMATION

Water Into Wine

For a few years, my wife Roberta and I lived in the town of Sonoma, in the heart of the wine country of northern California. I became marinated in the mystery that is the vine, the never fully apprehended wonder that is wine. I became more deeply appreciative of the central place that this mystical substance held in the imaginations of the writers of the Bible. The natural beauty of a vineyard distills itself into the taste of a grape. And in a fermentation tank, the juice of a grape, in stillness and quietude and darkness, unseen and untouched, sublimates into wine. What a marvel, what a miracle! In Sonoma, wine seems more plentiful than water. It's tough to get a water hookup if you are building a house outside of the city limits. Yet winemaking continues to be miraculous, commonplace though it may be. The grape juice in the vat just sits there and turns into something other than grape juice. It turns into a substance that tantalizes the tongue, dazzles the mind, lightens the heart.

It can happen to you, too.

Yes, you can sit there, in silence and stillness, and be transformed into a new being. And you don't have to drink wine to do it, either!

In the vat, fermenting, processes are underway in the juice of the grapes that cannot be seen with the naked eye. Uncountable trillions of yeast bacteria are going through their quick life cycles, eating the sugars and excreting them as alcohol, and doing other subtle and un-measurable things to add flavor to the wine. There is so much going on in wine vats and in oak barrels that no winemaker, no enologist, can possibly give it a full scientific explanation. One of my parishioners told me that the only liquid that is more complex than wine is human blood. That may have no scientific meaning, but it has the ring of truth to it! It's another reason to appreciate Jesus' words at his last supper, when he equated his blood with the wine in his cup.

Let awe overwhelm you, let a tingle run up your spine, as you consider this: your soul is fermenting and transforming right now. Out of your sight. Out of your conscious awareness. Change is going on in your soul of which you know little or nothing.

Jesus went to Cana because Mom wanted him to (John 2). He didn't really want to go. She shamed into going to the wedding party. Oh, how guilty I am of the same thing with my daughter, conning her into going to events she never would attend on her own, but will do just to humor me. Jesus showed up as the host was running out of wine, a huge faux pas in that time as well as ours. His mom shamed him into solving the problem. Oh, it's a myth, it's a fabulous tale, what happened. Impossible. Historically implausible, but spiritually as true as true can be. Jesus saw some big earthenware jars full of water. He turned them into jars full of wine. The party perked instead of pooped.

You are a jar of water. The Christ is turning you into wine right now. You don't know how. I don't know how. I daresay Jesus didn't know how either. Stuff is going on in that jar of yours that nobody can explain.

You may have been a jar full of anger. Somebody did you wrong, and you resented them, maybe resented them more than you knew. The hurt and the anger went deep. The Christ yeasted your anger and your hurt and without you even knowing it. Now it is being transformed into compassion and kindness. I don't know how. I can't explain how anger can turn into empathy and sympathy, but that is what happens. Let it happen, and it will.

You may have been a jar full of fear. Fear of being shamed or blamed, fear of failing or appearing to be a failure. Fear of losing your status or your looks or your youth. But the Christ passed over your jar of fear and without you knowing how, it is being sublimated into courage and strength. Let it happen, and it will.

You may have been a jar of selfishness. You may have strayed into the false assumption that you were put on this earth just for the purpose of satisfying your own desires and instincts. You may have come to define others as just entities whose job it is to meet your needs and cater to your preferences. You may have fallen into the seductive and currently fashionable belief system that says that greed is good for everybody. But the Christ has passed by your jar of selfishness and now, without your conscious intervention, you are being transformed into a being who seeks the common good. You are fermenting into someone who shares and sacrifices for others, who still seeks good for self but not at the cost of insensitivity to the needs of others.

You are changing, and maybe all it took for you to change was to be willing for the grace of God to enter your soul and ferment within you, in ways you don't understand and can't explain. You will be the life of the party. You'll be the best that was saved for last.

You are in these grapes, you are being pressed into the juice, poured into the vat, pumped into the cask, drawn into the bottle, poured into the cup that the Christ offers to all. From being sweet and simple, you are becoming fascinating and complex, a gift of God to yourself and all those whose lives you grace with your presence. Let it happen, and it will.

What's in your jar?
Into what is it fermenting?

Beyond the Fish Wars

We've seen the little symbols on the backs of cars. The "Jesus" fish and the "Darwin" fish. The "Jesus" fish eating the "Darwin" fish. The "Darwin" fish eating the "Jesus" fish. It makes for entertainment while commuting, but this front of the "culture wars" won't be won or lost on the freeway.

The evangelical Christian idea of "intelligent design" posits that the structure of life is so complex and delicate that it is unimaginable that it could have come into existence without having been designed by some intelligent force. Therefore such intelligence must be responsible for it. But this is a conclusion that can be reached only by assuming that it is true in the first place. It's a classic tautology, or example of circular reasoning, which has no place in science. It is not a theoretical alternative to evolution, because it suggests no other credible means by which this outside intelligence created the complexity of life. There is nothing in the theory of evolution, the only one that holds any water in explaining the origin of the species, to prove or disprove the existence of such an intelligent "designer." Even if one thinks of God as a separate, distinct being that manipulates the universe, "intelligent design" offers no intelligent reason to suggest that evolution wasn't God's chosen instrument of creation.

Circular reasoning doesn't belong in science education. "Intelligent design" is a thinly-veiled and inappropriate attempt to inject religious indoctrination into public schools. If it gets into school science textbooks, it will insult both science and religion.

The complexity of life truly is a wonder. It's staggering to ponder our own existence, to consider how we came into being over the eons. The theory of evolution is useful in making sense of the process by which life emerges. But it hardly is the last word on the subject. Religion does have something to say about it, and it might be reduced down to one word: WOW! Just because you have a tentative explanation for a natural process, that doesn't mean that you have "mastered" it. That doesn't mean you have usurped God's place. Evolution describes a process, but it doesn't offer a meaning or a purpose for it; such things belong to the subjective realm of our hearts and souls, the realm of religion and spirituality. The theory of evolution doesn't detract from our sense of awe and divine humility in the face of the miracle that is life. On the contrary. It's more awesome, more humbling, more divinely majestic to consider that all this living diversity emerged from something akin to random trial and error. To consider that a rose is a result of such a prosaic process: what a marvel!

And to think that trial and error, survival of the fittest, led to the human experience of awe! This, too, is divine. How amazing that a relatively simple function could lead to such a profound, powerful sensation? That is all the "proof" for the reality of God that I need. I associate God with my experience of holy wonder, rather than thinking of God as an "intelligent designer" who exists apart from the universe, tinkering with it from afar.

This "awe-wareness" gives spiritual expression its rightful place alongside scientific exploration. We don't need the non-theory of "intelligent design" to make the claim that science and religion are compatible. God is manifested dramatically in the processes of nature that science relentlessly strives to understand and describe.

What humbles you? What inspires awe?
Have you found God in these experiences?

Church and State

"Congress shall make no law respecting an establishment of religion, or prohibiting the free exercise thereof . . . ." —The First Amendment to the U.S. Constitution

This line in the Constitution is commonly known as the "separation clause," separating church from state. A better name for it is the "establishment clause." The Constitution doesn't bar religious people or religious institutions from intervening in matters of government. The Constitution just prohibits the government from "establishing" any particular religion or interfering with the free exercise of faith. It's a one-way separation: the government is "separated" from church, but church isn't "separated" from the government.

When Protestant churches and preachers started to agitate publicly for the government to abolish slavery in the early 1800's, that was a good thing. When in the 1950's and 60's the churches agitated for the end of segregation in the South, that was a good thing. Without the intervention of the churches, who knows? Those old racist laws might still be on the books today. Martin Luther King Day is a federal holiday celebrating a Christian minister who refused to "separate" himself from the affairs of government. His legacy reminds us of what "separation of church and state" does, and does not, mean.

But there are plenty of church interventions in state affairs that are more controversial today. Some priests in the Catholic Church deny communion to people who support the right of a woman to choose whether or not to continue or end a pregnancy. (I'm very proud to be ordained in the United Church of Christ, a denomination of churches that welcome pro-choice people, and everybody else, including the Pope, to our communion tables!) I don't like the way that Catholic leaders use their constitutional right to influence legislators about family planning issues. But I am grateful that they, and all other religious groups, have that right.

And with that right come consequences. If too large an amount of a church's time or money went into lobbying for legislation, or if a church endorsed a specific candidate, it could lose its nonprofit status. It could still be a church and do religion as it pleased, but pledges to the church would cease to be tax-deductible. Short of these limits, there is plenty of room for a church to influence the government while keeping its tax status. The real limit is not so much the law, but the conscience.

One of the many marks of the genius of our Constitution is that by banning the state from interfering with or promoting religion, our nation has become one of the most religiously observant on earth. This fact is forgotten by those who want to engrave the Ten Commandments on courthouse walls, or by those who so vigorously defend the words "under God" in the Pledge of Allegiance. This fact is forgotten by those who mistakenly claim that our "Founding Fathers" wanted this to be a Christian nation. They forget that the less the government is involved in religion, the healthier religion can become. Want America to be "under God?" Go back to the original Pledge of Allegiance, which didn't mention a deity. Want religious morality to thrive? Leave Bible verses off the walls of government buildings. Want children to commune with God? Don't require them to pray in public schools.

The Founding Fathers were not the traditional Christians they are purported to have been by so many conservative Christians today. Thomas Jefferson didn't believe Jesus was divine, didn't believe in the literal resurrection, nor did he believe in the Trinity. He produced the Jefferson Bible, a very thin book which excised all supernaturalism from the scripture. John Adams was a Unitarian. These Presidents, and the others of the Founding Fathers who were Deists or religious free-thinkers, would be thrown out of conservative churches today as heretics. Many of our Founding Fathers were religious mavericks, even as they valued religion. They understood that the way to wipe out faith was to have the state endorse it. That's what happened in Europe: many nations have state-sponsored churches, and the result is that only a minority of Europeans practice any religion at all.

So we can't hide behind the Constitution when it comes to deciding whether or not the church should be "political." For me, it's not whether, but how. How can we make our congregations places where respectful, honest, informative dialogue about political and social issues can happen? And how best can religious communities take stands on political issues? The church is one of the very few remaining contexts in which citizens gather to discuss anything of depth. Our society is atomized. We've hidden ourselves in living rooms, in front of televisions. Political dialogue by citizens has devolved into little more than rabid harangues on talk radio. If thoughtful, civilized discussion of political issues isn't possible in a church, where can it happen? And if religion doesn't interfere in the business of the state, which other social forces will take its place?

How does your faith inform your actions as a voter and citizen? How do you want religion to influence politics?

BUT or AND?

(A skit in worship: BUT speaks and withdraws from the communion table. AND speaks and approaches it.)

"I love you—BUT your habits annoy me to distraction."

"I love you very much, AND because I do, I'd like to work with you on our mutually annoying habits."

"I love you—BUT you are too fat or too thin or too poor or too rich or too imperfect or too perfect for me."

"I love you, AND I accept everything about you, AND I want to join you in growing and changing in positive ways."

"I would help you with your problem, BUT I'm way too busy right now."

"I'm busy with a project right now, AND when I'm done I will give you a hand."

"When you get sick, our insurance will cover you, BUT if you lose your job because you are sick and can't pay for the insurance anymore, you will be uninsured and your assets will be wiped out."

"Someday we'll all have health insurance when we get sick, AND we'll all stay insured if we lose our jobs because we're sick."

"I'll follow you, Jesus, BUT it's just too much to ask me to give up my status or my privilege or my comforts when following you leads to such sacrifices."

"I'll follow you, Jesus, AND that means I'm willing to risk it all for the sake of divine love. AND I hope you'll be there for me when the going gets tough."

"My religion is true, BUT yours will never lead to salvation. I'm going to heaven, BUT you're going to hell."

"My religion works for me, AND yours works for you. My religion AND your religion, working together, can bring heaven down to earth."

The Christ within us transforms "buts" into "ands."

**Which "buts" have been transformed into "ands" in your life?
And which need to be transformed?**

Against or Through?

AGAINST withdraws from communion table.
THROUGH approaches it.

I'm going to fight AGAINST my (diabetes/cancer/heart disease/aging process) with (money, prayer, medicine, exercise, therapy) and I'm going to beat it!

I aim to live in as much health as I can, and use every available approach to be healed, and I aim to get THROUGH what ails me gracefully, no matter what the result.

I'm going to put up an emotional wall AGAINST my partner or relative or co-worker so that he or she can't hurt or disappoint me any more.

I'm going to engage with my partner or relative or co-worker so that we can work THROUGH our conflicts.

The Christ within us transforms AGAINST into THROUGH.

The cross is the central symbol of the Christian religion. Yet I know a lot of Christians would prefer to ignore it or avoid it. And for good reason. It is strange to be part of a religion that puts an instrument of torture and death at its very center. I'm not comfortable with it, either.

And yet that might be the very point. To take us out of our comfort zone, and get us to confront the tough realities of our existence. Instead of ignoring the cross, setting it aside in our minds as an obnoxious thing that just detracts from an otherwise nice religion of love and compassion; we do well to face it squarely. To recognize that it's not just a strange symbol from 2000 years ago, but that indeed, each of us is on the cross with Jesus, one way or another.

So often, the only way out of that tough spot between the cross and a hard place is to go through it. I think of the cross in the same terms that St. Paul thought of it in his letter to the Ephesians. He said that salvation comes THROUGH the cross. It's no good to fight against the crosses in our lives. So often, fighting against things is what puts us on the cross in the first place. We are fighting AGAINST our mortality, our emotions, our friends and enemies who fail us, fighting against them so hard that we get stuck in the fight, stuck in a state of resistance and tension and anger and angst. But if we can with open hearts face the truth of our struggle, see it for the cross that it is, we can go THROUGH the cross to its other side.

What are you fighting against, that you really need to go through?

With or For?

(FOR talks on a cell phone, away from communion table.)
(WITH touches communion table, facing it while talking.)

Hi honey! So you want to plant a vegetable garden in the backyard! I'm all FOR it. Oh! Incoming call! Catch you later!

I'll plant that garden WITH you. When is a good time for both of us to start?

Hi! So you are running for city council! That is so great! I'm all FOR you! Oh! Incoming call! Catch you later!

I think you'll make a great city council member. How can I work WITH your campaign?

Hi, Billy! So you're having trouble with that term paper? No problem, Billy, I'll call your tutor and I'm sure that for a little extra, she'll write it FOR you. Oh! Incoming call! Catch you later!

Billy, I'd be happy to sit down WITH you and look over that term paper WITH you, and if you want some suggestions about how you might improve it, maybe I can help that way.

Thank you, Jesus for dying FOR my sins! All those years of acting like a jerk—you erased them FOR me! I promise that I'll never sin again, but if I do, it sure is nice knowing you've taken care of it FOR me and that I get off scot-free from any consequences for the bad things I do! Oh! Incoming call! Catch you later!

Thank you, God, for reminding me, through the example and words of Jesus, that you are WITH me no matter how tough it gets, that you are WITH me when I fail to do the right thing and need forgiveness, that you WITH me, giving me inspiration to seek and to do the right thing, and that you are WITH me when others hurt me and lead me into forgiveness.

The Christ within us transforms FOR into WITH.

When President Carter reinstated the draft registration for young men, the memory of Vietnam was fresh. Many were either afraid the draft might start again or were angry about having to register. I was the associate minister of First Congregational United Church of Christ in Palo Alto at the time, and I volunteered to become the area's primary source of draft counseling. My role was to explain the draft laws and procedures and to counsel young men who wanted to understand the system and make conscientious choices. A lot of my work was done on the phone, but some young men wanted to meet with me or our other draft counselors in person. One of those encounters is still fresh in my memory.

Although I suggested to him that its actual reinstatement was unlikely any time soon, this young man was very worried about the draft. He asked me a lot of questions about how the system worked, especially about conscientious objection, and I answered them. Finally, he asked me: "What should I do? I think I'm a conscientious objector. Should I register, or resist the draft and not register?"

And my answer was, "Conscientious objection is about just this: a personal conviction. It is up to you. Nobody can tell you what you should choose. It's between you and the inner voice of conscience within you. And in any case, I really don't have an opinion about what you ought to do."

And his response was, "But I came to you for advice! Tell me what I ought to do!"

And I said, I'm here to give you information and support, but I'm not here to make up your mind FOR you. This is what it means to be conscientious: to make your own choice, on your own."

And the look in his eyes, as he quietly pondered these words, was all the response I needed. I could see it sinking into him. I could tell that for him, at that very moment, childhood was over and adulthood had begun. For him, at that moment, a profound shift had occurred. I was there WITH him, but I didn't flip the switch FOR him. I never found out what he decided. But that wasn't nearly as important as what he had discovered in that moment. He found his conscience, and realized that it was up to him to listen to it and make his own choices.

A few years later, when I was working with homeless people, a couple with a little baby came to our drop-in center. The woman was young, but her face was worn. The man was a pretty rough-looking fellow. The baby was fussy. They sat down with me and the woman smiled toothlessly at me and said, "We come down to stay at his uncle's, but his uncle got mad at me and threw us out on the street. We ain't got no food. We ain't got no diapers. We ain't got no gas for the truck. We ain't got nothing!" And she cheerfully asked, "Whatcha gonna do FOR us?"

I remember being uncharacteristically speechless. Just what could I do FOR them? I could write them a motel voucher to keep them off the street for a few days; that was before we developed a half-decent shelter system in the area. But then they'd be back on the street when the motel money ran out. I could tap a fund to pay for some gas, but the truck was on its last legs anyway. I could give them food. That was no problem; we could feed them indefinitely, but it wouldn't solve their underlying problems of chronic poverty and homelessness and lack of life's skills that resulted in making so many bad choices. Where would they cook the food I gave them? They could come to our soup kitchen every day for the rest of their lives, but what kind of a place was that for a baby? I looked at that baby and wished to God that I could do it all FOR the kid, much less the kid's parents.

I did what I could. But the best I could do, besides vouchers and referrals, was to be WITH them. To listen to them, and show them compassion. To let them know I cared, and that I'd keep caring.

I tried to do what Jesus did with the people he served. His promise wasn't to fix all their problems. He could only do healings FOR a few folks; the rest of the healing work was theirs. He could only find food FOR a few thousand hungry folks, for a few times. The rest of the hunger work was theirs. But he promised us all: "I am WITH you always, to the end of the age." (Matthew 28:20)

How do you need others to be or do "for" you?
How do you need others to be or do "with" you?

Beyond Elsewhere

When the weather in Sausalito was particularly lovely, the town was overrun by tourists from all over the world. When I walked down the hill for lunch, I passed by hordes of people peering into the shops on the waterfront, looking for . . . what?

The tourists mostly came from the same place: a town called Where. It's the generic American community with its mall or downtown which has all the usual global chain stores. We all know what's at Where. Knowing what we all know, and bored with it, the people of Where became tourists looking for . . . what?

Looking for clothes in Sausalito? The town had much of the same clothes sold in all the Wheres of Ohio, Iowa, Omaha, and Oklahoma. Looking for ice cream? What Sausalito had to offer was essentially no different than what's available in the Wheres of Nashville, Asheville, Louisville, or Jacksonville. Looking for art? Much of what was sold in Sausalito was more or less mass-produced. Most of it repeated what is to be found in every other waterfront tourist town in America, from Sandusky to Sarasota to San Diego. Why do tourists shop at these places? They seem to seek tangible evidence to document their travels. But the evidence they bring home was made by the same factories in China that produce the items sold in every other tourist destination. So in a way, it was not Sausalito they were visiting. Rather, they came to make a pilgrimage to a generic Elsewhere. At Elsewhere, you can expect to find salt-water taffy stores, tee-shirt stores, stores that sell wind-up toys, ice-cream, and fast-food. At Elsewhere, so you don't feel totally lonesome for Where, you'll find several of the usual chain stores, and even a sweet little Presbyterian church to remind you of the one back home. There is a carefully calibrated distinction between Where and Elsewhere. The difference is just barely enough to make it interesting, but not so interesting that it would cause any anxiety about encountering the radically unfamiliar.

But having taken vacations there many times, the tourist may get the desire to seek out someplace beyond Elsewhere. The tourist may realize that a certain amount of anxiety with the radically unfamiliar might be a healthy thing. At that point, the tourist ventures further, wandering off Bridgeway Avenue and visiting with the grizzled guy who carves totem poles by the mudflats near the docks on the north end of town, and then visiting the studios of the local artists at Liberty Ship Way. The tourist then climbs up the public stairs to catch the amazing views, and from there, who knows? To the clubs where the local people hang out and listen to jazz? Instead of just snapping a picture of that pretty little church, the tourist goes inside, and after worship goes to coffee hour, and gets to know a bunch of people who might see the world differently than the way people see things back home.

The soul is like a tourist who gets bored with Where and decides to go Elsewhere for a vacation. The soul takes a prayer or a dream to get to Elsewhere, and once there, finds that things are not too much different than they are in Where. It feels like a pleasant break from the routine, but there are no shattering surprises. The spiritual tourist goes Elsewhere and there meets the 1950's Sunday-School God he or she expected to meet. This Elsewhere of the Spirit is a calmer and kinder place than Where. But after praying or meditating the way to Elsewhere many times, the soul-tourist begins to realize that Elsewhere is just a prettier copy of Where, an idealized projection of his or her own everyday reality, and that there must be more to experience than what is found Elsewhere. So the soul strays from the well-trod path and discovers that within the heart there is a realm that isn't familiar, that doesn't correspond to how he or she thinks things are or ought to be. The realm beyond Elsewhere is both beautiful and terrifying. In this place, the soul doubts its assumptions about itself and about the nature of God. The soul confronts its prejudices, questions its neat theological constructs, challenges its habits and beliefs. It's more work to go beyond Elsewhere, but it's also exhilarating and energizing. And as the soul travels further in this place, it begins to gain faith in its ability to live and love despite, and even because of, the uncertainty and ambiguity around it. In Where, the soul barely pays attention to God at all. In Elsewhere, the soul worships the God it thinks it knows. Beyond Elsewhere, the soul worships the God it knows it does not know.

All of us are tourists, trying to get a break from Where. May we all stray from the main drag of the soul, and seek out the less-beaten paths that take us beyond Elsewhere and into the mystery and majesty that is God.

What journeys beyond Elsewhere have you taken?
And which do you hope to take?

Word Yenta

Moon, I'd like you to meet Water.
Water, Moon.
Get to know.
Thought you might take a shine
To each other tonight
And maybe other nights, too.

Mountain, I'd like you to meet Sky.
Sky, Mountain.
Perhaps you can take a hike together
And see what comes of it.
Could be a breathtaking encounter.

Streetlight, I'd like you to meet Glasses.
An unlikely pairing, you might suggest.
But what do you expect
From a poetic matchmaker?
Together, on the sidewalk, you might hit it off
With a flash of reflected light
Brightening the night.

Grief, I'd like you to meet Rowdy,
For a far-fetched date,
And an unknown fate.
You might be much more
Than the sum of your parts.

Rose, I'm pleased to re-introduce you to Desire.
But after all your overuse, you should beware
Of each other's poetically transmitted diseases.
Watch for the thorns, the horny dilemmas,
Get into couples' therapy, prophylactically.
Oh, enough advice:
Have a good time, once again, you fools!

Words, I'd like to acquaint you with Deeds.
You are so far apart most of the time,
It has taken me some real effort to get you together.
Some would say you can never make it as a team,
But, really, what are you without each other?
I can't wait to see you burst out of this poem
And burn bright next to each other.

Faith Cleaning

Our house is quite small, so when it gets dirty, it's hard to ignore it. One day, when facing the obvious, I delayed the inevitable by asking myself a question. I've heard of faith healing, where people turn to prayer for cures for illness. Therefore, why not faith cleaning? Why can't I just get down on my knees and pray our house clean, instead of having to get down on my knees and scrub it?

Fact is, our bathroom doesn't have a prayer unless I bow down with a sponge and cleanser and do what needs to be done.

But then again, maybe there is such a thing as "faith cleaning." Maybe it begins with my own soul. "Cleaning" is a pretty good description of what happens to me in prayerful meditation. It's not about asking for the intervention of a supernatural force. It's about opening myself up to the awesome natural force that is God. This natural force manifests in the compassion and care I feel when I pray. Prayer is like sunshine and fresh air, blowing away the dust in my heart and burning away the grudges and anger that grunge my soul. I really do feel "cleaner" after I pray.

And when my soul is "cleaner," I seem to take better care of myself, others, and even our home. When my mind isn't cluttered, when it isn't "sticky" with unresolved resentments, when it isn't obsessed with unpleasantness, I'm liberated to take care of the things that matter, among them, cleaning the house!

So it seems to be with "faith healing", too. I don't expect supernatural intervention in my health or that of others. But for me there is no doubt that prayer sustains and even improves my health, and that of others. Prayer is an end in itself, but its by-products are also wonderful. Among them is the prospect of a cleaner home.

As the Psalmist says (Psalm 51:10), "Create in me a clean heart, O God, and put a new and right spirit within me." No more theologizing, then. It's time to get down on my knees to pray, spray, and scrub. Inside and out!

What needs cleaning in your life?
What faith do you need to do it?

Freedom of the Soul

Some friends of mine, outdoor enthusiasts from Albuquerque, moved for a few years to Oklahoma City. I visited them when I was driving across the country. They took me to a restaurant in a big mall. After dinner, we noticed a large wall made of faux rocks inside the mall. My friends rushed over and began to climb it. In the horizontal landscape of Oklahoma, it was exciting for them to find a place where they could exert themselves vertically.

But the people walking past them were offended. "You shouldn't do that," they muttered. "Get down from there!" There was no rule that banned rock-climbing in the mall. No city ordinance against it. But people were not used to seeing it happen there, so it seemed wrong.

In 1981, I went with a group of church peace activists to what was then the Soviet Union. One cool fall morning, I went running along the Moscow River with one of my clergy colleagues. Every head in each of the many trams and buses that passed by us turned to stare at us, as if we had dropped down to Earth from Mars. The fact that my running partner was a gorgeous young blonde might have had something to do with it. But we both realized suddenly that in that vast city, we were the only ones running along the river.

For all the many rules and regulations in that so-called "Evil Empire," a ban on running along the banks of the Moscow River was not among them. But people didn't exercise that freedom, any more than Oklahomans exercised the freedom to rock-climb in the mall.

Faith is recognizing our freedom and exercising it. We are free to see the world in many, many more ways than the media industry tells us to see it. We are free to interpret our own lives in many, many more ways than our egos think we ought to describe them. We are free to snap out of the humdrum existence we so often accept as life, and do it very differently, and delight in the vibrancy that surrounds us all the time. The spiritual path leads us not only to discover that we can write sideways on lined paper, but that we need to do so now and again.

Once there was a man named Zacchaeus, a wealthy tax-collector who wanted to see Jesus when he passed through his town of Jericho (Luke 19). He couldn't see over the crowd in front of him, so he climbed a tree. I bet that the people around him were annoyed at him. You can just hear them saying, "Get down from there! You are a grown man, not a child! Get out of that tree!" But there was no law against it, and Zacchaeus exercised his freedom. What did he have to lose? The people hated him anyway. Jewish tax collectors were considered "unclean" because they collaborated with the Roman occupying forces in Israel.

Jesus looked up in the tree and must have smiled at the sight of that little man waving at him. One exercise of freedom inspired another: Jesus invited himself to dinner at Zacchaeus' house. Every head turned on the spot! It was socially unconventional. It was not considered proper for a rabbi like Jesus to associate with such a sinner. But Jesus was a man who knew and practiced his spiritual liberty.

Zacchaeus was so blown away by Jesus' free-spirited choice that he decided to take a further liberty of his own. When Jesus came to dinner, Zacchaeus declared that he was going to take the money he had creamed from the local people in the process of collecting taxes, and give it to the poor.

We don't have to do life the way we've always done it. We don't have to think the same thoughts we've always thought. We don't have to categorize people the way others do. We don't have to do Christianity the way we thought it was always done, because people have been improvising ways of interpreting and practicing it since year one. We don't have to stay stuck in our ruts, not nearly as much as we think we must. And it would do us good, and do others good, if we actually employed our freedom a lot more. Use it or lose it, as they say. As true for our spiritual liberty as it is for our muscles!

What freedom could transform your life and serve others, if you exercised it?

Getting Oriented

A Muslim friend visited me at my office one day when I worked in Sausalito. It was time for him to pray, one of the five daily sessions traditional in Islam. He pulled his prayer rug out of the back of his car and I invited him to lay it out in the sanctuary of the Presbyterian Church.

Stephen is a freckle-faced Midwesterner who grew up Lutheran and started practicing Sufi Islam as a young adult. This mystical school of Islam has a long tradition of tolerance and openness toward other religions, so he felt right at home praying to Allah in my church.

He is in the Oriental carpet business, so as he unrolled his prayer rug, he apologized. "It's kind of cheesy," he said. It was made of synthetic fabric, with a printed image of the Ka'aba, the "cube" rock at the center of Mecca around which millions of pilgrims walk during the annual Hajj. And just below the image of the Ka'aba was a compass sewn into the rug. Its degrees were marked in Arabic numerals. On the compass was a dark arrow aiming at the Ka'aba, positioned so you could line up the rug to aim toward the east. A self-"orienting" Islamic prayer rug. My friend wouldn't be caught dead displaying a printed, synthetic rug in his store, but he does like the compass!

When he laid out his rug, I discovered that the church aimed to the northeast. Toward Scotland, homeland of the Presbyterian Church, appropriately enough. My friend and I went through the sounds and motions of the prayer, repeating the phrase "Allahu Akbar," God is great, many times.

Muslims pray toward the Ka'aba, but they don't pray to it. They don't worship the rock: they just use it to get "oriented" toward God. At Sausalito Presbyterian, we prayed toward the altar, facing toward Edinburgh. Tempting as it was because of its great beauty, the 1909 Craftsman-style building was not the object of the church's worship, nor was anything in Scotland. The altar was something physical which mystically assisted us in becoming spiritually "oriented."

There is plenty to disorient us from our ultimate Source and Goal. We can lose our bearings and head in the direction of pride or selfishness. We can go off course and get lost in the territory of resentment and disrespect toward ourselves and others. There are plenty of arrows aiming us at everything and anything except what really matters. Billboards and websites are replete with these arrows—directing us to spend, and often waste, our time and money and energy on things that don't get us any closer to the love that is God.

So it does take some effort for us to get re-oriented with humility, love, compassion, awe, and wonder. It does take some discipline to remember where we really want to be headed. Lining up in pews on Sunday morning, facing northeast, singing and praying; that can help. Bowing in holy submission on a prayer rug five times a day; that can help. Writing regularly in a spiritual journal; that can help. Making a habit of serving people who need our care; that can help. Silently repeating a sacred mantra as you hike up a mountain; that can help.

"Allahu Akbar." God is great. Greater than the Ka'aba in Mecca, greater than Mount Tamalpais in Marin, greater than any Presbyterian steeple. So let us pay attention to the compass, sewn into our souls, which orients us to the greatness of the divine.

What disorients your soul?
What orients it?

Getting Grafted

Once a year, the Presbyterian church I served celebrated the Kirking of the Tartans, a time to revel in its Scottish heritage. It was true that in our membership we had a disproportion, compared to the general population around us, of McThis's and MacThat's. But most of us were "grafted" into this Scottish patrimony by virtue of belonging to the congregation.

The Congregational churches I have served had a special bond to the Pilgrims of Massachusetts, giving Thanksgiving a special energy. But only a minority of the members had any "blue blood" from New England. The United Church of Christ (heir to most of the Congregational tradition) consists mostly of people who have "grafted" themselves into the lineage of the founders of Plymouth Colony.

The churches I have served celebrate Passover, a time to revel in the Jewish heritage out of which Christianity grew. Only a few in these churches have Jewish blood. Whatever "Jewishness" Christians have is mostly the result of "grafting." And it is well for us to stay aware that from the first, Christians tapped into Jewish roots against the strenuous objections of mainstream Judaism. The church chopped a hole into the trunk of Jewish tradition and pushed itself in as a branch, whether or not the trunk was willing for it to happen!

Jesus said "I am the vine, you are the branches" (John 15: 5). When my wife and I lived in Sonoma Valley, we walked by grape vines every day, and learned that almost all of them are the result of grafts. Certain vines have very strong roots, but have branches that yield less wonderful grapes. Others have weak roots but bear excellent fruit. Match the best qualities with grafting, and you have a tough-rooted, nicely-fruiting vine. Christians are people who graft themselves onto the vine of Jesus and his beloved community, so that their roots and fruits can thrive.

The grafting continues. I will always remember a weekend, back in my days as a minister with homeless people, when two volunteer groups came to do a gardening project for my organization. The first was a group of Japanese-American evangelical Christians. The next day, the group that volunteered consisted of Euro-American Buddhists. These two groups had abandoned the religions of their ancestries, and adopted each other's! The Japanese-American Christians prayed by pinching the bridges of their noses, bowing their heads, and saying the word "just" a lot, just like white TV evangelists, before starting their fast and thorough work. And how can I forget the Euro-American Buddhist volunteer in the garden, slowly picking up rocks and tossing them aside? He "counted" the rocks, Zen Buddhist-style: "One, one, one, one, one...." Both groups had chosen to graft themselves onto the religious roots that helped them to bear the fruits of service they were performing that weekend.

Whether New Mexicans liked it or not, I spliced myself into their culture a long time ago, after visiting the state annually for most of the last 30 years. I season my food with Chimayo red chili powder. I surround myself with photos and rocks and even jars of colorful dirt from there, and I do art projects that incorporate the old New Spanish, upper Rio Grande aesthetic. This identity is purely a matter of choice, since I have no roots in New Mexico, have never lived there, and don't plan to do so. It's an artificial connection, but one that has become integral to who I am. Meanwhile, my wife is grafted into French culture, after one extended trip to that country. Some part of her is now indeed French, despite the fact that she speaks nothing of the language and that her ancestry is Dutch and German.

It's good to respect the difference between a grafted-on culture and a native one. But when we get down to the roots of the roots, it's clear that every culture developed out of a process of grafting. For instance, the Jewish people were known as the Hebrews—and some scholars think the original word, "hapiru," didn't refer to an ethnic group at first, but rather to a lifestyle of semi-nomadism: part-time wandering behind herds, and part-time farming. The word "hapiru" meant something like the word "hillbilly" means in English. After centuries of people fleeing the oppression of Near Eastern city-states, heading for the hills around Palestine to live the "hapiru" way, twelve tribes of "hapiru" grafted themselves on to each other to become the Jewish nation.

It's possible to graft a tree into a cocktail, each branch bearing a different fruit. Christianity is something like this kind of tree; a wild array of spiritual additions and cultural accretions, adding disparate branches all the time. That's how it's developed its tough roots and good fruits.

Onto what or whom are you grafted?
Onto what or whom do you want to be grafted?

For All the Ways

Tune: "For All the Saints" Sine Nomine 10.10.10.A; words by Jim Burklo

For all the ways we help each other grow
As we share stories, moments high and low
The face of Christ among us now will show
We sing alleluia, alleluia.

For all the people that our church holds dear
For every precious memory made here
For those we serve in love, both far and near
We sing alleluia, alleluia.

For times when silence is the truest word
Or when the prophet's thund'ring voice is heard
For tears and laughter that our church has stirred
We sing alleluia, alleluia.

In all our struggles, God will lead us through
And give us strength to do what we must do
To gain the peace and justice we pursue
We sing alleluia, alleluia.

The Koan of Love

One night, at my church's Bible study, we had a conversation about Jesus' words in his Sermon on the Mount in Matthew chapter 5: "Love your enemies." What kind of love, we wondered? When I said I didn't think that Jesus expected us to have warm, fuzzy love for our enemies, one of our group members loudly said, "Whew!"

While we associate love with hearts and romance, there's much more to it than that. Jesus loved his enemies but I don't read in the gospels that he sent them Valentine's cards or heart-shaped boxes of candy. Indeed, he often gave his enemies doses of strong spiritual medicine, with no sugar to help it go down. He loved his enemies simply by being willing to engage in dialogue with them, even if the dialogue was testy. His love for them took the form of his trust in their ability to change their behavior. On the cross he asked God to forgive his enemies, saying "they know not what they do." Implied in his dying phrase was the trust that one day, they would know what they had done, and do differently.

Sometimes love is easy, and sometimes it's a conundrum of conflicting emotions. I can be deeply bonded to someone, and engaged in a struggle with them at the same time. The struggle is made harder if I expect that love must always be accompanied by a soft golden glow emanating from the heart. It helps to remember that even when it isn't easy, it still can be love.

And even when love's effulgence is bright and warm, there is more to its story. Love can be so astoundingly joyful that it is excruciating to contemplate its loss to conflict, betrayal, or death. Sometimes we avoid love altogether, because we can't bear the thought of losing it once we get it. Or our fear of loss leads us to over-react to any threat to love, no matter how minor, making it hard to love at all.

Jesus' challenge to "love your enemies" can be read as a "koan," one of those absurd Zen phrases intended to shock the consciousness out of its usual constructs and open the door into the deepest meditative state. The definition of an enemy is, in short, someone you don't love. So Jesus is asking us to do the absurd. And yet, this challenge is supremely worthy of engagement. We can't love our enemies, but if we try to do so anyway, this attempt to do the impossible is, paradoxically, a demonstration of love. And while it might not be the softest, warmest, fuzziest kind, it is a love that can take us a lot farther than we thought it could go. Jesus' admonition still inspires people to refrain from returning evil for evil, and leads them to resolve conflicts as non-violently as they can.

Jesus shocks us out of our assumptions about love. He ushers us outside the bounds where we thought it only could be found. If we follow, who knows how far love will lead us, and what surprising shape it might take?

What is it like, or what would it be like, for you to love your enemies?

Time for the Tiara

I called my mom and I asked her how she was doing. She said she was grumpy. This caught my attention, because that's not what I usually hear from my lively 80-year-old mother.

Her knees were hurting, and she had some annoying dental problems. And it was her day to vacuum the floor, a chore she dislikes. So she went into her closet, pulled out the tiara she keeps for just such occasions, and put it on. Thus ennobled, she found the fortitude to do what had to be done.

Picture, if you will, an octogenarian grandmother pushing a vacuum around her carpet while wearing a band of fake jewels around her head. That would be my mom. In our family, she is indeed the queen. I'm proud to be a member of her royal lineage.

In my grumpy moments and darker days, I would do well to follow her example. And to recall the words of the Psalmist: "When I look at your heavens, the work of your fingers, the moon and the stars that you have established; what are human beings that you are mindful of them, and mortals that you care for them? Yet you have made them a little lower than God, and crowned them with glory and honor." (Psalm 8: 4-5) Despite all that goes badly for us, and all that we do badly to others, we humans are still Godlike creatures. Especially when the going gets tough, it's time to take out our tiaras, dust them off, and put them on.

There are so many of us on this planet that we often take the human race for granted. Or we compare ourselves negatively to others, and disparage our dignity by thinking less of ourselves than our Source intends. This not only dampens our appreciation of life, but it can be a dangerous thing. What's more threatening than a person who disrespects his or her own life? What's more frightening than a community or nation of people who feel like their pride has been denied them?

But if we treat others royally, and if we are secure in the knowledge of our own nobility, then our homes and work-places can become palaces of peace. Even if we're the ones pushing the vacuum cleaners around their floors!

Thanks, Mom, for remembering who you are. And thanks, Your Highness, for reminding me of who I am, as well.

Grumpy Saints

Is faith a feeling? It's a good question to ask in Marin County, the capital of the "touchy-feely" culture that is the butt of so many jokes in the "red zone" of Middle America. On the "blue" coast, the left edge of the country, religion often is reduced to a therapy program, one of many techniques for achieving emotional and physical happiness.

But what about the person who knows he would feel great if he said something mean to someone who insulted him, and refrains from doing so, even though it hurts to bite his tongue? What about the person who knows she would feel wonderful if she bought a fancy car, but decides to keep driving her clunker and uses the money to help her struggling niece get through college? What about the man who works all weekend to repair the house of an ailing, destitute, and terminally obnoxious neighbor, knowing there will be no real thanks for the task, and that his help will probably be needed many times again?

Sometimes being faithful doesn't feel good. There are times when being faithful feels bad today but good in the future. There are also plenty of times when being faithful hurts today, tomorrow, and for a long time.

Jesus said that our intentions matter as much as our actions. He took the inner world of the soul as seriously as outward behavior. But often we do well by doing the right thing even with a wrong attitude! Maybe acting in a faithful way will be followed by a positive feeling. But there are times when that seems to be out of reach. It is better to be nonviolent and grumpy than to be violent and cheerful. It's better to be honest and frustrated than it is to be dishonest and carefree. At least the right action sets us on a faithful course. Maybe the attitude will catch up and harmonize with the action. But then, maybe not.

Lately I've been more acutely aware of how often religion is portrayed in idealistic, unrealistic terms. It seems out of reach to be a cheerful servant of others all the time, when being helpful or forbearing can be so annoying.

In Jewish tradition there is the belief that the continued survival of the human race depends on 36 righteous people, the Lamed Vov (the Hebrew letters for the number 36). Nobody knows who or where these people are, in any given age. They die, and others replace them. They could be anybody around you: your neighbor, co-worker, a stranger seen on the street. Their righteous acts are secret, but those secret good deeds keep human civilization going.

I have no doubt that at least a few of the Lamed Vov do good works with bad attitudes. Maybe this is on purpose, so that they will remain anonymous. After all, don't saints become famous because they are joyful in their self-sacrifice?

We all know a few. One might be you! Who knows? Human life on earth may depend on grumpy saints.

When have you been a grumpy saint,
or witnessed another one in action?

Ordination

So boundless bonds will grow
To make this human race a whole
Freely may your call be heard
To free obedience to your Word
To each of us our special tasks
Found by doing what you ask
By grace ordain us day by day.

A View from Utah

My daughter and I spent an evening at the home of a married couple and their two lively young sons who had identical shirts and butch haircuts. My daughter loved the wife, who worked in the main office of the independent, non-denominational boarding school my daughter attended for her last two years of high school. We had a great time with this kind, fun, and friendly family. The house was spotlessly clean, with a spectacular view out the dining room window of the Sanpete Valley and the snowcapped Wasatch Range of central Utah. On the kitchen counter were two copies of The Book of Mormon. One was illustrated for the children. The other was smaller, for the parents. A copy of a book by the president of the Mormon Church was propped up carefully on the windowsill of the bathroom. In the living room were copies of Mormon magazines and on the walls and fridge were pictures and quotes from Mormon literature. Years ago, the husband did his two-year Mormon mission (the men's version) in Portugal. The wife did a nine-month mission (the women's version) in Thailand.

How we see the world depends a great deal on where we are. That evening, I got a glimpse of how the world looks from central Utah, where the great majority of people are members of The Church of Jesus Christ of Latter Day Saints, better known to the rest of us as the Mormon Church. The spiritual "glasses" worn by these devout Mormon people are ones that work very well for many of them. As far as I could tell, the world looks pretty good from where they live, through those "glasses." Fabulous scenery, lots of nice people.

The spiritual "glasses" I wear are pretty different. Yet what I see from where I live and work leaves me as apparently satisfied as are the members of this Mormon family. I look out of my "glasses" and see fabulous scenery and very nice people in California, too!

And I suppose that is what brought us together in the kitchen of that home in Utah. This is what we share. We wear different glasses, see things through very different lenses, but we experience the same sorts of joy and beauty and compassion and kindness and just plain fun.

There was also a tension among us, because the man and the woman were not-so-subtly suggesting that I should check out The Book of Mormon and see that it's the truth. They wanted me to know that the way they read it is the right way, through the eyes of conviction in its factual veracity. They know I don't see it that way, much as I respect their religion and honor their practice of it. And to them, that makes me a Gentile, someone who has not yet found the true way that leads to eternal life. Unless I become a Mormon, this couple believes I won't experience eternal life; all I'm bound for is a dead-end, an empty void. (Happily, Mormons don't believe in hell!)

That hour in a Mormon home in Utah was a pleasure. I really liked and admired that family. And at the same time, our underlying uneasiness was a potent warning of forces at work far beyond that kitchen. At this point in our history, the United States is engaged in a period of cultural struggle. The country is split down the middle, split along the edges, and there are cracks everywhere else. Not just politically, but religiously and culturally, the tensions among us are causing friction that sometimes feels like it could blast into flame.

So it is even more important to sit in each other's kitchens and get to know each other, check out each other's religions and social and political views, and check out the reasons that we see things so differently, all the while making a real effort to enjoy our many similarities. Then we can look at our differences calmly and compassionately, and grope for better "glasses" through which to see the world together.

I hope that the church can be a place where people find more in common than not, and thus become a place where we can honestly and compassionately explore our differences. As Jesus put it in the Sermon on the Mount, God makes the rain fall on all of us alike. May the Spirit rain out the flames of the "culture wars," and soon!

What constructive and positive ways have you practiced or seen for people to talk about their religious and cultural differences?

Life and Death

My wife, Roberta, has a view of capital punishment that is grounded by tragic experience. When she was 16 years old, her father was killed randomly by a teenager with a sawed-off shotgun. That act of senseless violence left thirteen children without their devoted dad, a wife without her beloved husband, a Catholic parish without one of its most active members, and the US government robbed of a creative and productive middle-manager. The killer was never convicted, but if he had been, my wife wouldn't have wanted him to be executed. Roberta believes that capital punishment only adds to the culture of violence that contributed to her father's death in the first place.

I live in the shadow of San Quentin Prison in Marin County, where California's infamous Death Row is located. Its proximity poses a constant question. Just who does deserve to be killed by you and me as citizens? What kind of murderer is more or less worthy of execution by the state; the thousands of murderers who get life in prison, only because they had better lawyers than those who were sentenced to death? Or the murderers who happened to kill somebody of a particular race or socioeconomic status who got more or less sympathy from a jury? Who's more appropriate for execution, a developmentally disabled murderer who kills in cold blood? Or a fully competent murderer who kills only in the heat of passion?

There is no clear moral calculus used to decide which convicted murderers get the life sentence versus the death sentence. All manner of subjective and uncertain factors come into play in carrying out this most objective and certain of punishments. Differences in the way the death penalty is applied can be literally breathtaking, depending upon which side of a state line the crime is committed.

These mortally serious irregularities point to a conclusion. We are not competent to decide whether or not any other human being is more or less worthy of this one irreversible punishment. As a society, we have studied hard to pass the bar exam that would entitle us to condemn criminals to death, and we've flunked it, over and over again. We've executed people who later were found to have been innocent, an outrageous outcome that we can never be sure to avoid. We've enforced the death penalty in a manner that is perversely unpredictable. The one punishment which, above all others should be most clearly justified and consistently applied has been neither.

I do not ground this conclusion on a code ethic against killing. In my youth, I was absolutist in my response to Jesus' teaching against violence to one's enemies. Personal experience and growing historical awareness about the reality of sociopaths led me to a more nuanced view. Violence should be assiduously avoided, but, dreadfully, there are times when love gives us no real option but to use deadly force to protect others. But the death penalty is never employed in one of those times. Once murderers are jailed, the lives of others are usually protected.

The moral and spiritual weight of Christianity tips the scales away from the death penalty. Someone in jail, no matter what the reason for his or her incarceration, is in an exceptionally vulnerable position. Jesus and his followers had a strong bias toward protecting the weak, the marginalized, and the despised. Cherishing human life, especially the lives of those we are inclined to hate, is the most central spiritual discipline of the faith. It is the practice that liberates us from incarceration in our own selfishness and bitterness, freeing us from our basest instincts. It is the practice that makes us most divinely human and humanly divine.

We can't evolve into becoming fair, consistent practitioners of capital punishment. But we can evolve beyond our urge to avenge those who kill. This is the promise of the gospel.

How have you experienced the urge to take vengeance?
What have you done, or what can be done, to transcend it?

THE SOUL'S JOURNEY

The Ascent of Mount Tamalpais

In the 1950's, some literary figures were electrified by discovering the spiritual and cultural riches of Asia. Poets like Alan Ginsberg and Gary Snyder, and writers like Jack Kerouac, popularized "beatnik Buddhism." Much of the American practice of Buddhism, particularly on the West Coast, is a legacy of this phenomenon. Now there are many, many more Buddhas gracing the backyard gardens of Marin County than there are crosses or images of the Christ. Never mind that Jesus and Buddha shared much the same message of non-attachment, compassion, and spiritual awakening. Among spiritual seekers in my neighborhood, Jesus lost a lot of market share.

I want to do for Christianity what the beatniks did for Buddhism. I think it's time for progressive Christians to make our faith accessible and useful for people who have been turned off from it in the past. May Buddhism thrive, and may Christianity thrive alongside it, here and everywhere.

A group of "beatnik Buddhists," copying the practice of mountain pilgrimages among Buddhists in Tibet, began a periodic ritual of ascending Mount

Tamalpais in Marin while chanting mantras. This was memorialized in Gary Snyder's beautiful poem, "The Circumambulation of Mount Tamalpais." It reminded me greatly of that spiritual classic of 16th century Spain, "The Ascent of Mount Carmel" by St. John of the Cross. John drew a diagram of the allegorical mountain, with a path to its peak marked by the words "*nada, nada, nada, nada*": nothing, nothing, nothing, nothing. The path to the spiritual pinnacle was the "via negativa," the practice of abandoning attachment to anything, whether pleasant or unpleasant, that gets in the way of experiencing God directly.

So after my own ascents of the holy mountain of Marin, at the base of which our house rested, and in my quest to reclaim Christianity for those who seek the heights of the soul, I wrote this poem:

The Ascent of Mount Tamalpais

Pools in Cascade Canyon:

> Teenaged nymphs dip their toes into bubbling water in the stone bowls that hold the creek's oblation; squealing as they goad each other from the heat of summer into the cold water. Effulgence of sun on dusty air between the redwoods, their bark glowing deep brown-red in the light.
>
> "*Nada, nada, nada.*" To reach all, grasp at nothing. Not the beauty of the flesh, not the bliss of imagination, not the stimulation of the senses.

Myrtle Grade:

> Profusely, sweat breaks out. A fast scramble up a cliff of loose clay rock. Gripping the 'No Trespassing' sign at the top of the trail to make the last few steps onto the dirt road. Above, turkey vultures float in wide gyres over Cascade Canyon, away from their perches on the tall trees.
>
> "*Nada, nada, nada.*" To experience all, claim nothing. Not possessions, not pride, not happiness.

Tree Fort below Double Bowknot:

> Hands sticky with pitch. A grand view, sitting on the perch of

weathered plywood over two-by-fours nailed to the top of the fir tree on the ridgeline. The turkey vultures are circling specks below.

"*Nada, nada, nada.*" To enjoy all, hold onto nothing. Not achievement, not glory, not honor.

Falls at Fern Canyon:

Water drapes over stones, glides under stones, tumbles around stones, leaps over stones. The trail, a carpet of dried leaves. A stone stair. Redwoods yield to dense chaparral. The sky seems nearer.

"*Nada, nada, nada.*" To delight in all, be stuck at nothing. Not natural gifts, not human gifts, not gifts of heaven.

Tavern Pump:

Wooden stair rises through a thicket of manzanita. Lizard darts under blackened, twisted roots. Calves burn with exertion. Behind, an ocean gleams gold under the soft haze of fog.

"*Nada, nada, nada.*" To exult in all, expect nothing. Not insight, not wisdom, not revelation.

East Peak:

Boulders worn smooth by feet and hands. Scrub oak frames views of Diablo, the Bay, the City, the dimpled shores of the reservoirs to the north. Classical piano music emanates from the lookout tower. Taking long drafts of bottled water while leaning back on a sun-soaked rock.

"*To arrive at being all, desire to be nothing.*" (St. John of the Cross)

What attachments do you have, both to good and to not-so-good, things that get in the way of your connection to God? What helps you let go of those attachments?

Ask On A Starry Night

"So, Dad. I have never asked you this question, and I think it is about time. What is your theology?" I asked one day during a visit to my parent's house.

I had to ask, because he had never volunteered the answer himself. After all, it was Dad who mastered the fine art of sleeping soundly through the sermon in church without ever twitching a muscle. As a kid, I was very impressed at his ability to sleep sitting bolt-upright on a hard pew. Of course, he stays awake when he comes to hear me preach. He's proud of me, and makes that special effort no matter what I might utter. But my goal as a minister always has been to preach in a way that would keep him awake even if I wasn't his beloved son!

He never complained about what he heard in church when I was growing up, whether the sermon kept him awake or put him to sleep. That was true even when he wasn't as hard of hearing as he is now. For him, just being in the pew was an adequate statement of faith. His church is his community, an extension of his family, which is his highest value. In sleep and in wakefulness, Don Burklo is rock-solid in his devotion to the people he lives with and loves.

Dad never spouted dogma, doctrine, or beliefs about religion to me. His religion was simple. At night, when we kids were all asleep, or pretending to be asleep, he would open the bedroom door and worship us for a while and then quietly close the door. I caught him doing that many times, and it was all the religious education I ever needed from him. To this day, he still stands outside whenever we leave after a visit, and he smiles sweetly at us until our car disappears around the bend. His wife and kids and grandkids are all the evidence he needs for the existence of God.

I was infected, early in my life, by his sense of awe and wonderment in the face of the natural world during our camping trips and travels as a family. He made no attempt to wrap it up in religious lingo, as I tend to do, but he made it clear to me that in the beauty of earth and sky, he sensed the reality of God.

"So, Dad, what's your theology?" I asked.

"Well, that won't take long to answer," he laughed. "But you will have to ask on a starry night."

What's the theology of your way of life, and is it any different than the theology that you verbally espouse?

The Bible and Bob Marley

Nobody has let the Bible speak in a more creative and expressive manner than the Rastafarians, an obscure group of people from the mountains of Jamaica. The Rasta expression of Christianity is a unique one, and it might never have drawn much attention except for the amazing legacy of music that has come out of it: Reggae, made most famous by Bob Marley and his band, the Wailers. My daughter, in college, has a full length poster of Bob Marley in her apartment, and it isn't there because her dad likes the music! Young people are as fond of Bob Marley and the Rastafarian music tradition as people were in my generation. Marley has been dead for a couple of decades. He died young of cancer. But the love of his music endures.

One group of descendants of black Jamaican slaves called themselves Rastafarians. The name came from Haile Selassie, the last king of Ethiopia, who was formally known as Ras Tafari. The Rastafarians believed that the real home of the Christian religion was Ethiopia and that Ethiopia was their promised land. They came to believe that Haile Selassie was God in the flesh, an avatar of the Christ.

Haile Selassie was thought by Ethiopians to be a descendant of King Solomon and the Queen of Sheba. He was referred to with the honorific of Lion of Judah, an image found in Genesis 49:9 and elsewhere. He was thought to be the true steward of the historic Judeo-Christian tradition. Many of the albums of Bob Marley's music were decorated with the lion of Judah image and also with the red, yellow, and green of the Ethiopian flag.

The albums also have Coptic-style lettering on them, as well, hinting at the Coptic Orthodox Church of Ethiopia, one of the most ancient branches of Christianity. According to Acts Chapter 8, a eunuch, the treasurer to the queen of Ethiopia, rode his chariot up to Jerusalem. In the first century, Ethiopians came to Israel for Passover and for other occasions to steep themselves in its culture and spirituality. This eunuch met the apostle Philip, who converted him to Christianity. According to legend, the eunuch returned to Ethiopia and founded the Orthodox Church; over 40 million Ethiopians belong to it now.

Jamaican Rastafarians, oppressed by racial and economic inequalities, found great meaning and hope in the Bible. They looked at the story of the exiles of Israel in Egypt and Babylon, and found the image to describe being taken from Africa as slaves in the Americas. They saw themselves as Jah people, the people of Yahweh, bound to take action to get the justice they deserved, to flee from slavery of the body and the mind. To get liberation from Babylon, which Rastas use as the name for the social and economic order under which they have been forced to live. Hence Marley's song, Exodus:

Exodus - movement of Jah people
Open your eyes, look within
Are you satisfied with the life you're living
We know where we're going, we know where we're from
we live in Babylon - we're going to our fatherland

The song blends the land of Egypt with the land of Babylon, but both reflect the same experience of exile. In another song, Marley quotes from Psalm 137, in which the people of Israel are described as being asked to sing the songs of their homeland to the rulers of Babylon.

By the rivers of Babylon
There is a town
And there we wept
When we remembered Zion.
And the wicked carried us away, captivity,
Required from us a song.
How can we sing King Alpha's song
In a strange land?

Another song is called "Babylon System", a way of describing the whole political and economic system that made blacks into second-class citizens. Implicit in the Rasta lyrics is the expectation of the book of Revelation chapter 18, which also makes Babylon a metaphor for worldly oppression: "*Fallen, fallen, is Babylon the great! It has become a dwelling place of demons.*"

But to get Babylon to fall required not just passive belief, but forthright action. The Bible for Bob Marley was not some book that had all the answers, and that just predicted how God would solve all his problems for him. The Bible for Marley and the Rastas was full of inspiration to take matters into their own hands. Salvation required that people do more than just wait for God to save them; it required you to get up and stand up:

Get up stand up stand up for your rights
Get up stand up don't give up the fight

Most people think great God will come down from the sky
Take away everything and make everybody feel high
If you know what life is worth you will look for yours on earth
Now that you see the light, stand up for your rights

And in the song "Exodus", Marley paraphrases Moses from Exodus Chapter 14:10, when the people of Israel complain that they should have stayed in slavery in Egypt instead of suffering in the Sinai. "*Are you satisfied with the life you're living?*" the song asks. Time for a "*movement of Jah people*" to the promised land.

In the song "Cornerstone", there is the implication that the black race has been rejected, but will one day be triumphant. The song finds meaning in the phrase from Psalm 118 that the "*The stone that the builder refused — will always be the head cornerstone.*" Jesus described himself as this rejected stone that becomes the cornerstone in Matthew chapter 21: 42.

The Rastafarians and the music of Bob Marley creatively employed the Bible to craft a message of love, universal human brother and sisterhood, and active liberation from oppression. They are inspirations to us all, to bring the Bible alive in our own ways and for our own best purposes.

Which Bible stories best describe important incidents and experiences in your life?
Which Bible stories are metaphors for current events in this nation and in the world?

U-2: In the Name of Love

The rock band U-2 is unabashed about the biblical references and Christian values in their songs, and yet they anger and frustrate a lot of Christians. Why? Because they don't advertise themselves as Christian musicians. They don't work the Christian music circuit, from which they'd be expelled anyway because their lyrics don't mirror conservative orthodoxies. U-2's lyrics are reminiscent of the words of Jesus and the stories about him in the Bible. Their words are open-ended. Like Jesus' parables, they ask more questions than they give any answers, they grapple with the paradoxes of life, they are mystical and can thus be understood in more than one way. U-2's songs are about experience rather than dogma. They inspire visions of peace and justice in the real world, and wholeness for body and soul.

These people are not just nominal Christians. They are serious about practicing the way of the Christ. Bono, the lead singer, has had a major role in successfully pressuring the United States, Europe and other nations to write off a major chunk of third world debt. U-2 is a powerful force for eliminating third-world poverty, bringing together unlikely bedfellows in relief efforts, especially in Africa.

In Romans 8 there is a profound message of hope. "We know that the whole creation has been groaning in labor pains until now. . ." The early Christians believed that the world was going through an experience like childbirth, pain that would precede the coming new age of the kingdom of Love. U-2's song "Yahweh" riffs a litany that resonates with Jesus' words that "a city built on a hill cannot be hidden," a city that shines into a broken-open heart: "*Take this city, If it be your will, What no man can own, no man can take, Take this heart, And make it break.*" U-2's lyrics keep returning to this theme: that the heart must break so that love can come through. Just as the gospel reminds us that it was through Jesus' broken body that love came through, it is through broken bread that our souls can commune with each other and with God:

Take these shoes
Click clacking down some dead end street
Take these shoes
And make them fit.
Yahweh, Yahweh
Always pain before a child is born
Yahweh, Yahweh
Still I'm waiting for the dawn.

"In the Name of Love" is a hymn to all who lay down their lives for love: people who died in the struggle for justice, to overthrow the powers and principalities of oppression and domination and racism. One man named Jesus who was betrayed by a kiss, the very symbol of love, and died for the sake of love. One man named Martin Luther King who died when a shot rang out in the Memphis sky. Jesus said: "No one has greater love than this, to lay down one's life for one's friends." (John 15: 13). What more can a woman or man do for others? U-2's gospel is one of action that can be costly. The price of the love that is the Christ could be your life.

Love came to town one day. Jesus entered the city of Jerusalem and was greeted with open arms, and a few days later things were different. As U-2 sings it:

I was there when they crucified my Lord
I held the scabbard when the soldier drew his sword
I threw the dice when they pierced his side
But I've seen love conquer the great divide.

Love turned it all on its head, it conquered the great divide between life and death, love denied and love applied. And love didn't come to town just once, in one way. The gospel happens over and over again, every time love comes to town again, in a new and surprising way.

Some of U-2's songs express a central reality of our spiritual quest, the reality that sometimes we feel existentially alone and without meaning, that we experience hopelessness, that we experience the absence of God. This is part of the gospel story, too. After all, Jesus on the cross cried out, "My God, my God, why have you forsaken me?" Which were the very words of the Psalmist who wrote in Psalm 22: 1: "My God, my God, why have you forsaken me? Why are you so far from helping me, from the words of my groaning?" Even Jesus experienced what is described in U-2's song, "If God Will Send His Angels." The sense that God's phone is off the hook, and maybe he or she wouldn't answer even if it was on the hook. But this song isn't the last word, just as none of U-2's songs pretend to be the last word. This song is also a complaint against the hijacking of Christianity by those who think they do have the last word. "*Jesus never let me down, You know Jesus used to show me the score, Then they put Jesus in show business, Now it's hard to get in the door. . .*"

It's the blind leading the blond
It's the cops collecting for the cons.
So where is the hope and
Where is the faith and the love?
What's that you say to me
Does love light up your Christmas tree?

I pray that we open the door to the church once again, and make room in it with a full welcome for those who share U-2's awareness that there is more to the story, that life and love are bigger than any doctrine or ideology. We need angelic compassion more than we need simple answers.

U-2 believes in the kingdom come, when all the colors will bleed into one. A kingdom that is here, but yet to be fully seen. A oneness that is arriving, and yet not quite in our grasp. A Christ in which we can know faith, without pretending to fully comprehend it. A gospel that reflects the poetic, mythic, rocking and rolling truths of our souls.

How does your heart need to break?
How does the heart of society need to break?

Stupid-Head God

After the 2005 earthquake and tsunami that killed hundreds of thousands of people in Asia, I got the following email from the mother of a 6-year old child:

"After the tsunami, Molly told me that God was a 'stupid-head for letting that happen' and that he is 'mean'. I did as best I could to address her concerns and questions, but I really feel I'm lacking in this area. What have you said to children? How do you explain that this was a natural phenomenon and we can't know why everything happens? ANY light you can shed on this for me would be greatly appreciated."

I emailed the mother back and urged her to let her daughter get as mad at God as she wanted.

Young Molly is in excellent company, after all. Job was furious at God, Elijah wailed at God, the Psalmist decried God's negligence, and Jesus complained to God on the cross. When we're hurting, it's okay to get really angry at God, who answers to any name by which he or she is called, when we put our hearts into it. One of the names for God in the Bible is Love, and Love will answer even if we call her Stupid. Especially if a six year old girl is the one doing the calling.

Of course, all of us are youngsters compared to divine Wisdom. And Wisdom is yet another name of God to be found in the Bible, in the book of

Proverbs, where she's described as a woman. Mother Wisdom knows better than to punish her little children, you and me, when we get furious and call her bad names when we're upset.

I gave Molly's mom the following way of describing the "problem of evil," as it is known, to her daughter:

"Molly, I think that God is love. Love is what made the world and love is what everything and everybody is here to practice. But part of love is allowing for things and people to be free. Would it be real love if I forced you to love me? Would it be real love if you forced me to love you? I love you because I freely choose to love you, and that's what makes love so amazing and wonderful. All people and even animals and even rocks and trees and water have the freedom to love, in their own ways. They also have the freedom not to love. And sometimes that choice results in bad things. Part of the earth moves all of a sudden, under the ocean, very forcefully, and then an earthquake happens and the ocean rises up and drowns lots of people, and it's awful. But then, most of the time the earth is quieter and the sea is calmer, making a wonderful and beautiful world for us to live in. Sometimes people decide to do awful things, hurting other people. But most of the time, people choose love, and they cooperate with God and with each other in being kind and helpful. The more we love, the more we cooperate with God, the better this world will be, and the better we can protect each other from things like earthquakes and tsunamis."

How would you answer Molly?

Permission to Ask

If I had to do life all over again, I would do more asking. More than anything else, maturity for me has been the process of getting more and more comfortable asking people for things - for advice, for answers to my nagging questions, for help when I can't do something on my own, and for help in serving other people when I can't serve them myself.

I had a moment of maturity when I was working with my stepson during the remodeling of our house. I was doing a plumbing repair job and Nick, my stepson, said, "So, Jim, are you going into the plumbing business?" And I said quickly, "Absolutely not! This is the limit of my plumbing skill: capping off a water line. From here we ask for the people who really know what they are doing . . . the plumbers!"

Twenty years earlier I wouldn't have said that. I'd have kept plumbing ahead, headlong into some kind of expensive mistake that could have been prevented for less money by expensive professional plumbers that I would have been too stingy and stubborn to hire.

Sometimes we think that growing up is about doing things all by yourself; tying your own shoes, making your own lunch, doing your own homework. But growing up is, ironically, all about learning to know when you really do need help, and then to ask for it.

Jesus wanted his disciples to ask, ask, ask, ask, ask. He taught them what we call the Lord's Prayer, which asks for a lot . . . for bread, for forgiveness, for deliverance. In one of his parables he lifted up the example of the woman who wanted to get some justice from a judge and would not stop pestering him until he took action. He told his followers to knock on the door, to ask, and to keep knocking and asking. St. Paul said the same sort of thing, exhorting people to pray with persistence.

When you ask for help, you begin to create a personal connection with the person you are asking for help. And when you establish that there is permission for you to ask, that often results in establishing that your helper can also ask you for help. This takes the relationship deeper and makes it richer.

So often we hold back our true feelings, our true intentions, our real needs from each other and from God. But you've got God-given permission to ask. Permission to ask your neighbor to take care of your dog when you are going out of town. Permission to ask your mate for the kind of intimacy you want and need, even if it is embarrassing to talk about it. Permission for you to initiate a relationship, even if it seems a bit forward or nervy. Permission also to say no when somebody asks you for something that is not appropriate for you to give. It's really important to claim permission to say no. Because a lot of people don't ask for what they want because they think the other person doesn't know how to say no. If you exercise your permission to say no, then other people will feel more permission to ask things from you. And that is healthy for everyone!

You have permission from God not only to ask but to act. Permission to be wildly creative. To put other colors in the picture besides the ones that are numbered in your paint-by-numbers set! Permission to eat scrambled eggs for dinner and ravioli for breakfast. Permission to be extravagantly kind, extravagantly friendly, extravagantly playful. Permission to dance even if you don't know how. Permission to sing off-key even if you are not in the shower with the water running. And permission to ask God for absolutely anything.

If you need to show proof, then copy, fill out, and use this permission slip:

Permission Slip

I, God, give ______________________________ permission to

________________________________,

as a reflection of my divine compassion and creativity.

Signed, ____________, God.

For what do you need permission?

Getting a "Spiritual"

I went to the doctor and got a physical. It was the most thorough physical I've ever had. He asked me a lot of questions, poked and prodded all over. He said I was healthy, which was reassuring.

Afterward I got to wondering. You know, we all understand the idea of getting a physical. We need to keep our bodies in working order, and we need a regular checkup as part of that effort. But do we do the same for our souls? When was the last time you had a spiritual?

I'll bet you are overdue for one. So let's get started.

First of all, some basic questions. In a physical, the doctor checks your age. So in our spiritual, we'll start by asking how old your soul is. Are you a young soul, or an old soul? What do you think? Does it seem like the inner dimension of your being has been here on earth a lot longer than your body has been here? If you seem to have an old soul, you may need the help of young souls in staying loose and being creative. If you seem to have a young soul, you may need the help of old souls to make sure you don't fall into traps that wiser souls can help you avoid.

Moving right along . . . to your weight. What are you carrying around, spiritually, that drags you down? Is there some heaviness in your heart that is affecting the health of your soul, and your body, too, for that matter? Is it an old grudge, a festering resentment? An unfulfilled or shattered expectation? Are you schlepping around bad memories, lingering frustrations, unfinished business with others? Is there a way for you to lose that weight, to give it to God to carry around for you instead of you feeling like you must carry it? Jesus said that his yoke was light, his burden wasn't heavy. Maybe it is time for your soul to lighten up!

Your doctor checks your blood pressure, but in the Sermon on the Mount, Jesus checked his followers' spiritual pressure. He asked them to look at their own anxieties, and to let them go. Are you overly worried about tomorrow? Are you letting yourself become pressured by fear of failure or insecurity about how you appear to others? Have you become overly exercised about relatively trivial stuff? Make an inventory of your anxieties and consider whether most or even all of them might be good to release.

The doctor checked my eyes in my physical, to see how my retina looked. Kind of interesting, philosophically, isn't it? One eye looking into another to evaluate it. Caution is needed here. Lest, as Jesus says, you see a speck in somebody else's eye but ignore the log in your own. Your eyes may work, but can you see? Do you have insight into yourself and the people around you? Have you received any hints lately that might suggest that you have a speck, or maybe even a log, in your eye that prevents you from seeing something really important? When was the last time you saw deeper into something or someone, deeper than what met the physical eye? When was the last time you found beauty in something or someone that you might otherwise have overlooked, had you not seen with your soul?

And the same applies to checking the ears. They may function physically, more or less, but do they really hear? Is your soul receiving the messages it needs to hear? Or are you deaf to the needs of your own heart and of those around you?

The doctor palpated me during my physical. He checked my skin, but he also poked me to see how it felt under my skin. Does it hurt here? Does it hurt there? For your spiritual, it's good to check your inner feelings. Just how are you feeling these days? Joy, sadness, grief, happiness, fear, anticipation, ecstasy, misery, or a jumble of different feelings? There is a time and place for full-blown emotional honesty, and it's not always nor everywhere. But such honesty is appropriate more often than we tend to think. We need the presence and feedback of others in order fully to get in touch, to palpate, our feelings. We can give each other 'spirituals' every time we ask each other how we are, and mean it when we ask!

The doctor asked all sorts of detailed questions about my lifestyle, as it pertains to my health. Likewise in this 'spiritual' it is good to look at the lifestyle of our souls. Do you have a tendency to be forbearing and patient, or do you tend to blame others quickly when things go wrong? When was the last time you forgave someone who wronged you? Do you have anybody to forgive, anything for which forgiveness is needed? It's good to remember that forgiveness is more for your soul than for theirs. They may or may not be touched by your forgiving them. But forgiveness can liberate you from burdens that affect your spiritual and even your physical health.

And where are you on the spectrum of selfishness to generosity of spirit? I saw a sign on a church in Hollywood, of all places, that said "If you are all wrapped up in yourself you are overdressed!" Are you too wrapped up in selfish concerns and conceits? Or are you open-hearted and open-handed, looking for ways to serve the people you meet and to serve the needs of the wider society? A wise question was asked by Buckminster Fuller, the inventor and thinker: "If the success or failure of this planet and of human beings depended on how I am and what I do, how would I be? What would I do?"

The doctor wanted to know what kind of exercise I get on a regular basis. For our spiritual exam, we can ask the same question. Are we working out our souls? We can use St. Paul's list from Galatians 5: How much love, joy, peace, patience, kindness, goodness, faithfulness, gentleness, and self-control are we exercising? Spiritual virtues are natural to us as human beings. I don't think we are born as hopeless sinners. On the contrary, there is goodness, and a propensity toward goodness, in all of us. But more is asked of us than just our natural goodness. We are called to work out our souls with disciplined effort.

Just as the doctor listens to your arteries to see if there are any blockages, it's also time to inventory the blockages in your soul. What have you walled off from yourself, and from others? What defenses have you built around your heart?

Your doctor looks at the watch and takes your pulse. What's the rhythm of your soul? Do you take the time to look within yourself, to pray, to meditate, to write in your journal, talk at depth with a friend, or recharge your spirit through other means? Or is your mind pounding so hard and so fast that you don't have time for your inner life to express itself and discover itself? Sometimes we are moving so fast that we literally miss our lives. You can get so involved in your activities, work, sports, projects, distractions, entertainments—you can get so busy that your life happens but you don't live it. The doctor is hoping you'll have a slow, steady heart rate... not too slow, definitely not too fast. For your spiritual, we're hoping you have a life rate that is slow enough for you to experience your life consciously and reflectively. So you can really enjoy it, and fully appreciate this gift of your existence.

Till your next "spiritual," be well, body and soul!

What is the state of your spiritual health?

Original Zin

I sat in the window seat of a jet flying at 37,000 feet, and watched the sun set over Montana. I fell into a sort of trance, gazing at the colors: black over navy blue over turquoise over effulgent streaks of gold above layers of slate gray tinged with orange and pink. I wasn't just looking at the sunset. I was in it, and it was in me. I went into a state of what I can only describe as bliss. An hour of pure joy in which I found my mind repeating the words "thank you" over and over again, even after the sky went black over North Dakota. It was one of the rare moments in my life when I felt perfectly content in the moment, not needing anything else, feeling no push to do or think or feel something more. Time didn't matter: I was experiencing eternity in the moment. I was so joyful that I didn't even mind when the feeling passed and I went back to my more normal manner of experiencing things.

"The eye with which I see God is the eye with which God sees me." These words from the sermons of Meister Eckhart, the 14th century mystical Christian priest, ring true for me as I recall that sunset. Not only are we made in the image of God, but we also share the inner eye by which we and God encounter that image. The soul is like the mantle of a gas lamp, a thin surface where air, heat, and fuel meet to make light. The soul is where God, our selves, and the universe meet.

It is moments like that one at 37,000 feet that make it hard for me to accept the old Christian idea of "original sin." This doctrine presumes that human beings are fundamentally evil and thus in need of divine salvation through a bloody sacrifice. The good news is that Christianity offers an alternative to that time-worn concept. Christianity offers not only "original sin," but also "original Zin," as in Zinfandel. It offers a chalice of wine to everyone: a chalice that establishes mystical communion between God and human beings. Original Zin means that the lips with which we sip the wine are the lips with which God sips the wine, too. Zinfandel becomes the medium by which we know our fundamental goodness, the sacred essence at the core of who we are.

Thank you, thank you, thank you: these were the only words that came to me as I communed with God through that sunset. And they are the words before the sharing of the wine and bread in the traditional Eucharist, or communion, words called The Great Thanksgiving: "It is very meet, right, and our bounden duty, that we should at all times, and in all places, give thanks unto thee, O Lord." At 37,000 feet in a plane, or at ground level in a church: thank you, thank you, thank you.

When and how have you experienced mystical communion with God?

Old Twists

My old father and I took a long walk in Mill Valley. Dad and I stopped at Cascade Falls, a beautiful waterfall in the middle of the redwood forest. Looking above it nearby, he spotted a tanbark oak tree with a big bend in its trunk. "There was a mudslide there once," he said. "When I was a realtor, I could tell the stability of a hillside on a property by looking at crooked trees." He explained that when the tree was young, it slipped down the hill and stopped at a 45 degree angle. Then it began to grow upright again, leaving it with a big kink. The ground around it looks solid, but the bend in the tree reveals its soggy history.

My wife tells me that I'm crooked, too. She notices that one of my shoulders drops lower than the other. About 25 years ago, I went on a canoeing trip with a friend. We were lifting the canoe onto the roof of his Volkswagen bus when – zing! A tendon in my neck popped and instantly I was in a lot of pain. A careful look at my body reveals the lasting asymmetry, but its cause is not obvious. No canoe is in sight.

The kinks we see in others are almost always like that. Something slipped in their lives that the rest of us can't see. The death of a loved one scars a woman's face with asymmetrical lines of a grief that won't abate. Nobody can see the tears that carved those fretted creases. Some stray genes fall into the twisting lines of someone's DNA, forcing him to cope with a propensity for addiction. But who can see the microscopic impetus of his inebriation? A kid hears a peer call him "stupid" at school. It is exactly the wrong word at exactly the wrong time from exactly the wrong person. His parents and teachers can't tell what led his grades to plunge. It takes him years to grow upward after that sudden, sidelong blow to his ego.

It takes spiritual discipline to read the history in the kinks in our lives. That ability can give us insight and lead us to positive change, and it can inspire us to show compassion for the odd twists in ourselves and others.

What hidden stories are behind the kinks in your life?

On Being a Christian

I have been pleased to have been the minister of Christian churches which have included quite a few people who don't call themselves Christians. In progressive congregations, we have room for people to be fully involved in our communities without having to profess any particular religious label.

It also gives us an opportunity to reflect on what it means to be a Christian. It's probably no surprise for me to say that, indeed, I am one. I've been told repeatedly that since I do not accept the literal truth of the resurrection or the miracles of Jesus, it's impossible for me to claim to be a Christian. But such challenges really do roll right off of my Christian head, arms, hands, legs, feet, and toes. My religious identity isn't something I doubt.

But Christian as my chromosomes may be, I don't think of being a Christian as that big of a deal. This identity is undeniable, but it isn't what matters. What matters is how I follow the road of Jesus. What matters is whether or not I practice the compassion, seek the justice, and work for the peace of the Christ. What matters is whether and how I directly experience the love that is God. And of course you can do these things without being a Christian! Being a Christian is a relatively trivial concern. It's just a label, a shallow, transitory definition that says only a little about who we are. It's the wrapping paper, not the present. Christian identity is cheap. But Christian practice can cost you your life.

Cheap as it is, though, the identity has some utility. My Christian-ness helps me to learn much from Muslims, Buddhists, Hindus, and others. Being distinctly Christian has helped me discover the universal spiritual experience that transcends the boundaries of all religions. To claim your Christian identity doesn't have to prejudice you against other religions. On the contrary, it can be a useful starting point for discovering and exploring other faiths, and honoring the possibility that they could be as valid and good as our own.

And our religious identity offers access for others into the realm of the spirit. My Christian identity, at its best, is an invitation to others to explore what is good and useful in my tradition. Sure, there's plenty of baggage in my religion that is embarrassing and downright dreadful. But the mystical wisdom, the treasury of spiritual experience, the sublime music, art, and architecture, the layers of significance in the scriptures form a remarkable legacy. If I can be a doorway into the storehouse of these spiritual riches, let me swing wide for those who wish to enter.

I suggest that we make the best use of our religious identity, while wearing it lightly. For those who don't call themselves Christians, but are following the Christ as seriously as any of us for whom the label fits, I thank God for their living reminder that the contents matter more than the package.

Jesus wasn't much concerned with his religious identity. He was proud to be a Jew, but he was focused entirely on the path he was walking, not on the names ascribed to him because he walked it. So those who follow his way but don't think of themselves as Christians are in excellent company!

What's your religious identity?
How much does it matter to you, and to those around you?

Is the Bible Fit for Kids?

I once went to a Sunday school teachers' convention. It was a dull affair except for one workshop which I attended, entitled "How to Read the Bible to Kids." A disheveled fellow with broken glasses and shabby clothes came into the room with a stack of musty old illustrated Bible story books. He opened up one of the books, with its florid pictures of muscle-bound Philistines, heavily-bearded, grimacing patriarchs, and heavy-robed women kneeling in agonized supplication. He then read aloud some of the most gruesome and salacious of the Bible's stories, showing the pictures to the horrified Sunday school teachers.

The workshop leader then closed the book and declared, "Kids love this stuff!" He went on. "Throw out that namby-pamby denominational curricula for Sunday School, and go to a thrift store and buy an old Bible story book and read it to your kids. They won't let you stop reading it to them. They'll be riveted. They see violence on TV. It's in the Bible, too. They know somebody in their family or among their friends who has been molested or abused. Stories of incest are also in the Bible. They play computer games with action figures who perform amazing feats with miraculous powers, and that's all in the Bible, as well. The difference is that there's more to the story, there's redemption in the Bible that is lacking in the mayhem on television and in the movies."

His message stayed with me. Just because kids read that Samson slaughtered a thousand men with the jawbone of an ass (a fresh jawbone, the book of Judges would have us know), that doesn't mean they will go and do the same. Let kids see the many ways that the Bible describes the human and divine condition. Let them see God described as a hoary, jealous tyrant sitting on a throne on the other side of the sky, and also let them see God described as the mystical ground of being and unconditional love. Let them learn from the negative example of deceitful King David and oversexed King Solomon, as they also discover the wisdom of the Proverbs and the compassion of the Christ. Let them reflect on life in full as they read the Bible in full, including both the sickening and the sublime. I'm not in favor of emphasizing all the disgusting parts of the Bible. But I do think a certain amount of exposure to it is not only okay, but a good thing for kids.

When my daughter was little, she loved it when I read illustrated Bible stories to her. With trepidation I read her the story of the crucifixion when she was about 4 years old. I told her that some folks were mad at Jesus because he helped people that they didn't want him to help, so they killed him, and it was a terrible thing. She was transfixed by the picture of Jesus on the cross. I continued reading and flipping the pages, but she kept saying, "Jesus on the wood! Jesus on the wood!" because she wanted me to flip back to that picture so she could look at it some more. She was equally impressed by our visit to the old Spanish mission at Santa Clara, California, when she was about 5 years old. Inside, she stared for a long time, her mouth hanging open, as she faced the big statue of the beaten, bleeding Christ on the cross. I wanted to whisk her away from it, but then I realized that something important was happening inside of her. She needed to process that image of the tortured Christ in her soul, and begin to come to terms with the suffering and death that touches all of our lives.

During my "time with the children" in worship services over the years, I put the big, heavy pulpit Bible on the altar floor and gathered the kids around it. I asked them, "What were your first words, when you were little?" (My favorite of their answers: "Mommy's tired!") I then said that the first words in the Bible were a lot like those of little toddlers who learn how to talk with just a few simple words, and then as they get older they learn how use more complicated words and ideas. The Bible started out talking about God as if he were a man who ruled the world like an old-fashioned king. Then later on, the message of the Bible changed as people grew in faith and began to understand God as love that lives in our hearts. After flipping through all the pages of that big Bible, from start to finish, I flipped imaginary pages past the book of Revelation, illustrating that the Bible isn't the end of the story of our growth in love for God and each other. In the Bible, that growth process wasn't always a pretty one. But growing up isn't always so pretty for us, either. The Bible is a mirror that shows us to ourselves, imperfect as we are, but also evolving as we are. It inspires all of us, young and old, to add yet more positive chapters beyond its back cover.

How would you describe the Bible to a child, in one paragraph?

Complicated Simplicity

So many remarkable innovations in Christianity have been spawned on America's shores. Consider the Mormons, the Seventh-Day Adventists, the Jehovah's Witnesses, the Christian Scientists — to say nothing of the American manifestations of the Presbyterians and the Congregationalists. Despite the complexity of American Christian traditions, there are common themes that I notice. Foremost is the very American urge to return to what people define as the "original" church: what they presume to be the raw, uncut, unadulterated essence of Christian faith. But in this typically American effort to boil things down to the fundamentals (is this why we spell it "color" and the British spell it "colour"?). Christianity has become adulterated even further. This is evidenced by the elaborate beliefs of many uniquely American churches. To get back to the fundamentals took a lot of explaining, and then the explanations became sacred. When people started questioning the sacred explanations, the whole process of seeking the fundamentals started over again. This cycle continues to this day in our country. Europeans shake their heads at us in wonderment, boggled at the endless ferment and mutation in American religion.

It is sobering to read this history and see my own place in it. I, too, am on a quest to get down to the basics of Christian faith and abandon many of the unhelpful accretions to Jesus' simple message of love for God and neighbor.

I serve on the board of The Center for Progressive Christianity. A few years ago, at one of our meetings, we got into a discussion of whether or not to revise the eight points of our Welcome Statement, which is a description of the progressive Christian movement. Somebody said "No, we can't do that! People count on those eight points staying the same!" But all of us, the speaker included, started laughing at the prospect that our group, dedicated as it is to opening the church to people who can't deal with dogma, would develop a fixed set of doctrines of its own. The temptation to repeat history was strong.

This very American urge to boil religion down to the basics is a good thing, as long as we remember what can go wrong with it. Christian faith really is simple. It's about not much more than loving God and loving neighbor with heart, soul, mind and body. It's simple, but not easy. It's difficult to love God when bad things happen to good people. It's hard to love difficult neighbors, and even harder to love the basically good but sometimes impossible members of our families. It's hard to extend the concept of "neighbor" to people on the other side of the world, but more than ever, we are called to this challenge on our "globalized" planet. The practice of Christianity is plenty difficult. There's no need to make it harder with complicated theology and bewildering, illogical beliefs.

May history be our guide in keeping religion simple, so we can focus on the worthy challenge of living faithfully!

What's hard about following the way of Jesus, for you?

Confessions of a Padrasto

I discovered that I was a hangnail. And that being a hangnail isn't all bad.

This revelation came to me in the little village of Chetilla, a less-steep stretch on the side of a very steep mountain in the Andes. My stepson lived in a small room facing the road in a house near the center of the town where he served as a Peace Corps volunteer. We enjoyed sharing that cozy space, cooking meals together on a little gas stove and having long-overdue conversations with Nick, whom we had not seen in over a year.

We needed no more than to open the door of his room in order to get to know the warm, gracious, impeccably polite folks in the town of 1,200 Quechua-speaking indigenous Peruvians. Women in spectacular native dress, bright 'chales' (capes) and blouses, skirts hemmed with a distinctive band of color, and wearing huge straw hats, walked past us through the town, spinning wads of wool on long sticks into thread that they spun onto smaller, thinner spools. They tended donkeys laden with firewood, or herded sheep and cattle down the dusty road. Men on horses or on foot headed up the mountain to tend their patches of corn or potatoes perched on the heights visible from town. People speak unrefined Spanish there, too, at least most of them. So Nick was constantly introducing us to the local folks passing by. Roberta, he said, was "mi mama" and I was "mi padrasto," the Spanish word for "stepfather."

And also, I discovered, the Spanish slang term for "hangnail."

That made more and more sense with each introduction, because each Chetillan looked at me with bewilderment upon hearing that I was Nick's padrasto. They were polite to me, but clearly they were bothered by my identity. I wasn't supposed to be there. They had already met his father, who had visited earlier. In Latin America, people usually only have padrastos when their fathers die and their widowed mothers remarry. Divorce is rare here, particularly in the "sierra" where Nick lives. So who was I? An unwanted and annoying genealogical appendage. To make any sense of me, it would have been necessary to give a long lecture about Western culture, or the lack thereof, regarding family life and marriage. A lecture that they were no more inclined to hear than we were to give.

So I spent the week being a hangnail. Not only being strange by virtue of being one of only three gringos in an area at least the size of a state in New England, but also because of my implausible and somewhat scandalous marital status.

From my precarious vantage point, dangling from the fingertip of proper society, I was given a bit of extra distance from which to observe the goings-on in Chetilla. Listening to the loquacious Don Cruz, the buy-low, sell-high guy of the town, peddling a dose of anti-parasite veterinary medicine to one woman for her sick sheep, and peddling a dose of Panadol to the next woman for her headache, and insisting that we buy "cuy," guinea pigs, from him and not from the house where we were headed. (No, we didn't bring them home as pets. They became our dinner the next day. They're a local delicacy.) Jollying with the toothless old men drinking cañaso (bad rum) out of used pop bottles while standing next to their donkeys, while politely turning down their offers of shots delicately poured into the bottle caps. Gazing at the fields on the staggering heights, a piece-worked quilt of agriculture sewn with human sinew and sweat behind groaning oxen pulling ancient wooden plows uphill. Meditating on how people manage to make a home even in places where nature would seem to suggest we don't belong.

Meditating on this, our human condition. We are the padrastos, the hangnails, of the universe. We sense we don't belong here, yet here we are. Jesus said we "are not of the world, even as I am not of the world." (John 17: 16). It can be both curse and blessing to dangle off the fingertip of the natural world, separated from it all by our near-supernatural powers of insight and invention. It is faith to seize it as blessing, to make the best of our status as an odd-and-out branch on the family tree of life. It is a blessing to prayerfully, lovingly observe the world, being in it but not quite of it. It is a blessing to hang alongside the world, and to use that distance to honor the otherness of God, of others, and of ourselves.

When have you been an "outsider" in a way that gave you a helpful perspective?

Panhandling Pigeons

The Spirit arrived one day at Sausalito Presbyterian Church. The Bible says that the Holy Spirit descended on Jesus "like a dove" at his baptism at the River Jordan. In our case, the Spirit descended in a more prosaic form as a family of pigeons who nested inside the sanctuary, high up near the windows under the steeple. During Wednesday evening meditation, our prayers were sweetened with the high peeps of the babies and the low murmurs of the mother, coming from above us. We let their wordless sounds speak for the Spirit as we kept silence.

In his Sermon on the Mount, Jesus taught us to be like the birds and give up our anxieties. The birds, he said, don't worry about what they will eat tomorrow. They don't store up grain in barns. (I sure hope they don't store up food in churches, either!) Birds gather up what they need to eat, day by day. Today's troubles are enough for today—that's the lesson Jesus drew from observing birds.

When I was working with homeless people in Palo Alto, California, many of our regulars at the Urban Ministry Drop-In Center were panhandlers. One day one of them was feeding bread crumbs to the pigeons at our center. The bakeries gave us leftover bread to feed to the homeless, and what the homeless folks didn't eat, they sometimes fed to the birds.

The panhandler turned to me and said, "Jim, ever notice that you never see baby pigeons?"

I answered him, "You know you are right. I have never seen a baby pigeon. Why is that, do you suppose?"

He answered, "It's because pigeons send their babies to panhandling school until they are adults."

We have something to learn from pigeons and panhandlers, even if we do store up in barns, even if we have more productive and socially-acceptable means of making a living. We could use a short course at panhandling school, and learn how to get by in life without so much anxiety. We would do well to learn how to be birdlike, to let our spirits soar today, instead of getting overwrought about tomorrow.

"Holy habits" are the cause of a lot of anxiety. These are patterns that don't really serve us any more, if they ever did at all. Ways of doing everyday life, or ways of running organizations that clutter and complicate matters. They are unhelpful or wasteful habits, but their very habitual nature makes them too "holy" to change. "Holy habits" burn us out with excessive processes and misplaced priorities. That's when it's time for a visit by the Holy Spirit, who comes in on a wing and a prayer and reminds us to lighten up and let go of every unholy thing to which we cling.

What are your anxieties? What does it take to release them?

Seeker, Teacher, Friend
by Jim Burklo
Tune: "Fairest Lord Jesus"
(Crusaders' Hymn: 5.6.8.5.5.8)

Seeker of justice, turner of the tables
One who made sure that the poor were fed
Land for the landless, home for the homeless
And baskets filled with fish and bread.

Friend of the friendless, lover of the enemy,
Love that conventions cannot contain,
Boundless compassion, put into action
For peace beyond all selfish aims.

Mystical teacher, lover of the Holy One
Faithful beyond any rites or creeds
One with creation, in adoration
Revealed in humble prayers and deeds.

Storm-riding mariner, death-defying leader
With you in courage we seek to stand
Stilling the waves of fear, through chilling winds we steer
Till on that peaceful shore we land.

Hearer of children, healer of the broken ones
Finder of truth in what some despise
Touch the untouchable, love the unlovable
Till finally we see through your eyes.

Breaker of holy bread, pourer of the sacred wine
Ours are the hands that will serve your feast,
This bread is food indeed, this wine is what we need
To let the Spirit be released.

Sanctuary

In our travels in Peru, my wife and I admired a number of churches. Several times during our trip, I found myself kneeling in Catholic sanctuaries in the centers of the towns, pausing for moments of prayerful silence. The churches were havens of calm amid the din of street vendors' bells, honking taxis, the nasal falsetto calls of 'combi' bus conductors, and the rumble of flatbed trucks spewing diesel fumes. For a few minutes I was liberated from our itinerary, transported to a place that was independent of any national identity, aware of a divine realm beyond boundaries.

Those precious interludes reminded me that for many tourists from all over the world, the church I served in Sausalito had the same effect. Our building was a welcome break from the traffic and the multi-lingual chatter and the crush of camera-toting pedestrians down the hill on the main road, Bridgeway Avenue. Into our house of worship they entered with a hush, savoring the quiet, absorbing the warm light streaming onto the pews from above. Into our sanctuary they brought the deep hope implanted in every human heart, yearning for transcendent meaning and purpose.

What a gift to be able to enter such sanctuaries, houses of prayer of many religions, as we travel. And what a blessing to find such spaces in our own hearts.

Because a physical sanctuary is an expression of the inner sanctuary of our souls. Christopher Alexander's seminal book on architecture, "A Pattern Language," devotes a section to houses of worship. He says that a key feature of a religious sanctuary is the entrance. He said that it should have dramatic, narrowing stages of entry into the front door, opening into an expanding area for worship, reflecting the soul's journey to self-realization. The process of entering the sanctuary has much to do with its spiritual impact. Perhaps this explains why I am so often deeply moved by entering churches when I travel. The very process of going to a faraway place adds greatly to the effect of walking up the steps and entering the sanctuary doors. It is a reflection of the long and sometimes arduous spiritual journeys I take within my soul, traveling long and hard to get past fear and guilt, climbing up the steep stairs of anger and resentment, pulling on the heavy handles of the tall doors of ignorance and rejection. And finally entering into the sacred space at the center of my being, where I meet God face to face, and feel the glow of divine, unconditional, forgiving, redeeming love.

We who pay for the upkeep of our church buildings, and maintain them with the labor of our own hands, will never know but a fraction of the ways and times that our sanctuaries have awakened consciousness of the sacred spaces in the hearts of so many perfect strangers. Our pledges of money, and gifts of time and effort, grace the souls of people we will never meet. People who pause for a moment to stand in front of a church and remember that they are more than bodies wrapped in clothes, see that there is a realm that no camera can capture, know that there is a time that their watches can't keep, and recall that they have a destination that will not appear in any travel brochure.

Whether we fly to the other side of the world, or just sit quietly in a chair in our own living rooms, our inner sanctuaries beckon us to enter. The ultimate journey leads to the place of silence and serenity within each of us: the sacred space that opens in every human heart.

Where in the outer world do you find sanctuary?
What is your inner sanctuary like?

Treasure in the Field

We stood on the dusty street at sunset, my wife, Roberta, her son Nick, and me. Up the hill rode a thin fellow on an elegant salt-and-pepper horse with fine silver-tipped wooden stirrups. He was on his way to another Peruvian town over the mountains to be a competitor in a horse exhibition. He was visiting a friend in the town of Chetilla. The friend urged the horseman, whose name was Erasmo, to give us a show of his skills.

Erasmo, a gaunt-faced man with unforgettably intense eyes, nodded at us gravely and proceeded to guide his steed through its stepping-horse paces, prancing precisely up and down the dirt road as puffs of dust diffused the rich light. Making tight turns, and then leading the horse into a nearby pasture, Erasmo masterfully rode as we followed. Dismounting, he made his horse rest its hooves one by one in his hands, then with gentle but firm coaxing to kneel on its front legs on the grass. He ordered it to roll over, rise, and then allow him to pass between its front and back legs. Then he mounted and in the pink-purple glow reflecting from the mountains looming beyond, he guided his high-stepping horse around the pasture again.

Erasmo's face burned with the beauty of man and horse moving as one. His seriousness of purpose was as magnificent as the animal through which he channeled it. I was awestruck as the world around him took on a hyper-reality, refracted through his passionate, one-pointed intention.

It was the awe that strikes whenever I am in the presence of one who is fully present where he is, fully engaged in what she does, fully invested in what he creates, fully absorbed by what she sees and hears, empty of distraction. This intense engagement is contagious, releasing me from all else, overwhelming me with wonder.

After hearty applause from the handful of us who watched him ride in that remote mountain village, Erasmo took his leave with a solemn bow and we went back to Nick's house in the gathering dark. The show had been unannounced. There had been no tickets to purchase. This may be the only review of the performance to find its way to print. Yet the three of us knew we had seen somebody, seen something, distinctly significant. Ordinary time had been suspended, replaced by a holy, eternal moment, as Erasmo rode before us on that grassy field.

Perhaps it was the field of which Jesus spoke in his enigmatic parable about the man who gave up everything to buy a field in which he had found treasure (Matthew 13: 44). Erasmo in his joy had given up all else for the treasure of that moment, guiding his stepping horse in the setting sunlight. He delivered to us, in a flash of hooves, the divine realm itself.

What do you do that completely absorbs you? What is divine about it?

The Last Word

There are a lot of ways to read the Bible. It's a good thing, because the book is so long, and so many parts of it are so incredibly tedious, that reading it straight through from beginning to end is not the most thrilling prospect for most of us. We need to find other ways to read it. And there are plenty of options.

I had the privilege of getting to know a computer science professor at Stanford, Don Knuth, who wrote a book called *3:16*. Each page consists of a beautifully drawn copy of chapter 3, verse 16 of each book in the Bible (or chapter 1, verse 13 of those with fewer chapters). He chose this way of reading the Bible because John 3:16 meant so much to him. ("For God so loved the world . . . ") Each page is done in calligraphy by a different artist who had contributed to his earlier work in creating the original computer codes for letter fonts.

His method is so typical of a computer scientist, always trying to find ways to compress data through algorithms. So I tried his approach myself, using other chapter and verse numbers. Especially intriguing was the result for chapter 9, verse 11 of all the books of the Bible. Some of them spoke in uncannily appropriate ways to that unforgettable event in American history.

Here I explore the last verses of the books of the Bible, as yet another algorithm for appreciating the gist of the scriptures. What can these "last words" tell us about the whole Bible, or at least about the whole books that they finish?

Hopefully, last words are potent words, words worth remembering. They are the ones most likely to stick with us when we are done reading or hearing something. Hopefully they in some way sum up the whole of what has been said or written, or at least point back to them in a powerful and memorable way.

Here is a sampler, and I invite you to read the rest.

> Genesis: "So Joseph died, being one hundred and ten years old: he was embalmed and placed in a coffin in Egypt."
>
> Joshua: "Eleazar son of Aaron died; and they buried him at Gibeah, the town of his son Phinehas, which had been given him in the hill country of Ephraim."
>
> I Samuel: "Then they took their bones and buried them under the tamarisk tree in Jabesh, and fasted for seven days."

These last words point to the great importance that the people of Israel put on the places where their patriarchs were buried. Their bones became a kind of down-payment on the land, establishing Israel's ownership of the land.

So it was important that the last words of these first books not only rounded out the stories of the patriarchs, but also identified the places where they were buried, like signatures on the deed of trust to the land of Israel.

> Job: "And Job died, old and full of days."

Full indeed were his days! Full of wealth and woe, pleasure and pain. Job experienced the fullness of life and its emptiness too. He felt the presence of God, the absence of God. He had all the answers, then all the questions, then all the awe and dumb-foundedness that comes from a confession of the mysteriousness of God. His days, and his story, were complete. But for us, the questions he asked about the nature of evil and the will of God are still as alive for us as they were for him.

> Ruth: "Obed of Jesse, and Jesse of David."

The story of Ruth ends with a genealogy of David, which is then taken up in the first chapter of Matthew. Matthew might be considered the sequel to the book of Ruth. Jesus, a stranger in his own land, a rabbi who opened up Judaism to Gentiles, was a descendant of Ruth, the Moabite woman, who was a stranger in Israel.

> Zechariah: "And there shall no longer be traders in the house of the Lord of hosts on that day."

Surely this prophecy, pointing to a time when the worship of God would transcend worship at the temple in Jerusalem, with its sacrificial animal sellers and money exchangers. Surely this passage was on the minds of the writers of the gospels when they told the story of Jesus turning the tables on the money changers at the temple. It ought to be on our minds, too, as so much of Christianity is sold out to political and corporate interests that would deny protection to the poor, and would concentrate wealth into the hands of the richest.

> 2 Chronicles: "Thus says Cyrus king of Persia, 'The Lord, the God of heaven, has given me all the kingdoms of the earth, and he has charged me to build him a house at Jerusalem, which is in Judah. Whoever is among you of all his people, may the Lord his God be with him! Let him go up.' "

> Esther: "For Mordecai the Jew was next in rank to King Ahasuerus, and he was powerful among the Jews and popular with his many kindred, for

he sought the good of his people and interceded for the welfare of all his descendants."

Ezekiel: "The circumference of the city shall be eighteen thousand cubits. And the name of the city from that time on shall be, The Lord is there."

Daniel: "But you, go your way, and rest; you shall rise for your reward at the end of the days."

Amos: "I will plant them upon their land, and they shall never again be plucked up out of the land which I have given them, says the Lord your God."

Zephaniah: "At that time I will bring you home, at the time when I gather you; I will make you renowned and praised among all the peoples of the earth, when I restore your fortunes before your eyes, says the Lord."

The people of Israel knew all about exile, all about losing home and yearning to return. So many of the books of the Old Testament end on this theme — of yearning to return, of returning, of the promise of restoration of their land and their people. And these last words speak for all of us who have lost home, lost family, lost our place in the world, and want to get it back. In this lonesome world, where so many are strangers in strange lands, immigrants and exiles, these last words still speak volumes for us and to us.

Matthew: "And remember, I am with you always, to the end of the age."

Mark: "And they went out and proclaimed the good news everywhere, while the Lord worked with them and confirmed the message by the signs that accompanied it."

Luke: "and they were continually in the temple blessing God."

John: "But there are also many other things that Jesus did: if every one of them were written down, I suppose that the world itself could not contain the books that would be written."

The four gospels end with arrows that point ahead into the future. There was more to come. These books were just previews, just preludes, to an unfolding story of the relationship of God and human beings. They remind us that history isn't over, that the gospel is still being written, that the scriptures point beyond themselves, into and through and beyond today.

Psalms: "Let everything that breathes praise the Lord! Praise the Lord!"

> 2 Corinthians: "The grace of the Lord Jesus Christ, the love of God and the communion of the Holy Spirit be with you all."

> I Peter: "Greet one another with a kiss of love. Peace to all of you who are in Christ."

> Jude: "Now to him who is able to keep you from falling, and to make you stand without blemish in the presence of his glory with rejoicing, to the only God our Savior, through Jesus Christ our Lord, be glory, majesty, power, and authority, before all time and now and forever. Amen."

> Revelation: "The grace of the Lord Jesus be with all the saints. Amen."

Some of these last lines are used at the end of Christian worship. They are blessings, prayers for the well-being of the bodies and souls of those who read them. There is plenty in the Bible that teaches us by negative example, plenty that is distasteful and inhumane. But so many of the last words of the Bible are praises and blessings, hopeful signs that rise above the un-evolved parts of the scriptures.

> Song of Solomon: "Make haste, my beloved, and be like a gazelle or a young stag upon the mountains of spices."

Take a deep breath, compose yourself after that one! You get the feeling that the Song of Solomon is just a teaser. Please, please, tell us what happens next on the "mountains of spices!"

> Lamentations: ". . . unless you have utterly rejected us, and are angry with us beyond measure."

> Jonah: "And should I not be concerned about Nineveh, that great city, in which there are more than a hundred and twenty thousand people who do not know their right hand from their left, and also many animals?"

The Bible doesn't have all the answers. Some of its books end with good questions. God's question at the end of the book of Jonah is one we all could pose. Sure, Nineveh was a city of sin, but didn't those folks deserve a break after all? Isn't grace for all: good or bad, smart or dumb, human or even cattle?

Can you think of an "algorithm" for reading the Bible that would give you a useful sample of its contents?

A Parable

The kingdom of heaven is like a bluegrass band playing in front of a huge store. Four old men in cowboy hats and bolo ties are playing *Foggy Mountain Breakdown* in the overhang by the entryway to the store. The men used to work together at a locally-owned hardware store that was put out of business by the big-box chain store. An open guitar case is on the cement in front of the folding chairs on which they sit. A few crumpled bills and coins litter the inside of the case. A crowd begins to gather around the musicians. The growing audience starts to block access to the shopping cart rack. The box-store security guard is dispatched to quell the disturbance and move the old guys along. But as the guard listens to the music, tears well up in her eyes. She remembers her uncles and aunts sitting on the front porch of her home town in eastern Kentucky, playing this same music while the she and the other kids kept time with fiddlesticks. "Play *Orange Blossom Special!*" she begs, and the old boys nod and tune up their banjos and fiddles. The crowd gets bigger, and misplaced shopping carts begin to block traffic in the driveway in front of the store.

How has your life been surprisingly interrupted by a manifestation of the kingdom of heaven on earth?

Seeds of Listening

Jesus told a parable (Matthew 13: 1-9) about seeds cast on different kinds of ground. Some grew, some didn't, some that grew did well, and others did not, depending on the ground upon which they fell. Jesus then said; listen, if you have ears to hear.

His story is about seeds. And the story is a seed. Because Jesus cast the story on his listeners, to see if it would take. Some will hear the words, but the words won't take root. Their ears work, but they really aren't listening. Others have ears, too, and hear the words, but not only do they hear, they also listen. The story goes down deep and takes root in their souls.

When I'm writing at my computer at home and my wife tells me something while I'm typing, I say, "Yes, honey, sure." And an hour later, when she asks me why I didn't do what I agreed to do, I have no idea what she is talking about. My ears worked, I went through the motions, I gave her feedback, but I wasn't really listening. She cast the seed on me, but it didn't take root because I was preoccupied. I was hearing her but not listening. She cast her seed on me, it sprouted, but its roots were shallow and it dried up quickly and blew away.

Seeds are mysterious, no matter how much you know about biology. Open up a seed and inside, at its center, is yet another "seed," a little dot called the apical meristem, which consists of stem cells. How do all the different structures of a plant emerge from the identical cells of the apical meristem? Which part of the apical meristem corresponds to which part of the mature flower or grain stalk or tree? Answer: it doesn't work that way. Each of the stem cells has the potential to multiply into all sorts of different kinds of cells in the mature plant, and the kind into which one particular cell multiplies depends on timing and triggers outside of itself. All this can be explained by biologists, at least up to a point. But it is still a true miracle that a tiny mustard seed, looking nothing like a mustard plant, can expand into all its mature shapes and structures.

Likewise there is a mystery about listening. You listen to somebody's story with your full attention, you let it go deep, you let it take root. You remember what you were told. But the result of your listening is often a surprise. It has one shape as it goes into you, it has quite another when it sprouts. You listen, but your interpretation of what you heard may amaze you both. You might find something in the other person's story that they didn't hear when they heard themselves telling it. You share what sprouts out of you, and the person may find insight in it. Or the person may find no ring of truth in what you feed back to them. If you really are listening, you take this seriously and ask the person to plant more of seeds in your soul, until they sprout and bear fruit for you both.

Sometimes we plant seeds we don't recognize. I've done that before, finding a sack of seeds in my garage and not knowing what they were. Are those seeds of purple hollyhocks, or white ones, or carmine ones? Let's just put them in the ground and find out. So it is with people who truly listen to each other. They help each other find out what is going on inside of them. They plant seeds in each other and see what sprouts and help each other identify what is growing within them. Often, we need the listening ears of others in order to understand ourselves.

For years I served as co-director of Camp Cazadero, a United Church of Christ camp for high school kids. I found myself with a group of them at the waterfall one hot afternoon. One girl started telling me about how the scene reminded her of a camping trip with her family. She went into great detail about the trip, on and on, and for a moment I was getting bored, but then I realized that if I listened longer and better, something really interesting might happen. After a while the nature of her story began to change. I realized she was telling this story because it helped her understand her whole life story in an important new way. This self-discovery happened with hardly any of my intervention or direction. All I did was listen.

As the apical meristem of the seed has no agenda but growth itself; its cells can take any form in the mature plant. So we are called to abandon our agendas when we serve others by listening. Somebody is sick, and you go to visit them. You want to give them advice about how to handle the problem: what cures to seek, what strategies they can use to keep up their spirits, what words you think they ought to hear from you in order to feel comforted. But it's very likely that they need none of this from you. It's much more likely that they need your willingness to listen, without a scripted reply, to what they say.

Listening is what happens when the words of others go deep enough into our souls to take root. Like soil must be broken and tilled to be ready for seeds, our souls must be broken open in order to make way for what others need to tell us.

When have you planted a seed by listening?

Revival!

(Imagine: a tent with a sawdust floor, old wooden folding chairs, a rough wooden podium, an altar rail at the front, a beat-up piano, a preacher who needs no microphone, and a congregation of hungering, thirsting souls.)

Brothers and sisters, it's time for revival! It's time to get saved! It's time to get prayed up! It's time to get some religion! Because I believe everyone here is looking for some kind of conversion.

How about you? You, who need to be saved from fear. Fear of death or sickness. Fear of losing a business. Fear of losing a friend. Fear of losing your good looks to the aging process. Fear for others who are dear to you, who look like they are in some kind of danger. Fear that takes over your life and holds you back from having fun, having close relationships with others, having a close relationship with God.

How about you? You, who need to be saved from anger. Anger at those who have wronged you. Anger at you for having made a big mistake, or even a small one that still feels big. Anger at God for putting you in an impossible situation.

How about you? You, who need to be saved from addiction. An overdependence that hurts you and others. Addiction to food, addiction to booze, addiction to drugs, to sex. Addiction to perfection. Addiction to work. Addiction to gambling or risk-taking.

How about you? You, who need to be saved from meaninglessness. From shallow relationships that are going nowhere. Shallow thinking that prevents you from spiritual and intellectual growth. Crass desires. Surface-level activities that fill your time and your life like Styrofoam. You need to be saved from a life without substance.

How about you? You, who need to be saved from sadness. Overwhelming unhappiness that feeds on itself. Unhappiness caused by being unhappy for too long. Sick and tired of being sick and tired. You need to be saved from the pits of depression.

How about you? You need to get saved from a bad attitude. You might have let a series of small hurts and little insults pile up in your soul until your mood is weighed down with bitterness.

How about you? You need to be saved from unhelpful religion. You might need to be saved from a kind of Christianity, or other faith, that claims superiority over all others, that isolates you from people who see things differently, that warps morality, that oppresses the body and soul. A religion that is a set of handcuffs, when what you need is a set of wings.

The altar is waiting. God is ready for you. Just come on up, sisters and brothers, and get down on your knees, as you are able, and wake up to the reality of God in your life.

You need to come on up to the rail and ask Jesus to come into your life and fill you with the Holy Spirit. Jesus tells a story of how a house was full of demons, and the demons got driven out. But since the owner of the house didn't fill up the house with the spirit of God, the demons came back and brought a bunch of their pals with them, and trashed the house even worse than before. Oh, you can quit the sinning, but that isn't enough. You've got to fill up your life with something better! You've got to fill it up with the spirit of compassion. The spirit of creativity. The spirit of friendship. The spirit of gratitude. Once you have tossed out all the clutter in your house, all the junk, then you need to fill your house with simple, beautiful things. You've got to fill it up with the spirit of God, who is love. How can you fill up your life with God? Jesus believed that everyone could experience God the way he did:

> *"I do not pray for these only, but also for those who believe in me through their word, that they may all be one; even as thou, Father, art in me, and I in thee, that they also may be in us, so that the world may believe that thou hast sent me. The glory which thou hast given me I have given to them, that they may be one even as we are one, I in them and thou in me, that they may become perfectly one." (John 17)*

Brothers and sisters, Jesus wanted all of us to have what he had! He wanted us all to be one with God, through acts of compassion toward others, through prayer and meditation, through contemplation. You can have what Jesus had! And what he had was older than Christianity or any other religion. He had the original, universal, old-time religion!

Old-Time Religion (an adaptation)

Give me that old time religion, give me that old time religion,
give me that old time religion, it's good enough for me

It was good enough for Noah, it was good enough for Miriam,
it was good enough for Moses, and it's good enough for me

It was good enough for Buddha, it was good enough for Jesus,
it was good enough for Mohammed, and it's good enough for me

It was good enough for Gandhi, it was good enough for Martin,
it was good enough for Teresa, and it's good enough for me

Give me that old time religion, give me that old time religion,
give me that old time religion, it's good enough for me

It was good enough for Jesus, it was good enough for Buddha, it was good enough for Native Americans, and it is good enough for me! You don't have to say the right words. You don't have to believe a certain dogma. You don't have to belong to one or another kind of religion in order to get that old-time religion. It's free. Come on up to the altar and receive it! Heaven is right here on earth, if you have eyes to see it and ears to hear it. The trumpet of welcome has already sounded, the gates of the heavenly kingdom are already open, anybody can enter any time, there's unlimited parking, the views are fantastic wherever you sit or stand. The kingdom of heaven is here, offering you salvation from meaninglessness, from anger and resentment, from shallow living, from materialism, from excessive ambition, from addiction. Write your name in the book of life, sign your name in the book of life, and when the roll is called up yonder, you'll be there.

Come on up to the altar rail, and dedicate your life to building heaven right here on earth. Dedicate yourself to building a new life for yourself and for others. Dedicate yourself to clearing out all the junk from your spiritual house, and to filling it up with the Holy Spirit.

So let us walk the road of Jesus from the dawn till setting sun. Let us talk of all his wondrous love and care. As we bring the peaceful kingdom of our God upon this earth, and the roll is called up yonder, we'll be there. It's roll call time, brothers and sisters. If you feel God calling your name right now, then come forward to the altar to kneel and pray and get a blessing, come for anointing with oil as a sign that you receive the salvation that Jesus offers you. Come forward if you want to get some real religion, the old-time religion of all the great saints of all the great religions of all time.

Let us pray:

Thank you, Jesus, for showing us the way to salvation, showing us the way to the pearly gates of heaven right here on earth, free and open all the time. Thank your for leading us to the clear, cool river that runs through the middle of the heavenly city, the river running with the water of life. Dear One, we accept your salvation! With thanks we take up your offer to fill the emptiness of our lives, with thanks we receive your guidance to change direction. Right now, by the power of your Holy Spirit, we are converted from the way of death to the way of joyful eternal life on earth. Oh, Dear One, with humble hearts we come before you in prayer, and with joy we invite you to live in our hearts forever!

Let the congregation say "Amen!" Let the congregation say "Hallelujah!" Let the congregation say, "Thank you Jesus!"

Let us close with the words of that old-time hymn:

One by one our seats will empty
One by one we'll go away
But no matter that we're parted
We will gather back one day.

From what do you need to be saved?
To what do you need to be converted?

Spiritual Spam

A Sunday school teacher recounted to me a conversation he had with our church's high school class about messages from God. They were discussing the story of Noah. They read God's detailed instructions, down to the nearest cubit, of how Noah was supposed to build the ark. Why don't people get such detailed messages from God these days, the kids wondered? One teenager named Sean suggested that today, with so many messages bombarding us from so many directions, "if somebody got a message from God, they might think it was 'spam' and ignore it!"

I meditated on Sean's wise words. Just how do we sort out divine messages from the "spam" in our heads, much less from the "spam" sent to us by others? It's an old problem that won't go away. Early Christianity had a very difficult time distinguishing meaningful expressions of divine Spirit from those which were not. There were lots of Christians who claimed to deliver messages from God, and there was no institutionalized means of determining whether these claims were valid or spurious. St. Paul himself devoted much ink to this vexing problem in his letters to the first churches.

Later, once it consolidated its centralized authority, the Catholic Church simply declared the era of direct divine inspiration to be over. Any message seeming to come from God that wasn't approved by Rome was "spam."

This worked up to a point. After all, there was plenty within the bounds of Catholic dogma that did have the ring of divine truth to it. The authority of the church consolidated and preserved the Bible with all its spiritual riches. The doctrines of the church had some basis in the practical religious experience of everyday people.

But when the late medieval Catholic hierarchy became so corrupt, so hypocritical, so at odds with its own stated purposes it began to smell more and more like a spam cannery; people began to install the spiritual protection software of the Protestant Reformation onto their religious hard-drives.

One such anti-spam program was called the Wesleyan Quadrilateral. John Wesley, founder of what we now know as the Methodist Church, said that the way to discern whether or not an inspiration was authentic was by comparing it to four "corners"— the teachings of Jesus, of his disciples, and of the Bible, and the experience of Christians over the millennia since the Bible was written. In its time, the "quadrilateral" was a very progressive idea. It injected democracy into faith. It left room for questioning the supposedly divine utterances of the church, to see if they "squared" with the good common sense and practical life-lessons of everyday people.

Wesley's "quadrilateral" remains a useful rule of thumb, which can be generalized to many situations. When something purporting to be spiritually significant comes my way, I do well to ask the following four questions: What do or would the people I admire most have to say about it? Does it square up with common sense? How does it compare with the gathered wisdom of the great spiritual teachers of the past? How does it fit in my own wider experience? Just one of these questions might not be enough to sort out the spam from the Spirit. But together they put up a helpful firewall letting in fresh files of true inspiration, and gently clicking and dragging the rest onto the "trash" icon.

When have you received, or sent, "spiritual spam?"

"Postal Customer - Local" Writes Back

I throw most of it away. It's junk mail bursting out of the box as if it had springs, as if it yearned to leap into my hands and grab my attention. I try to ignore it. But its contents somehow get into my consciousness through the unopened envelopes. I don't want to admit it, but I know my junk mail. And my junk mail knows me. It knows my name, address, socioeconomic status, educational level, interests, hobbies, and habits.

Since my junk mail seems to be so intimate with me, perhaps it deserves a personal response:

> Dear Junk Mail:
>
> I receive about a quarter-pound of you every day, six out of the seven days of the week. So it is about time that you got at least half an ounce from me.
>
> I want to thank you, however grudgingly, for your many lessons. You teach me about acceptance and forgiveness. I can recycle you, but you will be back tomorrow, just like my bad habits and unresolved grudges. Every day, I must ask for forgiveness for my same old debts, and I, in turn, must forgive the same old debtors. Thanks for reminding me!
>
> And you teach me self-reflection. You challenge my values, and make me decide, over and over again, whether or not I will be true to them. Your catalog companies purchase computer listings of my name and address and personal characteristics. So, every day, you confront me with myself. The loan sharks know my vulnerability to offers of credit. The mail-order clothes companies notice that I like earth-tones and natural fabrics. The magazine companies know my political and life-style preferences. If I want to know who the rest of the world thinks I am, I need only look at you when you tumble out of my mailbox every day. Then I can decide if the person named on your mailing stickers is the person I really want to be.
>
> I've had years to think as I have sorted through you, separating the wheat from the chaff, sorting out your come-ons and requests. Junk mail, here is my answer:
>
> No, I don't want a second mortgage on my house so that I can go on a cruise. I would rather take other kinds of risks, for other kinds of rewards. I'd rather take out a second mortgage on my ego. I'd rather risk losing my cool, and take the chance of crying and laughing a lot more.
>
> No, I don't want a new and different wardrobe. I don't want to look like somebody else. On the contrary, I need to learn to be willing to look

like myself! As time goes by, I'll need to accept my appearance even more than I am able to accept it today.

No, I don't want a free three-month subscription to all of your magazines. I don't want to know everything. Sure, I like to stay informed, and my curiosity is endless, but after having tried and failed to be a know-it-all, I have decided to let God be God. You can send God all your trial subscriptions!

No, I don't want all of your gadgets, appliances, mineral supplements, and beauty products. I have been blessed with material abundance, and now my greatest challenge is to consume less of just about everything. Give me my daily bread, I pray, but no more, because there is no room left in my garage to store anything else.

I do not want my tires replaced, my carpets cleaned, my kitchen cabinets refaced, or my unsightly body hair permanently removed today. One thing at a time, if you please. Thank you, junk mail, for so overwhelming me with the things I need to do that it becomes obvious that I cannot do them all at once. Don't call me; I'll call you.

As years pass, I get more of you. It seems you know me better all the time. Thank you, junk mail, for reminding me of who I am, and who I am not, as I carry you to the recycling bin, day after day.

Yours most sincerely,

Jim Burklo

What don't you want? And what does that list say about what you do want?

Open Source Religion

Linus Torvalds created a computer operating system called Linux. He wrote a system that's very flexible, easy to adapt and improve, and he gave it away for nothing. He's a hero in the world of computing, for busting the near-monopoly of Microsoft. Linux is "open source" software; anybody can use it, for free, as a basis for their computer applications.

Likewise, Christianity is an open source operating system. Many would disagree with me, but there is a way to practice the faith without claiming a monopoly on the truth. The Christian faith is free, available to anyone, whether or not they buy into a particular belief system about it. Nobody owns Christianity, and there is no need to get a license in order to use it. It's an open source to which we can make additions and from which we can make subtractions, for the sake of following the way of love.

Organized religion doesn't have to be based on rigid theology that claims a copyright on the truth. Christianity is one of many operating systems that offer the free gift of divine compassion. Linus gave us Linux, and Jesus freely gave us his love. In order to know and share that love, we don't have to accept the whole package that evangelical Christianity defines as the faith.

The Bible's many books were never intended by their authors to exist under one cover. Contrary to the conservative claim that the faith is immutable, Christians have been picking and choosing which parts to take seriously, and which ones to ignore or downplay, from day one. By reclaiming this freedom to interpret the Bible and Christian tradition, we do for our faith what Linus Torvalds did for computer programming.

Ten Things In the Bible That Make Sense:

1. God's name is "I AM" (Exodus 3: 14)
2. The Ten Commandments (Deuteronomy 5: 7-21)
3. Loyalty and friendship (Ruth 1: 16-8)
4. Awe (Job 37: 14-24)
5. Humility (Psalm 8: 3,4)
6. Justice (Micah 6:8)
7. Love God and neighbor (Mark 12: 30, 31)
8. Love your enemies (Matthew 5: 43, 44)
9. Hope (Romans 8: 18-25)
10. Love, joy, peace, patience, kindness (Galatians 5: 22)

Ten Things In the Bible That Don't Make Sense:

1. God only loves Jews (Psalm 33: 10-12)
2. Gays should be stoned to death (Leviticus 20:13)
3. Women are men's property (Deuteronomy 20: 14)
4. Slavery is OK (Exodus 21: 7)

5. The world was created literally in six days (Genesis 1: 31)
6. God literally sent a flood to destroy the world (Genesis 6: 17)
7. Non-Christians will go to hell (Hebrews 10: 29)
8. We are depraved sinners who can be saved from hell only by believing that God arranged for his son to be brutally murdered in our place (John 3: 16)
9. Women should be seen and not heard (I Corinthians 14: 34)
10. It is best never to have sex at all (I Corinthians 7: 1)

What are your lists of things that make sense, or don't make sense, in Christian tradition?

Tanking and Tuning Up

They were eager to get them. One winter's day, during the free lunch we offered to the community at our church once a week, Gloria, one of our church members, handed out small tanks of propane. Our diners were delighted and grateful. Many of them were either homeless or are living on semi-seaworthy boats that are anchored-out in Richardson Bay. Cooking could be challenging in such circumstances. Our church's deacons bought a supply of small propane stoves which we had distributed earlier. On this day, Gloria offered refills for those who needed more gas.

I've heard people say they come to church on Sunday to recharge their spiritual batteries. But there was no doubt that people left the church that Wednesday with full tanks! There was even more power available in the church than I had presumed.

But the church isn't just about filling us up when our spiritual energy is depleted. It's a place where we can tune-up our souls so we'll be more energy-efficient. When we learn to practice compassion and patience in challenging circumstances, we aren't as spiritually drained as we would be otherwise. When we forgive ourselves and others, we save a lot of emotional energy that was wasted on resentment. When we return evil with kindness, we save all that power we would have wasted on the endless spiral of spite. When we calmly pause before responding to the difficult words of others, we save a force that we would have wasted by being verbally reactive.

Just as much of our nation's energy shortage could be met by conservation, our spiritual tanks will stay fuller longer if we don't waste our fuel on anger, repressed feelings, hidden expectations, gossip, and back-biting. The energy saved can be used for positive purposes.

We come to church to top off our tanks, but also to tune our souls to run smoothly and cleanly. We come here for adjustments so that our reserves won't drain nearly so fast, so that we'll have even more energy to spare and share with others who need it.

The Ten Amendments

The Ten Commandments endure as a foundation for morality, after thousands of years. But just like the American Constitution, from time to time we need to add amendments to them. The Ten Commandments are a short list, and that is a very good thing. They mostly tell us what not to do, giving us the freedom to do most everything else. But not everything else is so wonderful. In every time, in every life, we need to make additional lists for spiritual and moral guidance. Things we need to do, or to avoid, to amend our lives and mend our relationships. Here I offer my personal list of such amendments, my own ethical "marching orders":

1. *Thou shalt be amazed by the good in people.*
2. *Thou shalt avoid judgment of others.*
3. *Thou shalt not injure others with sarcasm.*
4. *Thou shalt not jump to conclusions.*
5. *Thou shalt attend to details in serving others.*
6. *Thou shalt make realistic promises and keep them.*
7. *Thou shalt have clear priorities for thy time and attention, for thy body, mind, and heart, and thou shalt act on these priorities.*
8. *Thou shalt wait 24 hours before doing or saying anything negative about another person.*
9. *Thou shalt not say "yes" when thou meanest "no."*
10. *Thou shalt ask before acting.*

Each one of these amendments reflects my own failure to follow it! The list reflects the ways my life needs to change for the better, in outward actions and inward intentions.

What's *your* list of ten amendments?

The Gravity of the Situation

Over the years, I have served churches that buck the current national trend toward dogma-based rather than fact-based science. I've ministered in churches that see no contradiction, for example, between our religion and the theory of gravity. When I worked in Sausalito, I was in a place where the law of gravity is particularly hard to deny. The town consists mostly of steep hillsides that plunge into the Bay. I got my aerobic exercise just walking from the center of town to the church, all of a breathless block away, up a steep set of stairs. One false move and I could accelerate downhill, tumbling head over heels, all the way below the Inn Above Tide. The gravity of the situation put real meaning into the "down" part of downtown Sausalito.

It's not a subject taken lightly in that town, magnet that it is for civil engineers who devise ways to dangle houses and carports from lots that have five times the vertical square-footage of the horizontal. Likewise, the church was founded on more than a solid faith in the spiritual realm. Have a look in the basement at the chunky concrete footer that was poured into the mountainside, to hold up the pretty pile of wood in which we worshipped! Isaac Newton's theory is proven daily in Sausalito. If that fateful apple had dropped on his head there, it would have bounced and kept rolling until it was applesauce floating in the Bay. And by the way, from the front door of the church to the pulpit, it's all downhill. There's a pitch to the floor in that sanctuary.

While honoring the hard science, the softer metaphorical possibilities of that vertiginous town invite us to meditate on deeper things. Sausalito is a good place to ponder this question: what keeps us grounded, and how? Because in this heady age when so much of our lives, and so much even of our economy, are consumed with words, images, and sounds, it is easy to get lost in the ethereal and forget the basics. Gravity is a good thing. It grounds our bodies. Without it, we would float away from the things we need and want, and it would get tough even to brush our teeth. (Just how do the astronauts do it?) Being spiritually grounded is a good thing, too. Maintaining carefully our most important relationships. Having plenty of face-to-face, unstructured time with friends and relatives. Taking plenty of time to cook and eat good meals with others (ever heard of the "slow food" movement?) Enjoying the low-tech exercise of walking to the store or doing a bit of gardening. Going to church and spending prayerful time with other struggling souls of all wages and ages. Blooming where we are planted, being in the here and now, instead of constantly focusing on where we're going or what we are doing next. Doing what we can to make our local communities better places to live for everyone.

The very loftiness of Sausalito brings to mind the dire consequences of not staying centered. Just as residents know to turn the front wheels of our cars toward the curb when they park, we know, in the heart of our hearts, that we need to ground ourselves in community with each other, lest we roll out of control, heady with the flighty passions and pressures of this world. As the church's steeple can't pierce the sky without the massive foundation hidden below to hold it up, so our souls cannot rise to their highest potential unless we are kept down-to-earth through fellowship with each other. As objects are attracted to each other in space, may we be attracted to each other in church, to keep ourselves grounded, body and soul.

What keeps you grounded and centered?

Traffic School for the Soul

My stepdaughter lives in Hollywood. One year, her birthday party was held at a bowling alley. We drove down to join in the fun. One of the partygoers was her hairdresser, a French fellow with spiky hair. Maurice was a very charming fellow who bowled in the oddest way. He'd scamper up to the line with the ball under his nose, stop, awkwardly drop it down, swing it and release it. Voila! A strike!

Between rounds of bowling, voila! the subject turned to religion when he found out I was a minister. He said "You know, driving is dangerous, no? So we make people get the driver's license. But the soul is dangerous, too, no? So that is why we have the religion. Religion is a driver's license for the soul."

I had forgotten his brilliant aphorism until I was sitting for eight hours taking driving school in a hotel ballroom. The teacher was a woman with a powerful voice, and had I known this I would have chosen to sit somewhere beside the first row. Had I known, I also would have avoided the Irish guy with cigarette breath who was sitting next to me, whispering bad jokes which only got worse when, voila! He, too, found out that I was a minister. I swear on a stack of New Revised Standard Version Bibles that I'll never go 45 in a 35 mile an hour zone, at least in Marin County, ever again.

The class was torturous, but about midway through, I finally came up with a way to redeem the experience. There's a sermon in this, I thought to myself: Traffic School for the Soul.

Maurice, the French hairdresser, had it right: The soul is dangerous if we are unconscious of its drives, or if we try to satisfy its urges in destructive ways. We are so often unaware of the power of the soul, its capacity for both positive and negative influence over us and others. We act like we don't even have souls, much of the time. We act like we have no inner life at all. Meanwhile within us our souls are seething and humming and steering us in directions we don't even know we're going till it's too late and - crash! Our relationships have fallen apart, our habits have morphed into addictions, our attitudes are making us miserable, our bodies have turned from temples into trashcans. Or worse!

We forget we have souls. Just like we forget we're driving our cars. We're unconscious of our driving because we're so busy talking on cell phones, using the rear-view mirror to put on makeup, eating McFood out of the bag stuffed in between the front seats. We forget our souls, lose awareness of how much substance and power are in our souls. Just like we forget we're driving these quarter-ton chunks of iron hurtling down asphalt roads at high speed, because we're so preoccupied with everything else. That's why we need Traffic School for the Soul.

It helps to know the basic metaphysics of the soul. If something is in your path, you need to see it in time to be able to stop. In a car, assuming you have good tires, good brakes, and dry pavement, at 55 mph it takes about 400 feet to react to something you see and to bring the car to a complete stop. At 35 mph, it will take about 210 feet to react and to bring the car to a complete stop. The force of a 60 mph crash isn't just twice as great as at 30 mph, it's four times as great! Likewise, the soul has a lot of momentum. Once it gets going in a certain direction, it tends to keep going that way. So if you get angry, you'll tend to stay angry longer than it does you any good. If you get sad, sometimes you'll stay sad indefinitely. You have to leave your soul plenty of room to adjust to the events that shock it. You have to compensate for your soul's momentum by taking long walks when you get mad, by giving yourself plenty of time to grieve when you lose a lover or friend, all the while listening to your soul and gently offering it alternatives. You need to give your soul plenty of time and space. If you overbook your life, packing it with activities all the time, end to end, bumper to bumper, your soul will have no room to adjust to the things that can collide with it.

Think of all the rear-enders you've done on others, because you weren't conscious of your soul's power and momentum. You snap at your mate in anger when he or she misplaces your shoes, an innocent mistake, but your anger isn't about your mate at all. It's about your frustration with your job, but since you weren't listening to your soul, weren't watching the road it was hurtling down, you crashed right into your mate. Most rear end accidents are caused by tailgating. To avoid this in a car, you use the "three-second rule." When the vehicle ahead of you passes a certain point, such as a sign, count "one-thousand-one, one-thousand-two, one-thousand-three." This takes about three seconds. If you pass the same point before you finish counting, you are following too closely.

Same idea for the soul, except it takes at least three minutes. When I counsel couples in preparation for marriage, I sometimes give them three-minute sand timers. I tell them that if one of them gets mad at their mate about something, they should take the timer and turn it upside down. That person gets the floor without interruption for three minutes. Then the mate gets to turn the glass upside down and say whatever he or she needs to say until it runs out of sand. It is a very effective way to stop bickering and start listening. The timer prevents spiritual tailgating!

We spend a lot of energy trying to get ahead. To be ahead of others in accomplishment, wealth, appearance, intelligence. Trouble is that a lot of others around us are trying to get ahead at the same time. And this is the main cause of spiritual head-on collisions. In a car at 55 mph, you will travel over 800 feet in 10 to 12 seconds. So will an oncoming vehicle. That means you need over 1600 feet (or about one-third of a mile) to pass safely. It is hard to judge the speed of oncoming vehicles one-third of a mile away. They don't seem to be coming as fast as they really are. Very often we act not only as if we don't have souls, but we act as if others don't have souls, either. We expect others to act like machines run by logical computers, when in fact they are run by messy, complex, sensitive, easily excited souls just like our own. We are in denial about the fact that their emotions and passions might be headed right at us at full speed and that if we don't handle ourselves skillfully we will crash right into them. We need to handle the souls of others with the same kind of gentle caution and sensitivity our own souls need.

Some people act as if Jesus was an airbag. You know, you have a head-on collision and the bag instantly pops out of the steering wheel and keeps your head from going through the windshield. Some people act as if this is what Jesus is all about: to save us when we do dumb things. They believe humans are hopeless screw-ups and Jesus died on the cross to make up for their foolishness. I offer another understanding of Jesus and the cross. The cross is something we make, and on which we crucify ourselves all the time. We crucify ourselves in traffic regularly. But Jesus didn't die on the cross to save us from the consequences of bad driving. Rather, the Jesus story awakens us to ways of driving better and preventing accidents. Jesus is not an airbag. He's our spiritual driving coach.

Blind spots: we all have them. There are two triangles on either side of your car that are not visible to you when your head is aimed toward the front of your car, not visible through your side mirrors. It is your fault if somebody or something is in your blind spot and you make a move that results in an accident. Turn your head and scan before you make your move in a blind spot area.

Of course our souls have even more blind spots. They say hindsight is 20-20, but let's get real! Even our hindsight is full of blind spots. The soul has unspeakably detailed vision of some things: awesome insight and vision. But in other areas it's completely in the dark. For instance, my soul is pretty attuned to group dynamics and to the nuances of how communities and social institutions work. I have good spiritual eyesight that enables me to be useful in community and organizational leadership. And I am sometimes pretty insightful as a pastoral counselor with individuals. But sometimes, with the people closest to me, I'm clueless. I tend to forget that, just because they are close to me, that doesn't mean they think like I do. When I miss something important going on in the souls of the people dearest to me, I sometimes say, glibly, "Oh well. It was in my blind spot." But that's no excuse. I could ask for help from others who have more insight than I do. If in your mirrors you can't see an area behind you where a car might be advancing, you have to turn your head and look. If you don't have immediate, obvious insight into a certain relationship, you have to find some other way of getting it.

Traffic School for the Soul is, more than anything else, about non-violence. It's about not returning evil for evil. When you are driving a car, never insist on taking the right-of-way. If another driver does not yield to you when he or she should, forget it. Let the other driver go first. You will help prevent accidents and make driving more pleasant. No different with the soul. If people do you wrong, Jesus has plenty of advice for you in the Sermon on the Mount, Matthew 5 and 6, where he says "love your enemies and pray for those who persecute you."

When you are driving a car, you quickly learn that you have to accept and adjust to the outrageousness of others, or you will wake up surrounded by twisted metal. Somebody just jetted out in front of you in an intersection when it was your turn to go? Oh well. Time to love that person and pray for them, because they're headed for Traffic School at best, or the hospital at worst. Life is not fair. The road is not fair. There are fair traffic laws, but if somebody else disobeys them, you still have to adjust to their bad behavior. All the rules of the road are trumped by a higher rule, the rule of good common sense and survival. The California Vehicle Code says, in many places and many ways, that safety IS the law. If the legal speed limit is 65, but a stake-bed truck loses its stakes and dumps a hundred thousand avocados on the road, suddenly the speed limit is no longer 65. It's whatever speed is safe to travel when the road is covered with guacamole. And if you go faster than what is safe, you've broken the law and can be ticketed and wind up in a hotel ballroom for eight hours of Traffic School listening to the big loud lady and sitting next to the Irish guy who smokes five packs a day and loves to whisper dirty jokes about priests and rabbis to you. This is pretty much what Jesus taught: there are all sorts of moral codes and rules in society and religion but all of them are trumped by the Law of Love. See somebody hungry on the Sabbath, and have the means to feed them, even though the Jewish law says you can't? Oh well. The Law of Love says you can feed them, and should feed them, anyway. The soul needs love more than anything else. The soul cannot live by following rules all the time. If a rule or a religious doctrine or dogma gets in the way of Love, then Love trumps that rule or doctrine or dogma every time.

So the last lesson of Traffic School for The Soul, while you are at the wheel of your life, is to hang loose and be guided by Love. Be a birdlike and barnless driver. If you are in too big a hurry to get where you are going, you won't make it. Jesus said "which of you by being anxious can add one cubit to his span of life?" And, we might add, which of us by being anxious can get where we're going in any better style than if we are patient and compassionate and forgiving?

What's your spiritual driving record? And how can you improve it?

Wishful Thinking

As I look back over my life, I feel a certain embarrassment at how often I've been wishful but faithless. Wishing I was omnipotent, I would take on projects I could never complete. I lacked the faith that if I worked hard while being realistic, I could accomplish more in the end. Wishfully I put on a happy face, denied disasters that surrounded me, and plowed ahead as if they weren't there. I lacked the faith that if I admitted defeat, grieved my losses, learned from my mistakes, and changed direction, it would have been better for myself and others.

At least I'm in good company. Is it any wonder that we avoid facing the chaotic, unpredictable, and unfair facts of life? We want to think that prayer or positive thoughts can magically fix anything that is wrong around us. We want to think that a loving God will supernaturally intervene in the soupy mess of the universe and make things good for us, if we just ask him or her in the right way. But even Jesus had to learn otherwise, and learn it the hard way. On the cross, he complained, "My God, my God, why have you forsaken me?" (Matthew 27:46) It wasn't fair. He'd lived a good life, prayed hard and well, shown compassion to others. Others were praying for him, too, asking God to step in and spare him. Jesus, like the rest of us, suffered from a surfeit of wishful thinking and a deficit of faith.

But on the cross, pie-in-the-sky religion died. And on the cross, the God of faith came alive.

Faith looks at reality with clear eyes, respects it for what it is, and chooses to live hopefully and compassionately anyway. Faith bases itself on facts, and then works hard to change them, even if the odds are against success. Faith doesn't expect miracles. But it gives us energy and perseverance to do the miraculous.

Faith is what happens when we stop pretending that we are entitled to divine exceptions from the laws of nature. Faith doesn't exempt us from the pain of this world, but it does give us an experience that transcends it and gives it meaning. Faith is the paradox of knowing our mortality and our immortality at the same time. Faith embraces the contradiction that we are separate, limited creatures and we are also one with God.

What ideas about God have you had to abandon?
What understandings of God replaced them?

Carrying On

Security at the airport got tighter. No longer can we carry on full bottles of shampoo. Nor full tubes of toothpaste.

Nor can we carry on protection from bombs or mayhem on airplanes, trains, or anywhere else. The US military, strongest in the world, armed with the most, and the most ingenious, weapons on the planet, can't protect us from a handful of determined people with mass-murderous intent and some box-cutters or nail polish remover and peroxide.

The likelihood of horrific terrorist incidents grows with each passing day. Airport security is an oxymoron, even at the highest state of alert. An open society, dependent on a torrent of commerce and travel and communication, cannot possibly interdict all the clever, persistent plotting of mass killers.

Yet we must carry on anyway. Otherwise, the terrorists get what they want, whether or not a lot of people die. We must carry on, or our souls will be held hostage to fear.

We must carry on with freedom, even though it's risky to defend the rule of law, to defend checks and balances against government power. We must carry on with pluralism, even though some people want to hijack religion and sow sectarian hatred. We must carry on with compassion, even though these are times that tempt us toward revenge.

We must carry on with a desire to understand deeply the motivations of those who want to destroy us. We must carry on with curiosity, with a genuine desire to comprehend points of view that seem utterly strange to us. We must carry on with empathy, even toward those who seem most repugnant. We must work harder to find common ground, to create means of dialogue, to give people all over the world more reasons to cooperate despite their differences.

We must carry on with faithful living, behaving as if life will go on, as if creativity will prevail, as if kindness will continue no matter what befalls us. We must be prepared spiritually for a long period of horrible events that will test our souls. We must train ourselves to be patient and forbearing, to resist the powerful urge to mimic the behavior of the people who aim to ruin us. We must show them a better way by our actions and attitudes, our words and deeds. They claim moral superiority with their willingness to die for causes they deem noble. The rest of us must occupy a yet higher moral ground, one to which terrorist sympathizers might aspire and thus turn from their bloody aims.

Tens of terrorists can kill thousands of civilians. Thousands of terrorists may kill millions of civilians. We'll want to even the score, even if most of our victims would turn out also to be innocent civilians. That would only recruit more people for the terrorists, and that is exactly what they want. So we must exercise an almost unimaginable restraint if we are to prevail in the long term. We must be willing to endure terrible losses without reacting in an ultimately counterproductive manner. We must be bigger, we must be better, than the rage we will feel each time these awful events occur. We cannot survive this challenge unless we create a far more spiritually advanced society than the one we live in today. Yes, we need a strong military and good police forces. But it is not a mere platitude to say that our best defenses will be purity of heart, clarity of conscience, and refinement of compassion. We must create a more just and caring society that is more worthy of preserving.

No matter what happens, we must carry on with joy, with reverence, with friendship, with community, with family, with creativity and with scientific advance. We must invest our hearts and our substance in things that will last longer than the long, painful struggle that lies ahead of us. Our nation and world is likely to suffer incidents of dreadful destruction in the near future. But we are called to carry on as if civilization is going to improve and flourish in the long term, because that is the only way it ever will.

How can you help to create a more spiritually advanced society?

Queries

The Quakers are small in number. There are but a few hundred thousand of them in this country. Worshipping in silence goes a long way toward maintaining their low profile in the public eye. But we could learn much if we listened to their still, small voices.

Today, most people associate Christianity with the loud pronouncements of the religious right. Most people, whether Christian or not, associate Christianity with belief in the literal factuality of the Bible, with belief that all other religions are inferior to Christianity, with opposition to abortion rights, with opposition to acceptance of gay and lesbian sexuality, with support for untrammeled capitalism, with unquestioned support for the state of Israel, and with male-dominated family life. These associations are the consequence of well-orchestrated campaigns in the secular as well as conservative Christian media to repeat slogans and statements that define the faith in a certain way, over and over again, associating it with a particular political agenda.

But Quakers have been allergic to such slogans and pronouncements for a very long time. Hundreds of years ago, the Quakers chose to ask questions instead of trumpeting positions. They called them "queries." Their regional assemblies would carefully refine these queries and pose them to the membership of their local Meeting Houses. They would keep asking themselves these queries or questions until, by consensus, they determined that it was time to ask different questions. The queries covered the gamut of personal spiritual practice, the conduct of silent Meetings, and social and moral issues. The queries activated the consciences of the individual Quaker and of the Community of Friends. They didn't result in any final dogma or doctrines, any answers that are binding forever.

What would happen if faithful people began to ask questions instead of arguing with answers they don't like? What would happen if we followed St. Paul's advice and stopped returning evil for evil? What would happen if we asked serious questions instead of behaving defensively in response to religious bombast?

I believe that asking good questions can change the world. I spent about a decade as the Protestant campus minister at Stanford. In that role, I was repeatedly impressed by the effect that students' questions had on me and on others. I led many field trips and events that put them in contact with policy makers and officials. The sincere, intelligent questions of students often embarrassed people in power, challenging them to rise to a new level of accountability and responsibility. When students asked questions, instead of making pronouncements, people in positions of power took them seriously, and were sometimes disturbed enough by the questions to seek new perspectives.

What questions could change the world for the better? Which ones transform anger into shared inquiry with those who take the "other side" on important issues?

What kinds of questions invite the calmest, friendliest, most constructive conversations with people who see the world differently?

Spiritual S.A.T. Question

man :: moon
?:: earth

Visionary Religion

Most of us do not go to a church or a temple in order to get a medical diagnosis for an illness. We don't go to the minister, rabbi, or priest to get advice about investments that will give a good return. We don't expect the church to explain in detail how to reform the educational system in America.

But religion can give us vision. It can help us see, with the eyes of the soul, a healthy and abundant life for ourselves and a just and peaceful society for all.

It can help us imagine a glorious future, and with faithful imagination we are inspired and energized to make it real.

I don't advise turning to the Bible for specifics about how to live. Even the last of its books and letters were written nearly 2000 years ago, in a world dramatically different from our own. In Paul's letter to the Colossians, 3:22, he said "Slaves, obey your earthly masters in everything." Yes, the Bible supports the institution of slavery, something unthinkable today. That's the bad news.

But the good news is that a few sentences later, Paul said "Masters, treat your slaves justly and fairly, for you know that you also have a Master in heaven." Written into the scriptures, in hundreds of such scattered lines, there is vision and there is hope pointing beyond the times in which they were written. Paul condoned slavery, since it was a socially acceptable thing at the time, but he also pointed beyond it to a future where justice and fairness would prevail, to a time when there would be no discrimination between Jew or Greek, slave or free, male or female (Galatians 3: 28).

In hindsight, I can read St. Paul and be full of righteous indignation that he could have condoned slavery at all, despite his admonition to treat slaves "justly and fairly." But there will be a day in the future when people will look back at us today, and say, "How could they have accepted, even for a moment, that tens of millions of Americans had no health insurance?" There will be a day in the future when people look back at us today and say, "How could they have imagined accepting such gross economic injustice, with the rich getting so much richer as poverty grew and the middle class shrank?"

Christianity won't tell us the cure for cancer. Christianity won't tell us how to set up a health care system that effectively and economically covers everyone. Christianity won't tell us exactly how to achieve a more civilized distribution of wealth and opportunity. Faith is often lacking in specifics, but it is rich with vision: it points beyond this present moment and toward a better and brighter world. Faith activates our imaginations, so that we can envision a future, and then work to fill in its details.

Jesus' first act, after his baptism and temptation, was to go into a synagogue and read aloud to the congregation some passages from the book of Isaiah: "The Spirit of the Lord is upon me, because he has anointed me to bring good news to the poor. He has sent me to proclaim release to the captives and recovery of sight to the blind, to let the oppressed go free, to proclaim the year of the Lord's favor." (Luke 4: 16-30) Isaiah pointed to a time beyond his own, offered a vision of a better future. Jesus continued: "Today this scripture has been fulfilled in your hearing." Jesus aimed to bring Isaiah's vision into reality, there and then. And today we can aim to make Jesus' vision real, here and now. And we can offer visions of our own, visions of a world with more justice, greater peace, and better health than we have now.

What is your vision of a just and peaceful society?
How is that vision informed by your faith?

Principalities and Powers

On television, on the radio, on the internet, in the papers, political polls are about the analysis of numbers. Precinct by precinct, county by county surveys. How many people will vote on the issues, how many will vote on their tastes? There is so much cold calculation, so much cynicism applied with such precision to manipulate voters and steer electoral outcomes.

That's how it looks through the lens of the media and political consultants. Then there is the view of an election as seen through the eyes of the heart.

With the eyes of the soul we can see what St. Paul saw in Ephesians 6:12: "For our struggle is not against enemies of blood and flesh, but against the rulers, against the authorities, against the cosmic powers of this present darkness." The eyes of the soul see that we contend with invisible forces in politics that are more potent than individual politicians or voters.

The real contention is with the power of fear. It's with the principality of vengeance. It's with the power of anger. It's with the principality of greed. It's with narrow-mindedness masquerading as morality. It's with chauvinism posing as true religion. It's with nostalgia for a glorious past that never was. It's with addiction to violence as the solution of first rather than last resort. It's with blindness to possibilities for promoting the greater common good. It's with shallowness that focuses on style more than substance.

Let us cling to a faith that shows us that no candidate can nullify the law of love. Let us cling to our vision of justice, which can't be bought off by rich special interests. Let us cling to our vision of peace, which can't be obscured by fear-mongering television ads. Let us cling to our vision of compassion, which can't be stopped with smear campaigns. Let us cling to our hope, which no politician can cut from the budget of the soul.

With love, with patience, with perseverance, without malice, without bitterness, let us name the powers with which we really contend.

What larger forces touch your life?
How do they touch the lives of people around you?

Meditations and Celebrations for the Sacred Seasons

ALL SAINTS' DAY

"Therefore, since we are surrounded by so great a cloud of witnesses, let us also lay aside every weight and the sin that clings so closely, and let us run with perseverance the race that is set before us . . ." (Hebrews 12:1

When my daughter was about 4 years old, she was sitting on her great-grandmother's lap one day. Nanie was about 85 years old and her face was a globe of happy wrinkles. Liz was poking around on her great-grandmother's face. And then, while pointing at a certain spot among the wrinkles, my daughter said: "We live riiiight here!" Fortunately, Nanie thought it was funny. Her wide smile spread on her face.

Nanie died when she was old and full of years, as the Bible said of the patriarchs and matriarchs. She lived long and well. And was blessed with that unforgettable smile until days before she died. A smile made unforgettable to me, because my daughter inherited it from her. A striking similarity, a distinctive grin, passed down a few generations.

We are surrounded, as the Bible says, with a cloud of witnesses, so many saints that have gone before us, from whom we've inherited so much. My daughter oriented herself with her great-grandma's face. She found her place in the world by poking around in her Nanie's wrinkles. Our saintly ancestors do just that for us; their memory orients us, gives us a sense of our place in the sweep of history. A history that isn't over with us, much as we might be in denial of the fact that one day, we'll join that cloud of saintly witnesses.

Sometimes I wonder at my own strong impulse to make myself memorable. To do things that will last beyond my mortal frame, to claim some fame that will outlast my body. When my first book was published, I had an especially happy moment when I went to my favorite independent bookstore, and found my book on a shelf in the religion section. That felt really, really good. Like there would be something that indeed could immortalize me, or at least less-mortalize me! It felt good for a few minutes, until I got bored by staring at my book in the bookstore rack. Until I started looking at other books, and considered that there were at least 10,000 books in the bookstore, and only one of them was mine. And the bookstore had but a tiny fraction of the books in print. Mine was but a miniscule speck of moisture in the fogbank of books in the world. Suddenly I felt mortal again. Immortality was nice while it lasted.

Jesus was said to have healed people miraculously. But if having the secret to immortality was the punch line of his story, what about the fact that all those folks are now dead? Including Lazarus, raised from the grave? There's got to be more to the story than the miracles themselves. I think the plot is about how death is a sub-plot of life, and how life is not a sub-plot of death. That my daughter's great grandmother died full of years, and her smile is very much alive and well on my daughter's face today. That the everyday kindnesses of forgotten people hundreds of years ago, including those with no physical offspring, those unsung acts of goodness created and maintained a civilization which you and I have inherited, a pattern of common decency that we barely notice until an unusual breach of it occurs. Those individuals are gone and their separate, distinct identities have faded into the cloud of witnesses. But they call us to account, inspire us to kindness and caring every day. The saints who have gone before are witnesses to the good news that life puts death in its place.

This is a day for all saints, a day to re-orient ourselves by remembering our ancestors, as well as the gifts we've inherited from those whose names are forgotten.

ELECTION DAY

Biblical Voters' Guide

The Bible won't tell you how to vote! Because the sacred right of interpretation of the Bible is ours. It is up to us as individuals to find the meanings and values in the text, and apply them as we choose. Each of us has the God-given authority to find the Word for ourselves among all the words in the Bible. We are heirs to a strong tradition that claims that individual lay people, not ministers or bishops, have the last word on matters of faith. As a result, there is always more wisdom to be found in the scriptures, as you and I find it and share it with each other. John Robinson, pastor to the Pilgrims, said to his people as they departed for the New World in 1620: "For he (Christ) was very confident the Lord had more truth and light yet to break forth out of his holy Word."

That attitude found further expression in American politics. Robinson's words are not only a foundation for religious freedom — they are also a foundation for democracy. As there is no last word in religion, neither is there a last word in politics. At every election, there is always a possibility for more light to break forth. It's up to each voter to seek it out.

So I offer to you a biblical voters' guide, not to tell you what the Bible says to do in the voting booth—only you can sort that out—but to offer some scripture passages that may give us direction:

Isaiah 1: 17:

. . . seek justice, rescue the oppressed, defend the orphan, plead for the widow.

Micah 6:

[8] . . . what does the LORD require of you but to do justice, and to love kindness, and to walk humbly with your God?

I Corinthians 12:

[4] Now there are varieties of gifts, but the same Spirit; [5] and there are varieties of services, but the same Lord; [6] and there are varieties of activities, but it is the same God who activates all them all in every one. [7] To each is given

the manifestation of the Spirit for the common good. [14] . . . the body does not consist of one member but of many. [24] . . . But God has so arranged the body, giving the greater honor to the inferior member, [25] that there may be no dissention in the body, but that the members may have the same care for one another. [26] If one member suffers, all suffer together with it; if one member is honored, all rejoice together with it.

Revelations 21:

[22] I saw no temple in the city, for its temple is the Lord God the Almighty and the Lamb. [23] And the city has no need of sun or moon to shine upon it, for the glory of God is its light, and its lamp is the Lamb. [24] The nations will walk by its light; and the kings of the earth will bring their glory into it, [25] Its gates will never be shut by day — and there will be no night there. [26] People will bring into it the glory and the honor of the nations.

May more light and truth break forth from these scriptures as we make critical choices for the future of this nation and of the world. And whatever the outcome of an election, may we ponder also these words from St. Paul: ". . . the fruit of the Spirit is love, joy, peace, patience, kindness, generosity, faithfulness, gentleness, and self-control." (Galatians 5: 22-23)

THANKSGIVING

Pure Thanks

I have unholy wants. Some things I desire are not so good for me, or for others. Even when I want good things, I sometimes want too much of them, harming myself and others. Or I want good things at bad times and in wrong places.

What I hope for isn't entirely pure. Some of my hopes are tainted by my selfishness and bitterness. I don't always wish the best for others, though I wish that wasn't the case.

What I worship isn't so holy, either. Because my religion, like all others, is a human creation. My idea of God is just that. My idea, colored by my prejudices, shaped by my preferences. I so often define God in my own image, rather than letting myself be defined in God's.

But through gratitude we come as close to divinity as we humans can get. We cannot fail by giving thanks. We fail only in forgetting to do so. To be sure, we are not thankful enough for enough of what we are and what we have. But every little "thank you" directed to other persons and beings and to the Divine Source of all - every silent or spoken expression of sincere gratitude - is perfection itself. It is an instant, if only in an instant, when we go beyond our limited, mortal selves and participate in the existence of a Source outside our egos.

Sincere gratitude is the very definition of holiness. It is the purest prayer we can offer. In gratitude, all people and things are equal. Perhaps I can muster thankfulness only for my most prized and valuable material possessions. It doesn't matter. It's still gratitude, just as much as if I had been grateful for something supposedly more virtuous. Divine gratitude overwhelms you when admiring all the signs of your wealth. Divine gratitude overwhelms you when looking at a beautiful fall-colored leaf on the ground. It's all the same.

God makes no distinction. Gratitude is gratitude. Thanksgiving brings everything up to a heavenly level. Thanksgiving creates spiritual equality for all beings and things. In thanksgiving, we can know what it means for all to be one.

Because in thanks, what once had been an "it" suddenly becomes a "you." We don't say "thank it"—we say "thank you"—recognizing implicitly that there is a transcendent YOU who is beyond us, blessing us with unspeakably wonderful gifts, none more wondrous than each breath we take and each beat of our hearts—as we gratefully contemplate the gift of life itself.

There is purity in gratitude.

Thank you, thank you, thank you.

ADVENT

Warless Christmas

Somebody once taught me that I should never eat anything that was labeled prominently with the word "food." If it isn't obviously food, but explicitly claims to be food, you wouldn't want it to touch your lips.

A major news channel should be presumed to be "fair and balanced," because that is the very essence of professional journalism. So when a news channel claims to be "fair and balanced," that's a strong warning to take what it says with a grain of salt. Or better yet, to soak it in a vat of brine for a few weeks.

One news channel made a large splash of the claim that there is a war against Christmas underway in this country. They presented as evidence a school district in Texas that banned red and green paper plates and napkins from a holiday party.

Yes, in an effort to do the right thing, and honor the separation of government from religion, there have been incidents when officials have gone farther than they needed to go. And yes, some businesses have taken their avoidance of religious preference to extremes.

But such incidents hardly indicate that there is a war against Christmas, against Christianity, or against religion. On the contrary, a religion-neutral public sector allows for the fullest flowering of religious sentiment. Religion has not been hurt by the decision to use white paper napkins and plates at school holiday parties. (What about "White Christmas", anyway?) Religion has never been more lively in this country than it is today, and strict separation of church and state is one of the main reasons for it.

Marin County, California, where I live, is about as far as you can get from the Bible Belt. And from my reading of local lore, it's always been this way. The long-time mayor of Sausalito in the 1970's was the retired Madame of a whorehouse. You'd think that if there was a war against Christmas, the front line would have passed through Marin first.

So why is Marin festooned with red and green? Why are supposedly Godless northern Californians surrounded by reminders that Christmas is approaching? If there was a war against Christmas, you'd never know it here.

I'm a Christian pastor in the part of America with the lowest percentage of people who attend church. You'd think that if there was a war against Christmas, I would be able to smell the gun-smoke. But on the contrary, I feel surrounded by the warmth and joy of the season, in public as well as in private. And I've found that spirituality is very much alive here. Just because some people would rather go mountain biking on Sunday than sit in a pew, that doesn't mean they aren't interested in experiencing mystical union of their souls with God, which the Christ represents.

We don't need red and green paper plates and napkins in schools to celebrate the story of the birth of the Prince of Peace. We don't need crèches in city parks in order to sense the joy of the coming of the universal Christ-consciousness into the world. We don't need chain stores to dangle Santa in front of us in order to sense the mystery of the divine Word becoming flesh. It hasn't happened here, and I don't hope it will, but if the stores and public spaces were denuded of Christmas decor, it would probably be a great thing for churches. Our famously irreligious citizens might well make more of an effort to seek us out, joining us in remembrance of the deeper meanings of the season: generosity, humility, conviviality, and peace.

From the land of hot-tubs and peacock feathers, here in America's Bible Shoestring, I wish you a glorious and warless Christmas!

Angels in Glitter

Some of the church kids were a bit iffy about participating in the Christmas play, until they were given a choice about their costumes. When a couple of the little girls found out that angels were allowed to wear glittery gowns, that sealed the deal. They were in.

But all angels deserve glitter, don't they? For all they do for us. Giving us gentle guidance, silent support, a few wise words whispered when we need them most. Giving us insight and inspiration. Giving us patience when it seems about to run out. Giving us courage when fear overwhelms us. And leading us in loud alleluias when we find the face of the Christ in the people around us, when we discover the presence of God in our souls.

Angels appear in many forms, some subtle, some not. Sometimes in the form even of unlikely people who for a time take on the role of heavenly messenger. Sometimes in the form of a still small voice within us, barely noticeable, but potent with assurance and strength. Usually, angels come to us in street clothes, if they wear any at all. Mostly they come to us without trumpet fanfares. But their gifts to us are grander than gold or silver, so why would we fail to celebrate them with glitter, when given a chance?

Thanks be to our glittery little angels, the kids who are messengers of the magic of Christmas, and whose dazzling robes reminded us of the un-heralded angels who surround us every day.

CHRISTMAS

Gifts of Christmas

For Christmas may you receive the gift of time
To enjoy and reflect in the moment and
To savor the future — yours, your children's, your grandchildren's —
The time that in our moments together
Transcends the time of clocks and calendars.

For Christmas may you receive the gift of memory
That does not dwell in the past, but rather
Adds flavor and sentiment to the present
And meaning and purpose to the future.

For Christmas may you receive the gift of perspective
That enables you to tell what is in front and what is behind,
That enables you to distinguish that which requires your attention
From that which will sort itself out on its own.

For Christmas may you receive the gift of vision
That is so focused on seeing beauty
That it finds it everywhere.
For Christmas may you receive the gift of God
Who is Love, already delivered to the door of your hearts,
Ready to pour in when you open it.

A Humbled God

God, outsourced to Heaven
To avoid domestic taxation,
Took no calls himself.
His staff offered a menu of options
That could be reached only
By pressing the right buttons
In the right order.
The prompts for the next touch-tone numbers
Were preceded by pre-recorded pitches
For dogmas du jour

And sacrifices a la carte,
The rituals required,
And the oblations expected,
Marketing hell
And advertising its antidote,
Packaging fear and ignorance
And selling them as family values.

God's liability was limited.
His acronym was listed on NASDAQ,
His identity managed by a top PR firm.
If you complained about his products,
If you questioned his policies,
You were told you were either for him or against him,
Either riding on his side or spinning on the axis of evil,
With hell to pay.

But within God was a stirring,
An urge that he could not deny.
There was something he needed
That his money could not buy.
Against the advice
Of his masters of divinity
And his tax accountants
And his media consultants
And his personal trainers,
The attraction of the carnal
Was more than he could resist.
The only thing missing from his omnipotence
Was finitude herself.

His lawyers tried to hush her up,
His board of directors met in secret,
His spokespeople made no mention
Of his little indiscretion
With a certain Mary of Nazareth.
But she was not embarrassed.
She went public right away.

She sang, magnificently, freely,
Turning down offers of cash from the tabloids.

Christmas is coming, she said, and soon,
God would have a face
Whether he liked it or not.
God, she said,
Was going to be outed,
And the whole embarrassing truth
About the incomplete creation,
The scandal of evil,
The rot in religion,
And the corruption of power
Would be revealed.
And, to add to the outrage,
This news would be delivered in a manger,
Wrapped in swaddling clothes, and
Would grow up to be a man
Who looked a lot like God.
Which would make it all the more surprising,
Since this man would be being kind and forgiving,
Just and faithful, caring and forbearing.
His divinity would embarrass his Father
Into behaving more humanely
Than anyone would have dreamed possible,
And inspire humans into behaving more divinely
Than they had ever imagined.
Three dark-suited agents
Descended on the manger
To buy her silence with gold and frankincense and myrrh,
And a corps of angels was sent
To sing loudly and drown out her every word.
A team of burly shepherds
Was hired to bounce the paparazzi and the press
Away from the manger door.

But Mary sang on, above it all:
Christmas is coming,

And heaven will come down to earth,
And there will be prophet-sharing,
And truth will begin to speak to power,
And justice will begin to prevail.
Christmas is coming,
And soon God's little mistake,
His brief fling with mortal me,
Will save God from himself,
And us from him.
Christmas is coming, she said,
And soon God's old idea of himself
And our old ideas about God
Will fly out the manger window
With the bathwater
And the baby Jesus will remain.
Christmas is coming, she sang,
And nobody and nothing can stop it!

Christmas is coming, and Mary still sings,
Sweeter now, and slow.
The wise men's faces have softened,
The angels merely hum,
And the even the shepherds have come inside,
Preparing to meet their humbled God.

The Last Candle

The last candle burns
The waiting's almost over
Soon we'll hear a baby crying
and we'll know that God is no mere idea
Soon we'll feel what Mary feels with the baby in her arms
And we'll know we've met God in person
A person among us, weak and wanting, wise and growing
Soon we'll know what is divine about being human
and human about being divine
One candle burning
One star shining in the night sky

One child lying in a manger's straw
One God, among us, Emmanuel!

Birth

Out of this house where there is no room
For the little ones that to him belong
(He is weak but he is God)
Let's get outside to hear the song
Of his birthing cry to this world of doom
(If she give birth to me, yet shall I love her)

The Calculus of Christmas

May we be enraptured
By overshadowing Love;
May our souls magnify the Lord
Through our widening eyes,
Through expanded lenses
and greater focal lengths,
By powers in geometric progression
In the parabolic curve that marks
the division of cells,
Of conception into gestation,
then birth,
Of Word becoming Flesh.
Oh blazing Star afar, come near!
Divine and human, arbitrarily close,
Oh ecstasy of Christmas, here!

Waiting for Christmas

A baby waits in a dark, warm womb
Lulled by the sway of a donkey's walk
Down a road in the night toward Bethlehem
A young man waits in a concrete cell
For the years of the curse of his crime to pass
What is left of Christmas now?

And what will be left of Christmas then?
A young girl waits by a lighted tree
Till her sleep can skip past the hours till dawn
When she will awake to her Christmas dreams
An old man waits for the phone to ring
And an earnest voice might offer a hint
Of a Christmas past, when his son was young
And a shiny train roared round the tree
A mother waits for the oven's buzz
For the cry of her child, for the call of her mate
For the time to write, for a chance to think
Of the deeper things that the season means
The officer waits in her darkened car
On the side of a road on a freezing night
For the squeal of tires, for a drunken weave
For the family fight, for the noise too loud
For her shift to end in peace tonight
The student waits in the airport lounge
Brooding against her travel bags
Till the blizzard ends and the runway's clear
Hoping to make it home in time
The trucker waits at the counter's edge
For a cup of warmth to heat the night
For the sight of a face to dull the pain
Of family lost, of lovers left
A truck stop Christmas must suffice
A soldier waits in the desert night
Ears alert for the slightest sound
Eyes strained into the fearsome dark
At home there's a chill in his young wife's heart
He feels her pangs for him this night
A father waits in a cobwebbed barn
By flickering light of a lamp of oil
Holding the hand of his struggling wife
As their precious child is born to the world
And we now wait in a darkened church

Ready to have our hopes fulfilled
Ready to kindle that holy light
Ready to find the Christ within
Each of us who has come tonight

Incarnation Meditation

I am what comes before sand and sandstone
Chickens and eggs.
I am the unproven truth
On which all proofs depend.

So why this stirring, this painful urge
To emerge through the cosmic pelvis?
Why this wanting to breathe thin air,
To play in the dirt, to shave wood, to cleave to flesh?
To make friends I could lose,
To share love that could break,
To mingle in blood and spit and mud?
On this side I am a wingless angel floating,
Sustained by all that surrounds me,
Breathless in bliss, in timeless sabbath rest.
On this side, I am someone else's idea.
All that without will or effort is, I am.

Out there are choices to be made:
Laments or laughter, caresses or crosses.
Out there are surprises —
Unspeakable horrors, ineffable ecstasies.
Out there is a Way,
Narrow or wide, slippery or safe?

Out there I dread, but yearn to go . . .
Out there is Christmas.

Dark Madonna

Gaze into her face, and listen. The Dark Madonna whispers to us from a realm beyond time.

The darker the soil, the more fertile it is. Out of the darkness of the earth, into which the seeds are planted, life springs up. We see it in this season, in this place. Green grass sprouts out of the darkness beneath the hills of gold. In the dark hollows of the redwood forest, lacy ferns explode into life. In the darkness of the womb, new life grows and then emerges.

In the darkness of a church, candles burn. Candles lit by hopeful faithful souls, generations after generations of people making the very signs of love and promise that they seek, by lighting votives in the hush of the sanctuary. The smoke of these numberless candles rises and slowly builds up on the surface of an image of the Virgin Mary in the monastery of Jasna Gora in Poland, darkening her face until she is known as the Black Madonna.

On a hill in Mexico, where once the goddess Tonantzin was worshipped, the freshly-baptized Indian, Juan Diego, kept a vigil, meditating deeply, and from the dark place inside him exploded a glowing vision that brought Meso-American and European spirituality together as one. In effulgence she hovered before him, La Morenita, the Dark One, the Virgin of Guadalupe, goddess and mother of God.

All over Europe, as people converted to Christianity, they found in Mary a figure that bridged the worship of the earth goddess of ancient times and the worship of the God of the church. And in dark images of Mary, they were comforted with a spiritual continuity, carrying the black-skinned earth goddesses into a new religious age. They heard whispers of the earth goddess as they gazed into her face in statues and icons.

Our Lady of Czestochowa. The black Madonnas of Switzerland, France, Germany. Of the ancient Coptic churches of Ethiopia. The deep copper skin of Mexico's Virgin of Guadalupe. The dark virgin's beatific gaze haunts us. Her voice emanates from the earth itself, asking us to pay attention to the state of the planet. The dark soil being washed to the sea by overgrazing and over-tilling. The air fouled with pollution, the water squandered and poisoned. The burning of fuels and forests that threatens the climate and the ecosystems upon which it depends. She whispers, reminding us that we are of the earth, we depend on the earth, that it now depends on what we do, the choices we make in what we buy and how we eat and how we travel. She whispers of the pain of the world which she took upon herself when she accepted the glorious doom of divine conception: Love the weak among you. Reach out to the lonely and lost and sick. Protect the most vulnerable among you. Show divinely humane kindness to the very people you are most tempted to hate.

She is with us now, in the gathering darkness of winter. Through her the hope of new life is born again within and among us. The dark Virgin whispers to us of a creative, peace-making, justice-serving Word that is about to emerge. A Word that energizes us to acts of compassion, to be willing to make sacrifices for the common good. A Word that seeks a justice beyond an eye for an eye and a tooth for a tooth and a war for a war. A Word that shows a love beyond the easy warm and fuzzy. A love that goes the distance, right into the hearts of our enemies.

In her image, holding the Christ child, the mysterious cycle of birth and death and rebirth is reflected. Her somber expression of fateful knowledge, her loving, caressing hands of hope. Grief and joy mixed, alchemically transformed. In her darkness the mystery of communion is consummated. Spirit and matter are united within her. Creator and creature embrace. She is the marriage-bed in which the eternal and the temporal, the divine and the mundane, wrestle into one. In her, the emergent property we call life arises out of the lifeless elements of the earth.

The dark Virgin whispers: You are my child. My precious child. And all those you know are my children. You are all brothers and sisters, flesh of my flesh, soul of my soul, so cherish each other as you cherish yourselves, and as I cherish you. Your pain is mine, in your victories I share. I am your Mother, and I need your love and your care, and more than all else I need your presence. I need to be with you, and you with me. So linger with me, let my heart be yours. Your gifts of compassion to each other, your acts of service, will be gifts to me. The respect you show to the earth and its living creatures will be respect you show to me. So may it be. Amen!

Christmas: A Joseph's-Eye View

For Joseph, the first Christmas must have borne a certain ambiguity. The biblical legend tells us that the baby Jesus was the son of God, not the biological son of Joseph. Standing there at the manger, what did Mary's husband feel? Pride in this new chip off, well, Someone Else's block? Maybe Joseph felt what an adopted child sometimes senses: uncertainty about the reality of his familial relationship. Jesus was clearly a wonderful Christmas present — but to whom was he given?

As the biological father of a daughter, with whom I clearly share morphology and even a sense of humor, I still wonder the same sorts of things that

Joseph must have wondered. Sure, I passed along a lot of my chromosomes to her. But is she mine? Well, not really. It is increasingly obvious that she is not just a gift to me and the rest of her family. She is a gift to the world. My job as a parent is to do no more and no less than what Joseph did: to love, nourish, and help her get ready to go into the world to which she is given. I find that in order rightly to do my job as her father as she matures, I must steadily retreat from behaving as if she were "mine."

Perhaps Joseph had an advantage, knowing from the beginning that this child was not his own. Perhaps this knowledge enabled him to give Jesus the kind of unfettering, unconditional love he needed to mature into the strong, compassionate, courageous person that we read about in the gospels. There must have been a poignant longing in Joseph's heart that blessed night, a wish that this boy could have been his own. But if I were standing by Joseph's side, I'd console him with the fact that even biological parents share that longing. If only my daughter were really "mine!" I'd never let her go. I feel that pang of sadness, knowing that one day she will leave home and be received by the world into which she was sent.

The gift of Christmas is not one to be grasped, not one to own for one's self. Like Joseph, we are but stewards and guardians of the Love that is given to the world at Christmas.

Christmas Eve

So often we act like our careers are God. Sometimes we put our work first, letting all else slide, letting our relationships, our families, take the back seat.

So often we act like our habits are God. We obey them so slavishly. Some of our habits are even good, but we still get so attached to them that they become holy, getting in the way of what matters more.

So often we act like our ambitions are God. We pursue them so relentlessly. We get a goal fixed in our minds, and we go after them to the exclusion of all else. Some of these ambitions are good, but when we get swept away by them. Well, that is not so good.

So often we act like our opinions and preferences are God. We hold to them so strongly. Maybe some of our opinions are correct, but when we act like they are God-given, well, that is not so good.

So often we act like our passions are God. We are so driven by them.

Sometimes a passion becomes an obsession, twisting a good thing into a source of torment for ourselves and others. At first we think we are in control of our passions, and then, so often, our passions drag us behind them . . . .

Tonight we have a chance to act differently. Tonight we have the opportunity to act as if God is not a career, or a habit, or an ambition, or an opinion, or a passion. Tonight we are invited to act as if God is . . . a baby.

That's right. A human baby. When God is tired, we let her sleep. And there is nothing healthier, nothing more relaxing and spiritually centering, than to hold a sleeping baby in your arms. When God is wet, we change his diapers. There is nothing more rewarding than service to another. When God is hungry, we feed her. What is more deeply satisfying than sharing an intimate meal with another? When God is fussy, we comfort him. What is more important in this life, in this world, than bringing solace to a crying baby? Nothing. Not career, not our habits, not our ambitions, not our passions. Nothing else.

Tonight we welcome this baby into the world once again, and tonight, by candlelight, and in song, we commit ourselves to this kind of God. One more compelling, more precious, than all else. This is what Christmas is all about. To you each, and to you all, may this dark and starry night be the start of a most merry and blessed Christmas. Amen!

The Mossy Compass

Norman Spiker, the scoutmaster of my Boy Scout troop in Columbiana, Ohio, taught me many useful and enduring lessons about nature. Norman would take us on winter hikes in the snow, and on one of them he taught us that if we ever got lost, we should look for moss on a tree. The side of the tree with moss on it faced north, because the north side of the tree got the least sun, allowing the moss to flourish in the damp of the dark. The radius line from the center of the tree to the densest strip of moss on the bark aimed north. This wisdom was much more useful in the flatlands of the Midwest than it is here in California, where we can reckon our location by mountaintops. But I still smile when I look out the window and see the moss on a cement wall, moss that faces north, just as Norman told us. The turning leaves of a Japanese maple glow in the sun behind the wall, while the moss grows in shadow.

So often we reject or deny the usefulness of our shadow side. We'd rather not even acknowledge our anger, pain, frustration, disappointment. We don't want to identify with our bad attitudes and potentially destructive inner tendencies. Yet it is the shadow side that can guide us when we are lost. The dark side of our lives can show us the way to go, show us the change of course that will take us in a better direction. If I can step back and lovingly observe my anger, I can let it direct me to its source, and resolve it. If I can step back and lovingly observe my pain, if I can calm down enough to let it inform me of its causes and the needs to which it can direct me, there is some chance I can find my way to relief. Pain is a perfect compass, if I can take the time to watch where its needle aims.

So it is with Christmas. At the darkest time of the year, when outer lights as well as inner lights are dimmest, we are best able to see the glimmer of the star that leads us to Bethlehem. If we are able to embrace darkness itself, it can guide us to the wonder that awaits us in the manger.

So if you find yourself stumbling in circles, remember my scoutmaster's lesson. Look for the dark side, and let it lead you out of the woods, and into the presence of the Holy One at Christmas.

EPIPHANY

The Three Wise Men's Boogaloo

High steppin' camels one by one
See the wise men boogaloo
Down to Bethlehem to have some fun
Rockin' this way, rockin' that
Camels strut to where it's at
All night long by the light of a star
No idea where they are
By a ragin' star, a flamin' light
And the sniff of a flarin' nose
Each camel seeks the blessed sight
While the wise men wisely doze

If you're hip to what's hap
You'll find your own way
To the funky old shack
Where the angels play
Hallelujah jazz on their saxophones
To the baby lying on the moss
That fell off the rolling stones
That the camels kicked free
On their winding road
From ancient history
With a load of frankincense and gold
And myrrh and the pyramids' plan
And Hammurabi's code of old
And all the poetry of ancient Iran
And drums and tubas to join the band
Rocking the manger
Mocking the danger from King Herod's hand
It's the three wise men's boogaloo
So join the choir with a tap of your shoe
They're coming to the manger nearest you.

A Prayer to Mother Wisdom

Holy Sophia, Mother Wisdom, through you I pray at this holy time of Epiphany, remembering the story of the learned men from the East who came to visit the Christ child.

I pray for the kind of wisdom that is deep happiness, so that I may remain joyfully boggled by the shocking beauty of the natural world that surrounds me. I pray to remain blissfully awestruck with fascination at the people I encounter every day. I pray that my feelings of frustration will be moderated by deep gratitude that I am alive to feel anything at all.

I pray for the wisdom of attentiveness, so that I can be awake to the ways that I can show kindness to others. I pray for the wisdom of imagination, so that I can transcend the confines of problems in order to discover solutions, so that I can perceive beauty even in places where it seems absent.

I pray for the wisdom of humility, to know my small place in the grand order of things. I pray for an acute awareness of my constant state of ignorance, so that I will be eager always to learn more. I pray for the wisdom of humor, so that I can enjoy the comedy of my own errors.

I pray that your divine wisdom will be revealed to others, as well. I pray that the leaders of this country will be motivated by compassion and genuine curiosity, rather than by fear and predetermined ideology. I pray that the people of this world will act on the wisdom of solidarity, aware that we have so very much more in common than the few things that keep us apart. I pray most fervently for the wisdom of forgiveness, so that the future will not be determined by grudges from the past.

Dear Mother Wisdom, make each neural pathway in my brain, each subtle structure of my mind, each layer of my consciousness, into a channel through which your creative and reconciling energy can flow. Amen!

Exile to Egypt

On a stony trail through the Sinai wastes
A little family headed south
Father, mother, little babe
A burdened donkey, head drooped down
Leaving home, might never come back
Might not return on the northbound track
Off to college, off to war
Off to travel or explore
Or kicked out of the house in a bad divorce
Or run out of town on a rail, or worse
Or just an urge to get out of Dodge
To find some other place to lodge
Some other way to live and be
Some other kinds of sights to see
The soul stirs and cannot rest
Until it makes another nest
For even should the exile end
Home won't be the same again
When it's time to leave, my soul will know
Will I follow? Can I let go?

LENT

Fat Tuesday

Jesus wasn't the only miracle-worker in the first century. Lots of people were purported in those days to be able to perform healings and do unnaturally wondrous things. He wasn't the only one whom people believed to have risen from the dead. Lots of resurrection was going on in those days, according to the popular culture of the time. Nor was Jesus the only wisdom teacher in Israel that caught people's attention. No, what made Jesus really different was this: he was willing to eat dinner with anybody. And in those days that was a big deal, because there were lots of folks who were considered unclean or outcaste or alien and it was considered outrageous to share a meal with them. But Jesus broke all those taboos, right and left, and sat down to dinner with them all. Lepers, women, Romans, Samaritans, tax-collectors, Pharisees, Sadducees, Zealots—he shared the dinner table with them. And nobody forgot it. The early Christian communities were built around dinner tables. They shared a meal called the Agape Meal, or love-feast. A big potluck, with room and food for all.

In this convivial spirit of ancient Christianity, to celebrate Shrove Tuesday, or Fat Tuesday, better known as Mardi Gras, the feast day before the fasting of Lent, I invite you to a virtual feast in the imagination.

Let's start with appetizers.

They are passed around on platters, a wide assortment of tasty and tangy treats. No two items taste the same. What are the appetizers of life? They are the ways we get opened to life's possibilities. They are our chances to try out far more than we can possibly fully accomplish, visit far more places than we can actually tap down roots. When we get a glimpse of another culture—that's an appetizer. When we take a drawing class for the first time, just to try it out. When we break our routine just for a day, to see what happens. When we volunteer for a special service project, to try it out. Appetizers aren't meant to fill us up, but they give us new ideas about how we could be filled. They awaken us to the abundance of this life, remind us to linger and savor over the tastes, whet our appetites for more to come.

After nibbling and talking for a good long time, it is time for soup. The tureens are brought out to the table and the steamy aroma inspires "ahhh's" from the diners. You taste a thick and creamy puree, and ask for the recipe, but when you hear the recipe you can't believe that this taste could have come from those ingredients. You are amazed to find that the soup is much more than the sum of its parts. The list of ingredients does not explain the taste that results from carefully combining them.

Roberta and I count ourselves blessed to be friends with a Sonoma chef by the name of John Littlewood. I once asked him about his favorite magical concoctions in cooking. He said that two things came to mind immediately: mole and curry. Mole is made out of chocolate, chili, and sesame seeds. We all know what these things taste like, but we could never predict how they would taste when mixed together carefully. Same with curry, which has a lot of ingredients, each with distinctive tastes, which when mixed create a new element, so to speak. If there was a periodic table of tastes, mole and curry would have their own squares on the chart! Human creations that stand alongside those that Nature has formed without us.

Life is so often like curry soup. It's alchemy, the medieval quest to turn base metals into gold, and to transmute the mortal into the eternal. Think of a person who had a painful childhood, full of traumas, but somehow grew up to be a healthy, positive, productive person. The ingredients of the person's life don't explain the person. Alchemically, all those bitter experiences were combined with other life-ingredients and transmuted into a sweet and delicious life. Your life and mine are a lot like mole. We're a jumble of seeming contradictions which, when carefully blended and tended, can turn into something wonderfully different than we could have imagined.

John also extolled the virtues of adding things at the very end of the cooking process. There's nothing like adding a garnish of parsley cream into a soup at the end, so that there is an uncooked texture to complement the taste of the cooked-down soup. Sometimes the rough stuff of life, which like parsley isn't much good by itself, can surprise us by adding texture to our lives, and be redeemed and transformed by the delicious soupiness of our stories.

Now it's time for salad. And unlike soup, salad is all about distinct, crunchy experiences. I think of the churches I've served much more as wonderful salads than as soups. The members are as distinct and different from each other as carrots are from lettuce, as cranberries are from pecans. And yet, tossed together, they're really something to enjoy and talk about! John Littlewood says that salads are all about pairings. You take one bite, and you experience what a pecan with a piece of romaine is like. The next bite might be what a cranberry and an apple slice taste like. And he says one of his favorite pairings is

Roquefort cheese and pear slices. An unexpected surprise, he says: alchemical in the salad sense, rather than the soup sense. A different manner of being more than the sum of the parts.

Then there's the main course. John told me that it is important to present the main course, with the meat, the vegetable, and the starch, on a plate that leaves room around the outer and inner rim of the plate, so that it isn't cluttered on the plate, so that the food doesn't look overwhelming, so that you can have a visually calming experience, and distinguish what it is you are about to eat. He said that in the restaurant business, a big part of doing it all well is not so much what you do, but what you don't do. Don't clutter the plate. Don't jangle the senses with too many colors and shapes in the dining room and on the table. And I mused that this is what spiritual practice is all about, too. It is more about un-doing than doing. It is more about removing mental and emotional clutter than it is about doing something special. God is already here. We don't have to do anything high-tech or fancy to reach her. Mostly what we have to do is get things out of the way of our experience of God. Let go of the things that obscure or interfere with our knowledge of God. John says this is the high art of a good eating establishment: doing things very well, but keeping many things simple and crisp, only giving service when it is wanted, and staying away when it is not wanted, not chatting up the patrons with distractions. God is already here, and the high art of religion is serving her up on plates where she can be seen and appreciated most thoroughly.

John also said that food items look best on a plate not in twos, but in threes or other odd numbers. Which I suppose is where we got the ancient Christian notion of God in three persons, the blessed Trinity. God looks better on the plate that way. It's just a way that our minds find beauty and a sense of completeness.

The main course is where we get the most vital nutrients of the meal, the protein and the minerals and vitamins. John is on a quest to get as close to the source as possible, buying local organic produce and righteously raised and slaughtered meats. In that quest a few years ago, he, as someone averse to hunting and fishing, decided he needed to experience what it is like to kill and eat on the spot. He went fishing off Baja California and said it was a holy, sacred experience to catch a fish, watch the light fade from its eyes, and then cut it up for sashimi so fresh he could taste the iron in its blood. It was an experience he'd never had before or since. He felt such awe and respect for that fish, such a sense of responsibility, in that act of killing and eating. He said if we all did more of this, more of us would become vegetarians, or at least would have a lot more respect for the animals we eat. Stay close to the source: that is his mantra these days in his cooking. Stay close to the source: isn't that what spiritual practice is all about? Remembering that the Divine Presence, is closer to us than our own blood and our own breath. Staying close to the source of our food, maintaining as much personal connection with the land and its produce as we can, is a sacramental approach to eating that keeps us closer to our Divine Source.

Ahhhh! That was a divine main course! After a bit of a rest, it's time for dessert. The exclamation point at the end of the meal. You don't really need it, but what's Fat Tuesday without it? Just like every story needs an ending. Which is the way John describes a good meal. It's like a symphony that has movements, a beginning, middle, and end, and if it is a great meal, like a great piece of music or a great story, you finish it knowing deeply that there is not one part of it you would change. It all belongs together as it is. And so it is with a life well-lived. It all makes sense in the end. We all deserve those dessert moments in life, which sweetly resolve all that's gone before into a deep sense of fulfillment and completion. In worship, the benediction is the dessert, the last word that crystallizes or caramelizes the whole experience that precedes it.

I can't even imagine eating a thing, now that I've imagined such an incredibly satisfying meal. The mere thought of it seems enough to get me through Lent!

Ashing Questions

Ash Wednesday is a time for ashing, and for asking questions.

> Where is love leading you today?
> Who is hard for you to love, and why, and might there not be a way for you to love them anyway?
> What is the difference between your highest values and the way you actually live?
> What unfinished spiritual business do you have that ought to be completed?
> What are you running away from, and what would happen if you stopped avoiding it?
> What is below the surface of the image you present to the world?

and what would happen if you revealed what was below the surface?

What can you discover by taking time to keep silence, and finding the courage to look within?

What is getting in love's way, for you?

What kind of help do you need, and are you willing to ask for it and receive it?

What gift do you have to give today to others?

How do your decisions about what you wear, buy, and eat affect others you don't know and will never meet?

What can you do to make life better for poor people and other vulnerable people in the wider world?

What message do you need to hear, but don't feel ready to hear?

What can you do to get ready to hear it?

It is our humility to realize that we don't have all the answers. It is our glory to be able to ask the questions, including the ashing questions of Lent.

It's What's Inside That Counts

In my line of work we have a phrase called "the edifice complex." A take-off, of course, on Freud's Oedipus complex. The edifice complex consists of all the ways that people in churches become obsessed with their church buildings, sometimes to the point of forgetting the mission of the church to love and serve human beings, and reducing it to an architectural preservation club. The cure for this temptation is to bring to consciousness our deep, visceral, visual, even olfactory resonance between sacred architecture and the design of our own souls.

Enter a church with me in your imagination, and as you go with me, enter also your own heart. For this building is an especially clear mirror for the soul. Otherwise our hearts would not be so moved by it.

The entrance to the sanctuary is dramatic. A brick staircase leads down to a curved, covered alcove that leads to the heavy, curved doors. The entry is impressive, strongly conveying the sense that this is a place to be approached with awe, with humility, and with respect. So it is with the soul. When you enter your own heart, or someone else's heart opens to yours, you pause—you stop your normal patter, hush your usual way of speaking. You snap out of your normal way of being, recognizing that you are entering an extraordinary state.

I was meeting with a couple that was preparing to get married. The bride and groom were handsome, put-together folks. He was a lawyer and she was an airline pilot. They did normal life really well. Our conversation was chatty and informative and friendly at first. Then I asked what I thought was not a particularly deep question. The bride choked up. And then started to cry. I reached for the box of Kleenex, and in doing so, I realized we had come to the doors of the sanctuary of her heart. Half a box of Kleenex later, we were all the way inside that sanctuary, the three of us, sharing a sacred moment.

The church season of Lent is an old spiritual discipline of opening the door of the inner sanctuary of the soul and going inside. It's a time to rediscover the chapel that exists in the heart, and enter it deliberately and intentionally, and meditate and worship there. Sometimes we stumble upon its doors when something happens that moves us to tears or moves us to awe. But now we take time to purposefully enter that holy of holies within us, and take the time to explore what is inside.

Because it's what's inside that counts! So much of the architecture of our lives is pretty prosaic. I'd say a substantial square-footage of the structure of my life could be compared aptly to a strip mall consisting of tilt-up concrete buildings spangled with garish neon signs enveloped in a soulless parking lot. The Egg McMuffin ambience that occupies so much of our lives, the gas-station aesthetic that permeates so much of our waking consciousness; we take it for normal, we feel comfort in its predictability. Then along comes an experience that is orthogonal to all of that.

In one of my churches I had a parishioner who had recently been present at the birth of her first grandchild. She said it reduced her to nothing. She felt like she didn't exist. She just wanted to get down on the floor and prostrate herself, the moment was so awesome and overwhelmingly beautiful. That is what people do in sanctuaries. They look up into the soaring steeple and their jaws drop and for a moment, they don't exist as the selves they usually know. They are humbled and they kneel in the pews and some even prostrate themselves on the floor. It's an out of ego experience to enter the holy sanctuary of a beautiful church, and also to enter the holy sanctuary at the center of your own being, that place where your everyday idea of who you are falls away and all that is left is God.

The ancient Jewish temple in Jerusalem was, in a way, nothing more than a series of entryways. You went up to the Temple Mount, and entered the Court of the Gentiles, where anybody could go, Jewish or non-Jewish. Then you entered the Court of Women, as far as women could go. Then you entered the Court of Israel, as far as normal Jewish men could go. Then you entered the Court of Priests, as far as normal male Jewish priests could go. Beyond that was the Holy of Holies, an area enclosed with a heavy cloth curtain reminiscent of the tent in which the first altar was set in the early days of Israel. Only the High Priest could enter it. If he were to make some kind of mistake in presenting the offering to God to redeem the sins of the people, a jolt of divine electricity might strike him down, and the lesser priests wouldn't be able to enter the Holy of Holies to drag him out. So he entered the Holy of Holies with a rope tied around his waist, so that in case of emergency, his lesser priests could drag him out!

So it is when we enter the Holy of Holies in our own souls. It can be a shocking experience to leave everyday, comfortable reality and suddenly find yourself face to face with what's inside you. For so many of us for so much of the time, what's deep inside us is a mystery to us. A Stanford student told me once that a seemingly random event triggered a memory from his childhood, a moment in the church his family attended when he was asked to read out loud from the Bible. The memory of that moment flooded back to him in an instant, by surprise, and he said he cried for days. He had a strong need to return to his spiritual roots, enter into the sanctuary of his soul and pay attention to what was there. That set him on a journey of spiritual discovery that, among other places, delivered him to my office door.

It's what's inside that counts! Or should I say, it's who's inside that counts! Because if we go all the way in through the heavy doors, go to the center where the axes of the church meet, and look up, God is there. May you accept God's invitation to enter the holy of holies within your own heart, a place you can visit any time, whether or not you are anywhere near a sacred edifice!

The Sanctuary: A Guided Meditation

You are walking toward the church on a bright morning.

Your mind is abuzz with lists of things to do, people to meet, places to go.

You are just doing life, and church happens to be part of it, and that's good.

There's nothing any more or less special about this day than any other.

Whatever normal is for you, you are doing it and thinking and feeling it as you approach the little wooden church with its high steeple.

You approach the front door, through the arched, shingled entryway.

You hold the wrought iron handle and pull open the door.

Light streams onto the pews from the windows.

And you know you have entered a holy place, a place set apart.

Whatever was normal for you have been set aside, and you can feel it.

But to your surprise, none of the usual people are in the pews, though the pews are full.

It's quiet in the sanctuary; the music hasn't started to play yet.

And nobody is talking.

And then it hits you.

The church is full of what's inside of you, the aspects of yourself you have neglected, forgotten, avoided.

Just as you start walking down the aisle, you see a talent of yours, a gift that you've never used. She glows with a greeting. "Remember me?" she says. "I'm still here! Please call me and let's get together soon!" And you remember. She's an innate ability that you have had all along, but have never taken the time to develop. You've known about her since you were a child. And you know that she could be such an incredible blessing to you and the people around you, if you made the sacrifice needed to develop this relationship and exercise this talent.

You take another step and you are shocked to see an old resentment of yours, sheepishly acknowledging your presence as you sheepishly acknowledge his. An unresolved relationship, an unforgiving incident, a grudge held way too long. "I suppose it's time we made peace," he says, barely audibly. And you respond. "Yes, I suppose it is." You both shed tears to release the pain, and then the tears become expressions of your gratitude at liberation from it.

You hold the side of the pew and take deep breaths. You offer a prayer: "Dear Lord be with me as I face what I find here."

Your next step brings you into the gaze of an outdated belief. An idea that guided your life for a long time, but no longer serves you nor anyone else. A pattern of thought that is very much in your way, but one you've avoided confronting. "I guess we ought to let go," she says to you. And you respond, "Yes, be free of me, and I'll be free of you." And with a prayerful gesture she bows to you and you bow back to her.

Not far from her is an insight. He is winking at you, and has a grin on his face that wraps from ear to ear.

"You have got to be kidding!" you say to him. "You've been in here all this time, and I never noticed you before!"

He laughs quietly, then puts his finger to his lips. "Sacred place here!" he whispers. "I'm so happy you finally found me. I've been waiting for you all this time, while you have struggled to understand and solve your challenge. I'm ready to serve you when you are ready to put me to work."

You are awestruck at this insight which now gives you another way to see your problem, another approach that is so different than the other ways you've tried and failed at your difficulty. Now he sits and grins at you, clear as can be.

And just then there is music—an old woman singing a lovely chant. Her voice seems to ride the air like a gently rocking boat on the sea. It's a song of thanksgiving. She is gratitude herself. And as she sings she looks at you and smiles, the folds and wrinkles of her face amplifying her happiness. And you know she is grateful for your life. And you can't help feeling it yourself. And as she sings her alleluias, you are awash in gratitude for all the large and small gifts that surround you every day, things and people that you take for granted, beauties that you barely see any more. Now as you gaze into her eyes and let her voice surround you, you are swept away with thankfulness, gratitude you didn't know you were capable of having.

She finishes her song and sits down.

You turn your head and there is a man gazing up into the vault of the steeple, muttering something and twitching. You know he's either very disturbed or he's praying his heart out. Or both. He's out of control, flailing, scared, upset. You know exactly what is terrifying him. You've hid from him for a long time, avoided him, let him flail all alone. But now that you are inside the sanctuary you approach him and face him. "It's okay," you say. "I'm willing to look at you, finally. Yes, you're scared, yes, you're frightened. I'm with you, I'll sit next to you." And you sit down next to him and hold his hand, and that is enough to settle his breath and calm his body. He leans back, sighing. "Thank God! It's still hard, but I know I'm not alone!"

Next to you on the other side is a young boy, scribbling on the back of the church bulletin. You know who he is. He won't look at you. But you know. He's your social responsibility that you've avoided. He's the poor person, he's the person without health insurance, he's the forgotten inner city dweller of America, he represents the suffering people of the world that you decided were too much trouble even to think about. Now you look at him and realize that in your own way, within your resources and energy, you can do something important to help him, to act as a caring citizen and voter and volunteer.

A woman stands at the front of the church with a vial of olive oil in her hand. She invites you to come forward. You approach her, and as you do, you realize who she is, and you stop. She is grief. For all those broken relationships, beloved ones you've lost to death or disappointment. All the lost opportunities and broken dreams of your life. But she has a kind smile on her face. You catch your breath and come forward to her, and she marks the sign of the cross on your forehead. "It's safe. You can feel your sadness with me. It's sacred. Feel it and through it you will be made whole." You feel the grief swelling and rolling through you and it hurts but as it passes you feel a powerful sense of relief, as if you've been given a great gift. She embraces you and releases you and points to the altar.

There on the altar is bread and wine, and behind it is a framed picture. What's in the picture? You cannot tell. You step up, carefully, to the altar and look. In the frame, to your great surprise, is—a mirror. You gaze at your awestruck face for a moment. Light emanates from behind your head. The bread and wine are before you, and you look at them, and you reach down and take a bit of the bread and dip it into the wine, and eat it as you look at yourself in the mirror. And suddenly you realize you are looking at the Christ, the face of God in human form.

And as you look into the mirror, other faces appear behind you. The whole congregation has come up behind you and placed their hands on your shoulders. And you see that you are all one. Each member is a part of you, part of the Christ who makes you whole. Those you had neglected, forgotten, avoided: every one is an essential part of you with whom to be in harmonious relationship.

You turn and find that the church is empty. Worship is over, and you are the last one there. Slowly you walk down the steps of the altar, down the aisle, and out the heavy wood doors. Turning once as you depart, to look again at the glowing shafts of light coming down from the vault of the steeple, and then gently closing the door.

PALM SUNDAY

Over Here, Jesus!

Jesus! Finally you have arrived! I've been waiting so long for you to come. Now that you're here, everything will be different! As you surely know, the decor in the temple is so out of date. So first-century BC! Certainly the first thing you'll do is get rid of those dowdy curtains in the holy of holies, and put up something with more class. Can you believe those lamp-stands? Nobody's polished them in decades. And the smell in this place is horrendous. Surely you'll get right to work on hiring a new staff of janitors to come in twice a day to clean up all the blood from the sacrifices. Thank God you have finally arrived!

Jesus! The nation needs you more than ever. You're our savior! We need your endorsement to get some legislation passed so that our moral agenda, which we are absolutely certain is your agenda, too, will become the law of the land. I know you're all hung up about justice and peace, but if you'd just take a moment now to tell the country that you want abortion to be banned, that would be terrific. Also if you could—yes, that's right, aim your mouth toward the microphone—yes, if you could also endorse prayer in the schools, creationism in the science textbooks, and engraving the ten commandments on courthouse walls, that would have such an impact. Everybody's listening, Jesus! Come on, give us some air time!

Jesus! So glad you made it! This country has gone crazy! Right-wingers are misquoting you all the time! So if you could just speak now on Air Israel radio, that would be great. Now's your chance to tell it like it is, Jesus! Get specific, would you? Tell the people that God wants them to vote the left-wing ticket. Tell them the war is against God's will. Tell them that God wants an end to global warming. Tell them God wants serious efforts to end poverty. Save us, Jesus! Stop giving us vague references to peace and justice—people don't want to think for themselves, Jesus, they want you to give them all the answers! Come on, Jesus! You can do it!

Jesus! Would you help me, please? My mommy lost her job and can't pay the rent. My daddy is sick and can't afford a doctor. My little sister is sick, too, and we can't afford her medicine. And my monkey is losing his stuffing. Everybody says you can make things better for us, Jesus. Won't you help us?

Jesus! Welcome to town! Now if you'd just step this way, the limousine will pick you up and take you straight to Nob Hill where a gathering of local business and government leaders is holding a luncheon for you. We have a lot to discuss. Economic revitalization, infrastructure improvements, trade agreements with Asia, tax breaks for research and development. I'm sure you're aware of the influence you have around here. We think you could assemble a coalition of financial, political, and technological leaders that could make this region the pre-eminent force for global progress. If you could just dust your sandals before getting in the limo, that would be wonderful.

Jesus! Help me, and help me quick! I can't stop myself from drinking and drugging! I'm killing myself and only you can stop me. Every time I see the fridge, I open it and eat something—I can't control my weight. Jesus, you have to help me! I'm addicted to sex and it's destroying my relationship with my partner. Jesus, just say the word, and it will all stop, and I can get sobriety and sanity in an instant! Jesus, help!!

Jesus, Jesus, would you stand over here? Smile, Jesus! Oh, come on, smile! You can do it! Lift your chin a little, would you? And straighten up. You, behind Jesus, could you crouch down so he looks a lot taller? Great. Thanks! Don't worry, I'll use PhotoShop to fix that bad tooth. I always wanted a smiling Jesus, full of sunshine and light and niceness, to put in a frame on my wall. You're wonderful, Jesus! What a sweetie!

Jesus! We're all so glad you arrived. Yes, we're the Jesus Seminar, the Bible scholars who have been trying to figure out who the historical Jesus was. And here you are! If you could please step this way, we have a lot of questions to ask you. First of all, what did you really say in your Sermon on the Mount? And please, please, tell us what the parables really mean, if in fact you really told them at all! Please come with us! We have a week-long conference here and we need you to lecture every day!

Jesus! Don't listen to these people! Their priorities are all wrong. Come with us. The helicopter is waiting over there. We have a trip planned for you to go to Africa. With a wave of the hand you could stop the horrific genocide and starvation going on there. We'll visit areas where drought is about to kill millions. With a nod you can bring them rain and save their crops and prevent children from dying. After that, it's off to fight AIDS, and then to Southeast Asia to end repression, and then . . . .

Jesus! Jesus! Jesus! Jesus!

True Humility

First thing one morning at the Urban Ministry drop in center for homeless people in Palo Alto, a gleaming stretch limo pulled up. Everyone's head turned. People came to our center on foot, often walking for miles to come enjoy a cup of coffee and comradeship every morning. Or they came by bus. A few owned beat-up cars, in which they camped at night. So this was a most unusual occasion. Everyone at the drop in center fell quiet and stared as the driver, wearing a natty looking cap, leaped out of the limo, swiftly came around and opened the middle passenger door, and closed it behind the passenger. He was one of our long-time homeless people, a fellow who was addicted to crack cocaine and had been in and out of jail and rehab programs. With a sheepish grin he came up to our drop in center as the limo sped away. The homeless folks were all smiles. I congratulated him on such a magnificent arrival. But he said "No big deal, Jim. The limo driver is homeless. He lives in the limo. He just let me sleep in the back seat last night!"

Jesus wasn't a suit, he wasn't a swell. He was a homeless guy, and his ride wasn't even a stretch limo driven by another homeless guy. His ride was an ass, the lowly cousin of the horse. Palm Sunday matters not because of the style, or lack thereof, with which Jesus entered the city. Instead, the story of Jesus' arrival in Jerusalem illustrates true humility.

Fake humility is pretending to be less than one really is. It happens when people want to avoid looking like they are overly proud of great achievements. If you win the Nobel Prize for physics, you have nothing to be humble about when it comes to doing science. If you are the best golfer on the planet, you have nothing at all to be humble about when it comes to swinging a club. Did you know that there is a world's champion barista? Well, if you are the world's champion barista, then you have nothing whatever to be humble about when it comes to making double espressos.

Jesus was the world's champion humble person. When it came to humility, he had us all beat. And how did he master humility? By practicing, like all world's champions must do. Here was his humility program:

He started by going out into the desert for forty days and forty nights to do nothing but pray, meditate and stare at the scenery. Well, I've done enough of that sort of thing to be able to report what it is like. If you sit quietly in the desert for any length of time you will notice that you are a puny speck in the midst of an enormous landscape. If you stare at rocks in the desert long enough, you realize that they are really, really old, and you aren't. You find rocks out there containing the fossilized bones of creatures a lot bigger than you, creatures that went extinct a long time ago. Someday you, too, will be nothing more than the dust of the desert. If you spent forty days and nights in the desert, looking at the star-studded sky every night, you'd begin to recognize that you are a fleck on a speck on the hair of a flea compared to the majesty surrounding you. This is true humility: to know how tiny, how flimsy, how miniscule even the most powerful and memorable human beings really are. Go ahead and be proud of your achievements, the victories you've won by dint of your own effort. As long as you remember that as glorious as you are, you are not that much more glorious than the bacteria that live on the fuzz of moth-wings, when you are compared to this gargantuan universe.

Jesus practiced this kind of true humility. He knew he was an ordinary human being who, in St Paul's words, fell short of the glory of God. But by staying conscious of this humility, he was able to be as godly as any human being has ever been. He fulfilled so much of his human potential because he understood his small place in the grand plan.

If all beings lived from this true humility, their will-power could become better aligned with the loving purposes of their Creator. Jesus' humility was contagious. He inspired others to do as he did: shedding false egotism, becoming conscious of their true place in the cosmic order. If all of us were truly humble, we'd have a lot more compassion for each other. We'd be a lot more patient. We'd be more tolerant of each other's mistakes and differences, knowing that the difference between our best and our worst is infinitesimal compared to the difference between our best and the cosmic goodness of God.

So you are a champion weight lifter? Wonderful! Be proud. Enjoy the glory. Delight in the envy of millions. But remember: God flings the earth at 66,000 miles per hour around the sun, and the earth weighs 6,000,000,000,000,000,000,000,000 kilograms. That's six with 24 zeros behind it. The best weight lifter on earth is a wimp compared to God. Understanding this, and behaving accordingly, is true humility. The more we live from this humility, the better for us all.

The glory of a fine Palm Sunday service with lovely décor, outstanding choral music, and a rousing sermon is pale in comparison to that of the God we worship. So at best, our worship restores us to true humility. It's a time for us to rejoice in being the best we can be, and at the same time, a time to be boggled at how much grander is the divine drama in which we play our brief parts.

GOOD FRIDAY

The Gift

(Numbers 21: 4-9, John 3: 13-15)

No one's raised who did not fall
No one saves whom God did not send
No one stands whose knees won't bend
No helper's not been helped at all

While being raised we each shall die
The poison has an antidote
God may sleep in my storm-tossed boat
But when he rises, so shall I

Here where nothing grows which cannot bear the windy blast
And serpents live because they hug the ground
A person lives by eating what he's found
And gazing at the victims of the missiles he's cast

The one who knows heaven as well knows earth
The victim and convict of our crime
Will raise the veil of space and time
She plumbs the grave who fathoms birth
It finally made us face our spite
So lift God's gift above the plain
With our blood its teeth and skin are stained
To remind us of our hope and plight

The Stations of the Cross

The practice of re-enacting or visually representing the Stations of the Cross is very old indeed. The fourteen traditional Stations mark the passages from the moment Jesus was condemned to death until his burial in the tomb. To experience the Stations is not only to remember the gospel story of Jesus' crucifixion, but also is a way for us to reflect on the human condition of evildoing and suffering. By looking into the mirror that is the Passion story, we see truths about ourselves that are not only painful to behold, but also, paradoxically, are the means of our salvation. Transformation begins with a clear-eyed encounter with difficult reality.

There are many ways to describe and interpret the Stations of the Cross. The Stations are archetypal, mythical and evocative rather than simply historical. Some of the Stations correspond to passages in the New Testament accounts of the Passion. But other Stations have no corresponding verses in Scripture. Jesus' encounter with Veronica, for example, at Station Number 6, is based on a legend that developed long after the biblical era.

Here I offer the Stations accompanied with reflections and questions for meditation and with suggestions for illustrations. I have displayed them on church walls with photos, paintings, and sculptures. I also used these meditations on a website that corresponded with fourteen locations in a downtown district. Participants printed out the fourteen meditations and a map with a route to fourteen locations that correspond to the Stations, and then made a one-mile walk to experience them. For instance, Station Five, where Simon of Cyrene is forced to carry Jesus' cross, was a corner where Mexican-American day laborers gathered to be picked up for jobs.

Station One: Jesus is condemned to death by Pontius Pilate.

(Image: A finger pointing at the viewer.)

It's a shame game. Jesus was caught in a tangle of blame. The Romans were threatened by anybody who caught the attention of the masses and might lead them to rise up against their foreign oppressors. The Jewish authorities were trying to keep as much independence of the Jews from control by Rome as possible, without getting crucified themselves. Jesus was blamed for upsetting the Roman occupiers and their balance of power with the Sanhedrin, when in fact he had done nothing to deserve his condemnation. Pilate washed his hands to deny his own guilt for condemning an innocent man. One of the enduring values of the Christian faith is its emphasis on forgiveness. Jesus forgave the Romans for doing what they did to him. The Way of the Cross leads to liberation from guilt, ending the cycle of blame and the game of shame.

How have you been tangled in a web of blame? When and how have you suffered by the accusations of others? When and how have you subjected others to blame and shame? Who are the "I.S.'s," the "identified sinners" who routinely get blamed for social problems around you? What can you do, spiritually and practically, to get out of the thorny tangle of blame and shame and guilt? How can you forgive, and be forgiven?

Station Two: The cross is laid upon Jesus.

(Images: a cross made out of soldiers and tanks and fighter planes; a cross made out of pills; a cross made out of bottles of liquor; a cross made out of money)

The cross is anything that we think will save us, but which crucifies us instead. The cross is any temporal thing in which we put our ultimate trust and faith and hope, which in turn betrays us. Our nation (like the Roman Empire) so often thinks our military might will "save" us, but instead we become entangled in quagmires in foreign countries, and our use of our weapons ends up recruiting new enemies to make war on us. Our medical technology seems like it can "save" us, but then addicts us or torments us with bad side-effects. We think more money will "save" us, but then we become enslaved by the process of getting it and keeping it. The Romans thought the use of the cross would save their Empire, frightening people into submission. But this brutality contributed to the fall of the Empire. The early Christians did something very radical: they turned a symbol of torture and state power into a symbol of personal and social liberation.

What is your cross? What did you think would "save" you, but turned out to "crucify" you instead? How can you let go of this cross, and be liberated?

Station Three: Jesus falls for the first time as he carries his cross toward Golgotha.

(Images: statues fallen from their pedestals)

St. Paul said: "I have been crucified with Christ; it is no longer I who live, but Christ who lives in me." (Galatians 2:19-20) One way to understand the Way of the Cross is to see it as an "out of ego" experience. Jesus fell—he fell off the pedestal of admiration that so many people had for him. The crucifixion was a total humiliation, an "ego-buster." This is a painful process but also a liberating one. Think of the many things that trip us along life's way — we are "busted" as we fall over desire, greed, ambition, lust, anger, prejudice. It hurts to be separated from our egotism, but it takes us down to the very core of our being where we can find oneness with God, where we can find that "it is no longer I who live, but Christ who lives in me."

From which pedestals have you fallen? What has "busted" your ego? What pitfalls have you fallen into, and what, if any, positive things have resulted from those experiences?

Station Four. Jesus encounters his mother, Mary, as he carries his cross.
(Image: mother with hand on soldier's coffin)

Imagine the agony of Jesus' mother as she encounters her son on his way to his death. Remember the inevitable pain of parenting and being parented, the shared suffering that always comes between mother or father and child. Take consolation in knowing that this suffering is universal; it is inseparable from the human condition. To love our children, to love our parents, will someday and somehow bring us pain. Yet without that pain we would also be without the love that this most basic of human bonds brings with it. At this station, remember that despite its sometimes terrible price, love is worth the suffering that comes with it. And remember also the ways we can honor and give relief to our parents and children.

How can we be instruments of healing and reconciliation in our families? What has remained unsaid, and undone, between you and your parents or siblings or children? What would you say, what would you do, if you could?

Station Five: Simon of Cyrene is ordered to carry the cross for Jesus.
(Images: cross made out of shovels, cross made out of dishes, cross made out of vacuum cleaners)

Simon of Cyrene was visiting Jerusalem from Africa — he was there to celebrate Passover. The Romans built their empire on slave labor. They had a law that allowed their soldiers to press anyone into temporary service, to carry a load for a soldier or to do day labor for imperial purposes. Simon was drafted on the spot to carry the cross for Jesus, who, after being beaten severely, was too weak to carry it himself.

Who does our dirty work in America? And what is our responsibility as citizens to them? What would happen if "illegal aliens" disappeared from our community tomorrow? Who would do our dishes, wash our laundry, dig our ditches, lift our loads? And who else carries our cross? What of the people who work under terrible conditions in third world countries to produce the goods that stock the stores? Are we giving them what we owe them, for all that they do for us?

Station 6: Veronica wipes Jesus' face with a cloth as he passes by.

(Image: mirror with vague form of Jesus' face imprinted on it)

This legendary story says that Veronica, whose name in Latin means "true image", wiped Jesus' face with a cloth, and in so doing an image of his sweaty and bloody face was left on the cloth, which became a legendary religious relic in the Middle Ages. Can you see, in the mirror, the true image of the Christ in your own face, your own body? Can you see the Christ in everyone? Because the Christ is the human encounter with God, the human expression of divinity. Within each of us, through each of us, is to be found the spark of God's flame.

How do the people around you look to you now, as you intentionally seek to find the Veronica, the true image of Christ's face in each of their faces? Can you see the image of the Christ in your own face?

Station Seven: Jesus falls a second time on his way to Golgotha.

(Image: a house with a big rock holding up one corner)

Jesus said (Matthew 21:42-44) that the stone of stumbling - referring to himself - would become the cornerstone, the most important stone in the building of the new Kingdom of Heaven. We all trip on the block, and get busted — and while this is painful for us, it is also what "levels" us all, rich and poor, strong and weak, famous and unknown, and puts us in our place. But there is the promise that our stones of stumbling can be transformed into cornerstones of new life on the other side of the cross.

What is now getting in your way, laying you low, preventing you from going where you want and need to go? How might it be transformed into the building block of a new life for you?

Station Eight: Jesus meets the women of Jerusalem.
(Image: Destruction of World Trade towers on 9/11)

Jesus met a group of women from Jerusalem, who were weeping for him, but he told them they should instead be weeping for their city; he predicted its destruction, which happened in 70 AD when the Romans destroyed Jerusalem after a Jewish revolt. Jesus saw his own story, his own suffering, in a much wider context. He had a sense of history, and of his place in it. Something much larger than the fate of his own life was at stake.

What is your place in history? What social suffering do you witness or experience? What larger drama gives context for your life? What is your part in shaping the story of your society, bringing greater harmony and justice, now and in the future?

Station Nine: Jesus falls a third time.
(Image: chart of tumbling stock prices)

Jesus fell on his way to Golgotha. This third fall was the antithesis of his triumphal entry on Palm Sunday, a week before. How could he get this low, when he was riding so high only days before?

When have you gone from high to low? And low to high? What have you learned from those dramatic changes in your life?

Station Ten: The soldiers strip Jesus of his garments and draw lots to see which one gets his clothing.
(Image: gambling casinos)

The Roman soldiers who executed Jesus played a game of chance to decide who would get his garments. It was an insult added to his injuries, to leave him naked on the cross.

We can be so cruel, both purposefully and unwittingly exposing others to humiliation, because of our own pride or jealousy or anger.

When have you been stripped of all that protected you? How did it feel? In words or deeds, how have you embarrassed or insulted others, and made light of their suffering?

And what can you do to right your wrongs, to restore these people to dignity?

Station Eleven: Jesus is crucified on the cross.
(Image: lethal injection chamber on "death row")

Jesus was subjected to death by torture, a slow, agonizing execution that was meant to frighten Roman subjects into obedient submission. The Romans intended the cross to be a symbol of the consequences of defying the power of the empire. But Jesus transformed that symbol by dying on the cross. And the early Christians understood what it meant: that the Roman Empire showed its weakness through the cross. The Christians turned the cross into a symbol of the impotence of Rome. Through the crucifixion, an alternative empire was established on earth, in direct contradiction to the empire of Rome. Through the crucifixion, God's empire of peace, justice, equality, and charity came into being in a new form, a new way.

What are the crosses of today? How can your actions change them from instruments of fear and death into signs of hope?

Station Twelve: Jesus dies on the cross.
(Image: caduceus, the symbol of medicine: a pole with intertwined snakes)

The Christian gospel tells us that the death of Jesus was the turning point, the moment when salvation came to humanity. Somehow, by facing death, we come to life (John 3:14). The people of Israel, wandering in their desert exodus, began to despair of their fate and were then punished with a plague of snakes that bit them and killed some of them. Moses cried out to God for help, and God told him to put up a bronze serpent on a pole and have the people gaze at it, and thus be healed of the snakebites. The gospel of John says that as the serpent was lifted on the pole to save Israel, so would Jesus have to be lifted up in order to save humanity. The image of serpents on a pole, the caduceus, is still the symbol of medicine. The bronze serpent was spiritual homeopathy for snakebites. Likewise the cross is spiritual homeopathy for the human condition of suffering and mortality. By gazing at the death of Jesus, we see our own death, and are thus liberated from it into life.

What kind of spiritual homeopathy do you need now? What do you need to be lifted up on the pole, to gaze upon, so that you can recover from it? What social problems need to be lifted up, seen clearly, and faced honestly, so that they can be addressed and transcended?

Station Thirteen: Jesus' body is taken down from the cross by Joseph of Arimathea, a powerful Jew who risked his reputation and even his life to offer respect for Jesus' life by honoring his body after death.
(Image: a flowing shroud of cloth)

Joseph of Arimathea arranged for Jesus' body to be lovingly wrapped and buried. Legend has it that Joseph of Arimathea had the cup that Jesus used in the last supper, and that he put the cup under Jesus' wound when he was speared by the soldiers, and gathered Jesus' blood. Jesus died a profoundly shameful death, naked on the cross, but his body and blood were treated with the greatest care and respect after his death.

Do you show respect to your own body, and the bodies of others? What would it be like for you and others to treat the body as respectfully and lovingly in life as Joseph treated Jesus' body in death?

Station Fourteen: Jesus' body is placed in the tomb.
(Image: spot of light surrounded by darkness)

Ashes to ashes, dust to dust. Jesus' body returned to the earth from which it came. But that which was put into the earth came out of the earth three days later, transformed. As St. Paul said, "It is sown a physical body, it is raised a spiritual body." One need not believe that Jesus physically rose from the dead in order to fully experience the meaning and power of this story. The three days correspond to the three trimesters of human gestation. Jesus' physical body went in, but the eternal, universal, and ever-present Christ came out. The pain and terror and horror of crucifixion went in, but hope and promise came out. Jesus' body went into the tomb, but a new and wonderful kind of Christian community came out, three days later.

What new life comes from the parts of you that have died, or must die? What new life is growing inside this dark place at the end of the Passion? How is humanity being transformed through the dark passages of our history?

EASTER

Working It Out

Each of us has to work it out in her or his own way.

Some of us go through years of therapy to get there. Others become fitness fanatics and try to run or swim or weight-lift it out. Others plunge into artistry, trying to paint or sculpt our way through. Sometimes we go through nightmarish addictions to get there, nearly destroying ourselves in the process.

But one way or another, we must do it. Somehow we must resolve the mighty struggles raging within us.

God went through it, too. The Bible, in all its verbose majesty and travesty, might be reduced to the following short, mythical synopsis of God's inner struggle:

Before the beginning, God was alone, and desperately lonely. So he decided to create a friend, and a world to sustain this friend. But as soon as he created humanity, God was ambivalent about us. God was afraid we would get the better of him, get too clever and take his place. God wanted to keep us below him, but intimacy requires the risk of being an equal, or even being a servant, to one's friend. We wanted to go farther than God would allow, and this angered God, who kept changing the rules and limits he placed on us in his ever-more-frustrating attempts to manage us. So God "acted out" against us. He heaped terrible pain and loss on Job, who had been a loyal friend to him, punishing Job for no good reason. Job complained bitterly to God, whom he had loved and honored. God hated himself for what he had done to Job and to so many others. So finally God could stand it no longer and gave up and became a human being himself, a human being who suffered the full weight of God's anger, so that God would know what it was like to be cursed by God. (4) And as a human being he realized he needed to become better than the God he used to be. As a human being, he became more God-like than he had been when he was God. And as a human being, he showed other people that they could rise to a higher level of divinity, as well.

He suffered and died, and then he was reborn as a new God, a God of mercy and forgiveness and compassion. And this is the moment we celebrate at Easter. Easter was the time when the old-fashioned God of vengeance and jealousy and ambivalence and rage was buried with Jesus in the tomb, to be reborn as a new form of divinity that would dwell in every human heart. The God who died on the cross was reborn as the God of unconditional love, the God who rejoices in us just as we are, the God we can't embarrass no matter how foolishly we behave, the God who is not afraid to be our friend no matter how clever or ridiculous we may be. This is a reborn God who decommissioned his thunderbolts and dried up his floods and quenched his hell-fires. A God who died on the cross as a domineering male, and rose up as both male and female, heterosexual and homosexual. A God who died on the cross as a tyrant, and rose up as a servant. A God who died on the cross as a rage-o-holic, and rose up as a gentle friend.

We all have to work it out somehow, even in the strangest of ways. Approaching Easter, we celebrate the moment when we leave our inner turmoil behind, when we rise from the death of bitterness and resentment and frustration and disappointment, and take up the new life of peace, patience, kindness, hope, and creativity. God got there at Easter, and so may we!

Never the Same Again

A few summers ago, a young girl I knew went to Camp Cazadero, our church camp in Northern California. Her family belonged to College Heights United Church of Christ in San Mateo, where I was the pastor. She was twelve years old, a tomboy who loved to play rough and wear levis and flannel shirts. The Sunday after church camp, she came to worship wearing pretty clothes and a little bit of makeup on her face. I asked her, "Betsy, what happened to you? Is that you in there?" She flashed me a big grin and said, "I had a great time at church camp!" There, she had taken interest in boys, and they in her. In just seven days, she had become a new person that I hardly recognized. She left the old garments behind. She's never been the same as she was before.

Mary Magdalene found the stone rolled away from the tomb. She ran to tell two of Jesus' disciples, Peter and John, who then ran to the tomb and looked in and saw the burial cloths lying empty right in the spot where Jesus' body had been laid. He had left those garments behind. He's never been the same since.

I once knew a homeless man named Randy. He was always a sweet-natured guy, easy-going in his manner, though he seemed depressed. Randy smelled bad, wore filthy clothes, lived in the bushes, panhandled for money, and spent it on crack cocaine. He came to our drop in center for the homeless to get some coffee and leftover bagels from us and to face another day. Then he stopped coming around, and I worried about what had happened to him. A year or so later, I ran into him on the sidewalk in Palo Alto and we warmly greeted each other. He told me had been to a drug rehab center, he then got a job and a little place to live. He was sober, healthier, and much happier. He was wearing clean, nice clothes. He had left his old garments behind. He was not the same as he had been before.

After I met my wife, Roberta, I left a lot of my old garments behind. She has wonderful taste, and an eye for excellent, low-cost clothes. She also has a good eye for the changes I have needed to make in my ways of thinking and acting. I have more old garments to leave behind, as I am further transformed through our marriage. After I met Roberta, I was never quite the same, and I (and others!) have been grateful for the changes she's introduced in my life.

The life-changing, consciousness-expanding myths of Passion Week and Easter tells us that the Roman soldiers gambled for the right to strip him of his last bit of clothing while he died on the cross. The story tells us that he was wrapped in the cloth strips of death before his burial. Gone was his painful crown of thorns, replaced with a linen shroud around his head. And the story tells us that he left the shroud and wrappings behind, lying empty on the stone, when he rose. And then it tells us that after resurrecting, Jesus showed up on the road between Jerusalem and the town of Emmaeus, and that he met up with a couple of his disciples, who thought he was just another traveler along the way. If he had been naked, they would have noticed, and the story would have told us. So we can presume, for the sake of the consistency of the story, that Jesus was wearing clothes as he walked to Emmaus. Somewhere, somehow, he got himself a new set of threads after he left the old garments of his previous life and death behind. Hmm... wonder how they looked?

And later he appeared to the disciples again, for the last time, and he said to them, "I am sending upon you what my Father promised; so stay here in the city until you have been clothed with power from on high."

From then on, whenever the disciples broke bread, there was Jesus, known to them again. To this day, this is one of Jesus' favorite outfits: a loaf of bread, the bread we share in communion. And when we are clothed with the power of the Holy Spirit of love and creativity and positive energy, we're wearing another of Jesus' favorite outfits.

At Easter, so many of us wear our finest. Wondrous is a new dress, or a new suit, or even a really nice-looking $50 used Brooks Brother's suit like the one Roberta found for me in a thrift store. How much more wondrous is the new set of clothes that Jesus got at Easter, clothes that made a mere mortal man into someone divine! How yet more wondrous is the new set of clothes he offers us now, wrapping us in spiritual gifts of peace and patience and hope and forgiveness and faith!

But to put on these new clothes we must strip ourselves of the old and cast them aside. I'll never forget my daughter's room in her high school years. She would change clothes and toss the dirty ones on the floor and not do her laundry for weeks, until finally the clothes would become a slow-moving glacier, scouring across the floor and pouring out the door. When the glacier of stale clothes started to calve into the living room, that was where I drew the line and made her do her laundry.

Likewise we need to cast aside the old clothes of addictions, cast aside the old clothes of fear and hate and petty jealousy, cast aside the old clothes of greed and callousness to the suffering of others. Easter is about a lot of things, and one of them is about changing our wardrobe: clothing ourselves in passion for justice, commitment to peace in word and deed and thought, embracing the mystical unity of all beings and things.

Jesus is wearing new clothes for Easter. Can you see them? He's wearing the bread and wine we share in communion, the food we lovingly share with each other in our homes and our churches. He's wearing the oil of healing. He's wearing love so beautiful and so flexible that it even fits on your enemies. He's wearing the smile on your face when you greet a lonely stranger. He's wearing the empathy you share with someone in pain. He's wearing the strength that keeps you clean and sober. He's wearing the grace with which you face your illnesses and injuries. He's wearing the patience that you have with the people with whom you are in conflict. He's wearing the bliss you feel when you make love or music or art or poetry. He's wearing the truth you tell to others, he's wearing the truth you receive with an open heart from others. He's wearing the common good your promote through your job, your citizen activism, your service in your church. Check out his new threads. Admire the new hat that crowns his head, and let his hip new outfit be yours, as well.

The Easter Code

Typing onto punch cards in 1972, I crafted my first computer program at the University of California, Santa Cruz. It was an algorithmic version of a board game I had invented. I was excited at the prospect of turning my low-tech game into what was, at the time, a high-tech manifestation.

I handed my stack of cards to the computer operator. After I waited in that neon-lit basement for quite a while, he emerged from the back of the computer center with an expression of disgust on his face, as he lugged a pile of continuous-feed paper. Only after he retreated did I dare to approach the counter where he had slapped the pile down on the Formica surface. Indeed, the pile was mine. It was supposed to be just a few sheets thick. But I had written an endless loop into my code, a mistake that caused the computer to print the same subprogram over and over. The computer operator saw what was happening, and turned off the program before it used up all the paper in the building! Garbage in, garbage out: that was the lesson I learned in my computer programming class that afternoon.

But, thank God, what is true in the realm of computers is not the last word in life.

Betrayal, judgment, prejudice, persecution, abuse, terror, pain, killing, death. These were the inputs in the program that led to the tomb where Jesus' body was laid. Yet what came out of the tomb was completely different than what led into it. What emerged from the tomb, after three days of processing, was not garbage at all. Despair in, hope out. Isolation in, community out. Terror in, courage out. Violence in, kindness out.

Clearly, the algorithm of Easter is of a higher order than any computer program yet devised. It's an elegant code written in a special language with mysterious, metaphorical elements.

The cross. It is a code that tells us to focus our attention and intention on something beyond it, to go in a positive direction instead of scattering ourselves in a negative entropy. You don't focus on the cross-hairs in a surveyor's scope: you use the cross-hairs to focus on something far beyond the scope itself. The cross is an x-y coordinate, an intersection, that aims toward the best we can be, toward the highest service we can render, toward the most wondrous love we can feel and share. The cross aims beyond the fear and dread that the Roman soldiers wanted people to see in it. The Christians made the cross a pointer toward a life that defies death itself.

A tomb. A womb dug in the ground. For countless millennia, the earth has been a goddess to human beings. Planting seeds was a sacred act, an insemination of the divine mother. In dreams, we go underground and then reemerge above ground with new knowledge or new being. Three days Jesus lay in the ground, corresponding to the three trimesters of human pregnancy. On the third day, re-birth. The tomb emptied. Jesus, the human being, went in. Christ, the divine encounter with human beings, came out. St. Paul said that the Christ was sown physical, and raised spiritual. With Jesus, we go into the dark. Depression, despair, grief that seems to have no end. Meanwhile, within us, we are changing in ways we barely can tell. Then the stone rolls away, the womb opens with a groan, and we come out transformed. And we barely know how or why. Ponder this: how do you learn? Can anybody really teach you anything? A teacher can't go into your head and put something there. He or she can point toward it, describe it, talk about it, demonstrate it, but the teacher can't make you know it. Somehow all that input goes into the darkness between your ears, behind your eyes, and somehow it gestates in your brain until the stone rolls away, the lights go on, and you know.

Bread. Jesus appears after the tomb is found empty. He walks down the road to Emmaus with his disciples, who don't recognize him until, as the unknown guest, he is invited to bless and then break the bread. And when he breaks it, suddenly he becomes known to them. And then immediately he disappears. Haven't we heard about bread in the gospel before? Feeding thousands on repeated occasions with only a few loaves and fishes? Didn't he say he was the bread of life? Didn't Jesus break bread with all sorts of people with whom a good rabbi was not supposed to commune? Didn't he say the bread was his body at his last supper with his disciples?

And there's something fishy about this Easter Code. Why did the story say Jesus ate fish after his resurrection? What about his saying that the fishermen he recruited as disciples would be fishers of human beings? What about his multiplying of a few fish into a meal for thousands? And what about that mysterious story in which tax collectors asked Jesus' followers if he would pay tax to the Romans? And Jesus said that the rulers of the world don't ask their sons to pay tax, but rather ask it of everyone else. But to keep the tax collectors happy, Jesus told his disciples to go to Lake Galilee and catch a fish and look in its mouth, and find a coin in its mouth to pay the tax. Why did the fish pay Jesus' tax? It's dreamlike: fish that live underwater, that powerful symbol of the unconscious realm, fish that navigate the hidden realm of the soul. Jesus is in touch with the fish; they work for him, pay his taxes, come at his bidding and fill the nets of the disciples who hear a man on the shore tell them to lower their nets in a certain place, and they pull up a huge catch of fish, and when they get to shore, the man is Jesus. And strangely, he's already cooked a breakfast of fish for them to eat, and in amazement, they eat the fish. Jesus represents the power to dip down into the realm of dreams, the realm of the unconscious, and find value there for living on the land, above the deep, to dip down into the soul and pull up that which will give us life and strength.

Can this be a key to the Easter Code: that the story of Easter points beyond itself? Jesus' followers slowly re-gathered in their state of fear and shock after his death. They continued to catch and eat fish together, and break bread with each other, as they tried to make sense of the seemingly senseless death he died, and to make sense of the powerful acts of caring and healing of body and soul that he did while he was alive, days they wished had not come to an end. Meanwhile, without knowing it, they were doing what Jesus had done. The nurture and intimacy and care that Jesus had shared with them over these meals, they were continuing it. After a long gestation, a period of despair in not knowing, suddenly, light! The stone rolled away. At some point, perhaps over a period of weeks or months or even a year or so, they understood, they knew, that the life they had known in their days with Jesus was a new life that they were now living. The stone rolled away and they then knew who they were and what they needed to do. They suddenly were able to celebrate what they had grieved until then. They suddenly saw hope in the same things that led them to despair. Jesus' soul, his spirit, his essence, the essence beyond his body or ego, what they came to call the Christ, was there, every time they broke bread.

With the breaking of the bread, the loop of fear and anxiety that made their heads spin at the crucifixion was broken. The broken bread broke the Easter Code, and its message of transforming hope overwhelmed them. The broken bread inspired them to create and sustain a community of unconditional love. Every time we break bread in communion, we decode Easter once again.

Easter Prayer

> *Dear One who meets us on both sides of the stone that guards the tomb, who makes new lives out of the ones we lose, we hang on to the old lives we are losing, and hesitate to embrace the new ones you make for us. We hang on to immaturity, to habits that have become holy to us, even as they drag us down. We hang on to ways of thinking and living that we have outgrown. We hang on to political and economic systems that result in gross inequity, just because we hate to give up what is famil-*

iar. We let our homes become museums instead of shelters for a living love. We linger at the tombs where we store our embalmed images of ourselves, even as you are transforming that image into yours. In the silence of prayer we wait for you to roll away the stone and reveal to us the new life that you are creating for each of us. Amen!

TAX DAY

A Prayer for April 15

(I pray in worship with my hand on a copy of my income tax return resting on the pulpit, on the Sunday before taxes are due.)

Dear God, bless my taxes! Give me peace of mind as I struggle to fill out the forms and determine the right amounts I should be sending to the government. Keep me calm, I pray, as I write out those fat checks on April 15. And whisper a reminder to me, Lord, of all the good reasons that I send my money to my government every year.

Remind me of the fact that I could not write this prayer if I had not received an excellent tax-subsidized education. My parents couldn't have afforded fancy private schools or colleges. Gently show me that the Internet, through which I send this prayer to others, was created with taxpayer dollars. Help me to recall that my freedom to pray as I wish was purchased with the lives of soldiers and the tax payments of other citizens who defended liberty before I was born. Reveal to me, Lord, in my mind's eye, the roads and the airports, the water systems, the magnificent parks and wilderness areas, the public health workers, the regulators of the environment and of commerce, the scientists, and all else that my taxes make possible. They provide safety and comfort, protect natural resources, and enable capitalism to flourish for the benefit of all. Remind me of how hard and scary life was for the sick and elderly before citizens paid Social Security taxes and received its benefits. Remind me, dear One, just how expensive, difficult, and unpleasant life would be for us all without all the services and protections that are funded by my tax payments.

Dear Lord, remind me that for all the good things that I and others receive back from the government, my tax payments are a bargain. Redeem me from selfishness and give me a spirit of gratitude as I write those tax checks. Inspire me to see that this is a sacred duty, and is a way that I serve others who are vulnerable, poor, or sick, and are especially dependent on public assistance.

O dear One, there are so many ways I wish my taxes could be spent differently. There are many things I don't like about what my government is doing, and there are many very important things it leaves undone. I'm very distressed that my taxes fund an immoral war, I'm disgusted at the diversion of my tax money into political corruption. I'm embarrassed that my government doesn't take the needs of the poor seriously, and I'm outraged that my taxes aren't paying for a health care system that guarantees coverage to everyone. I'm willing, O Lord, to pay even more in taxes if it would work for the common good: it could save us all even more money and trouble, in the end. More than ever, dear God, give me the strength and the vision to take action as a voter, pressing my government to act for peace and justice at home and abroad. My sacred duty as a citizen is only partly fulfilled as I write my tax checks. I ask for your guidance, God, as I join with others to change the priorities and values of our government, so that it reflects your loving will more closely.

May your blessing rest on my Form 1040 this next week, dear Lord, and may my taxes well serve you and my fellow citizens! Amen.

PENTECOST

Grief's Gift

"Absalom, Absalom!" cried David after the death of his son (2 Samuel 18). "Absalom, Absalom." David was the king of Israel. There was a war on. He had to be on, he had to work. But David was despondent. His whole vocabulary had been reduced to one name, reduced to three syllables: Absalom. Other people had many other things that they wanted to be on King David's mind. But King David had only one thing on his mind: Absalom, his son, was dead. David's advisors tried to snap him out of his grief. They tried to shame him out of it. But for David, everything else was boring wallpaper, everything else was refrigerator hum, everything else was tasteless, odorless, meaningless. Only one devastating reality mattered to him: his son was dead. Absalom.

Those of us who tend toward the feel-good version of Christianity, and I include myself in that number, can be tempted to think that holy equals happy. Grief is awful. It is terrible. People sometimes say they would rather get a root canal or a bone marrow transplant than to suffer the inner, invisible pain that overwhelms them in grief. And yet grief is sacred. It is devastating and dreadful yet it is a holy thing. Terrible as it is, it is a gift.

The therapist Joanna Macy reminds us that the word "apathy" doesn't just mean disinterest. Apathy is worse than that. Apathy comes from the Greek word apatheia, which means non-suffering. So apathy is the unwillingness, or inability, to feel one's own pain or to feel the pain of others. In other words, apathy is numbness. Joanna Macy says that perhaps the worst problem in modern post-industrial wealthy societies is that people have become numb, unwilling to suffer pain themselves, unwilling to co-suffer, to empathize, with the suffering of others near or far.

The gift of grief is that it snaps us out of apathy. Its wrenching agony makes us feel when we become numb. And if we weren't numb already, if we already were able to empathize, to feel the pain of others, our grief invites others to snap out of their apathy, their numbness, and feel with us.

Are we willing to grieve? And willing to let others grieve, and to honor the sacredness of their grief, and to create a safe and loving space around them to protect and honor their grief? Or are we like David's advisors? Do we try to talk grieving people into being happy again, when they aren't ready to do so?

Do we expect their grief to be over when we think it ought to be over, according to some arbitrary schedule we have decided is normal? When loved ones die, they leave holes in the hearts of those who loved them. Do we presume that somehow these holes can be filled, as if with some kind of caulk or expanding insulating foam? As if your beloved wife or husband or father or mother somehow could be replaced?

No. Grief's awful sting reminds us of something that we so often wish we could forget. It reminds us that each human being is endlessly precious and unique and of supreme value, and that no other human being or thing or activity will even come close to replacing that individual. When a human being dies, a universe dies with that person; which is why grief seems so eternal, so overwhelming, so unfathomable, so utterly unacceptable. When we grieve a death, we are grieving the loss of a whole cosmos.

It's a paradox. For the grieving person, nothing appears to be able to come to any good; the loss of that precious person takes away the taste, smell, and texture of the world. Yet life does go on, and joy and pleasure do go on, as well. Somehow in grief we must hold the tension of this contradiction, not letting one experience deny the other its coexisting place.

There are cultures in this world where a woman puts on a black manta or kerchief when her husband dies, and keeps it on in grieving for the rest of her life. These cultures make plenty of room for grief and honor it as sacred. I know someone who wishes she could wear black all the time, after the death of her beloved, but she thinks that a lot of the people around her wouldn't get it, because they don't get it about grief. They want to cheer her up, they can't stand it that she isn't happy and hasn't gotten over her loss. They just don't have room in their hearts for her grief.

But let us pray that the church is a place and a people that make room for grief. In a way, the Christian religion is based on grief. A much-loved man named Jesus died, long before his time, and those who loved him were beside themselves with sadness. It took a long time for them to grieve. It didn't happen on a schedule, either. According to the gospel myth, they drifted in depression and confusion until the day we call Pentecost, fifty days after Easter, when they gathered together and discovered a new way to be a community. The Christian church grew out of a fully-observed, fully-honored grief. The church is a community that makes plenty of room for grief, gives it the time and space and the comfort that it requires when we suffer a terrible loss. The symbol of the church is a cross, after all. A death brought us together and taught us how to show compassion to those who have suffered terrible loss. The church itself is a gift of grief.

So let us abandon our apathy, rise above our numbness, and honor, tenderly and patiently, the sacredness of grief.

Thank you God for love I've lost
For love is worth the pain it cost
For giving me this heart to feel
The gift of grief that you reveal

The Spark of Pentecost

In that story in the Hebrew Scriptures, humans started out with but one language. Everybody understood each other. So they could cooperate together to get a lot accomplished. Like building a tower out of bricks at Babel (Genesis 11), so tall that it reached almost up to the outermost heaven where God was said to live. But God did a NIMBY—"Not in my backyard!"—on them. Like so many people today who object to anything built next door to their houses, God didn't want this tower in his neighborhood, so he decided to stop the project. He caused people to start babel-ing in all kinds of different languages. They couldn't understand each other so they couldn't get their act together to finish the tower project.

So the story of Pentecost in the book of Acts chapter 2 is a very hopeful one. It creatively expresses the idea that there is a way for people to understand each other across their cultural, religious, political, ethnic, linguistic, and even personality differences. It promises that a Holy Spirit of love will blow through like a wind and get us talking and cooperating, and help us to accomplish much for the common good. At Pentecost, God went from being a NIMBY to being a YIMBY—"Yes, In My Back Yard"!

Tongues of fire over the heads of the disciples, like the tongues in their mouths, fired up to share the promise of a new world where people can understand and respect each other despite their differences. This amazing mythical story is another of the many in the Christian tradition that suggests that things don't have to be the way they are. The world can change; human beings can change in profound and deep ways. Human society can change. Human nature itself can change, for the better. Even I can change! Fancy that; a mighty wind can blow through and fire me up with a new spirit and a new way of doing life.

Imagine a fire, outside in the night. The wood crackles, the flames lick up into the darkness. Imagine that the fire itself is something that came down from the outermost heavens long ago, and was locked into the wood. A spark from a flint against tinder caught fire, and the tinder released the fire inside the wood; let it go up into flames. Imagine that the fire cannot wait to return to the outermost heaven from which it came. Imagine one of the glowing sparks from the fire, rising up. It is so willing to get to the fire of God that it is willing to disappear entirely in the darkness above the fire on earth. It wants to get to heaven but the only way to get there is for it to disappear for a while. And rise through unknowing, un-being, non-existence, up, up, and away. In order to reach God it must give itself up. Then, once it has risen to heaven, it accelerates eagerly into its divine Source in a burst of light.

Imagine that you are that spark. You are a bit of God, living on the earth. You yearn to return to the Love from which you originally came. You want to get back to God, but you know you must give yourself up in order to get there. You are afraid, you are torn between your desire for divine love and your fear of what it will take to return to it. To return to your loving Source, you must abandon your attachments to this world, your attachment to your ego, to your old ways of being. You must take the ultimate risk of non-being — releasing your desperate grasping onto the transient things of this world.

This image comes from the 14th-century German mystical preacher, Meister Eckhart. He compared the soul to a spark that disappears as it rises from a flame, on its way to the divine Light far above the darkness here below.

Like that spark, locked inside the wood, you are stuck in your fear, but then suddenly something is lit under you, like flaming tinder. The heat releases your attachment to your accomplishments as well as your failures, releases your clinging to possessions and to your identity. You stop clutching onto the people you love, and you let go of your resentments against others. The flame of Pentecost fires you up, and you let go of who you thought you were and what you thought you could and couldn't do. You rise, you rush, you accelerate into the warm and glowing heart of God, where you are inflamed with divine love. God put a spark of divine love in your heart, and that spark wants to be reunited with its source, and the only way to get there is to risk disappearing into the darkness of uncertainty and unknowing.

MOTHER'S DAY

Dear Mom

Writing a prayer may not be as spontaneous as a spoken or silent prayer, but the very process of editing it is a prayer in itself. It is a peeling-away of the layers that get between us and God, hopefully revealing our highest intentions, deepest sentiments, and most refined hopes along the way.

In addition to honoring my physical mother, Barbara Deemy Burklo, whom I adore and enjoy, one Mother's Day I decided to write a letter to my spiritual Mother God. The result was a letter I could have addressed to either of them:

> Dear Mom:
>
> Happy Mothers' Day! For the gift of my first breath, and every breath since, I thank you. For always being there no matter what, for your patience in my childhood and in my extremely long and no doubt trying and tedious adolescence, I thank you. You really are the best.
>
> Remember that time when I told you that you were an especially cool mom because you evolved, you changed with the times? Well, now that I'm a bit older and, by your grace, perhaps wiser, I realize that it was my idea of you that evolved and changed with the times. I was the one developing, while you patiently nudged the process along. Maybe parenthood has helped me understand this. You know how it goes. One minute my child thinks I am a nerd, and the next minute either I've changed remarkably more than I perceive, or, in an epiphany, my child has discovered that I'm worthy of respect. Well, you are certainly worthy of my respect. If you've changed, I cannot say, but now I realize how much I have changed.
>
> I am so grateful for the times when you've stayed close, times when I've been in crisis. Yes, I have friends who also stood with me in a very trying time a few years ago. But friends can't be there all the time. When they couldn't listen, you did. When they weren't around, you were. You received my blubbering complaints, you heard my blatherings as I played the victim in that messy conflict. You didn't judge, you didn't intervene, you didn't fix it for me, you just stayed with me and paid attention and gen-

tly directed me toward growth and strength, so subtly that I hardly noticed what you were doing. As I look back, I see that while that crisis took a few years to resolve, I needed all that time to understand it and gain the wisdom to take a higher level of responsibility for my situation. Looking back, I see how you stilled the storm inside of me, time and again. Thank you.

Right now I am challenged to maintain my integrity and pursue the calling you have given me, and at the same time satisfy the sometimes conflicting preferences and expectations of others. I'm being challenged to be much more tactful and carefully-spoken than I've ever had to be. I'm being challenged to be patient and forbearing and as you know, Mom, this hasn't been my strong suit. You've been nudging me sweetly toward this all along, but now I need to get serious about it, and it doesn't come naturally to me. I always prided myself on being blunt and direct, but that's not working for me nor others these days. I need your help to make this change!

I need your support in my marriage, too. I have so much more to learn from you about it. After all your years of marriage to the human race, with all the ups and downs and highs and lows in your relationship, the intimacy as well as the frustration you've experienced, you are a fount of wisdom about how to stay committed while being true to yourself. I look to your example in doing my part in my marriage. Will you help me to be honest but gentle with her, to remember to ask her lots more questions, to be better at anticipating her needs and desires, to be a more complete partner to her in every aspect of life? I need to be less selfish in our marriage, and you are the least selfish person I know.

Mom, there are some things about our relationship that I miss. There were times when I was younger when your presence was like magic. When I felt your soft embrace all around me. I think I used to appreciate your creativity a lot more than I do now. I'd get goose bumps looking at your sunsets, a thrill up my spine gazing at the layers of your distant mountain ranges, a burning sensation in my chest as I walked through your vast deserts and alluring forests. I still feel all those things, but not as often as I did before. I want to go back to those places again with you. Let's get together soon—I want to have a good long look at your artistry, the new stuff as well as the old, really soon! And I look forward to a good hug from you, and I hope you are up for a hug from me.

For this day, and for your abiding love, I celebrate you with all my heart. I love you, Mom!

Your child,

Jim

ST. BUDDHA'S DAY

Once there was a Christian saint by the name of St. Ioasaph. In the medieval era, there was a popular story, now clearly seen to be a legend, that a Christian missionary named Barlaam went to India and converted a philosophically-minded prince to Christianity. For this, both Barlaam and Ioasaph were canonized into sainthood, and August 26th was declared St. Barlaam and St. Ioasaph's Day. Later, as historical knowledge and accuracy became more important in the Western world, it became pretty obvious that Ioasaph sounded a lot like Bodhisattva, a name for Buddha. Once it became obvious that the Catholic Church had accidentally made Buddha a Christian saint, he was demoted and his day removed from the church calendar.

Gautama was indeed a philosophically and spiritually minded Indian prince. That was about the only accurate part of the St Ioasaph legend that brought us St. Buddha's Day. One day, Gautama decided to step outside the walls of the palace where he had lived a secure and pampered life. He witnessed the terrible suffering of ordinary people in his kingdom, and it affected him so profoundly that he dedicated his life to helping people overcome suffering. He discovered that the primary cause of suffering is desire. Transcend desire, and suffering is alleviated. He followed this path in meditation and reached a state of enlightenment, at which he took on the title of Buddha, one that applies not just to him but to anyone who reaches that state. In the group of his sayings called the Dhammapada, he says: "This is the only way, the only way to the opening of the eye. Follow it. Outwit desire. Follow it to the end of sorrow."

In my own experience of practical life, as well as meditation and prayer, I've found his words to be true. The mind is a sort of monkey trap. The monkey trap is a banana in a jar that is just big enough to let in its hand, but the mouth of the jar is too narrow for the monkey to pull out his hand with the banana in it. So the monkey's hand stays stuck in the jar, trapped by his own desire for the banana. There's a wonderful image from Christian tradition that illustrates Buddha's point very well. Dante, the Italian poet, described Satan in his Inferno. Satan is stuck headfirst in a pool of ice at the very bottom of hell. The ice is created by his flapping wings, which he is flapping wildly in his desire to fly out of the hole. On the other side of the icy hole is the opening to Paradise. So near, yet so far! He can never get there because of his desire. If he'd let go of the desire, the ice could melt and he could get out of the pit of hell. The Buddha taught that the mind plays tricks, and the source of most of those tricks is our fixation on our desires.

At least in my own experience, I find that through prayer I can't really get rid of my desires. And it's not really about ceasing to want things, especially good things. It's fine to have desire for love, for the joys and pleasures of this life. But when I start wildly flapping my wings at the thought of those desires, when my desires take control of my mind and my life, I become a slave to them and get stuck in suffering and sorrow.

We're never going to get everything we desire, not even close. Meditation and prayer can put us into a different relationship with our desires. A new relationship in which what we want does not control us.

When our dog, Kai, was a puppy, he once got curious and stuck his head in a plastic jug that had a wide mouth. It was an opaque jug, so it was dark inside. Thank God we found him in time, because Kai assumed that, all of a sudden, it was night. So he just peacefully curled up in the middle of the yard, on a bright sunny day, and started to sleep. We ran to him and removed the jug. Suddenly, it was daytime again for him, and he scampered happily away. Illusions can be deadly. Our minds can, as Buddha says, make mischief with us and convince us that day is night and night is day, that our desires are all that matter, convince us that slavery is freedom, make us so blind that we don't even know we've gotten our heads stuck in plastic jugs. We fall asleep, even though it's the middle of the day and our eyes are supposedly open. As Buddha says, "For he who is awake has shown you the way of peace. Give yourself to the journey."

Let us give ourselves to the journey that St. Buddha took, the journey that led him to Buddha-hood, to spiritual awakening. Let us give ourselves the journey that Jesus took, the journey that led him to become the Christ, that led him to spiritual awakening. Let us go beyond, beyond, beyond, utterly beyond, our attachments to the things of this world, become liberated from our bondage to our desires.

Rites and Sacraments

COMMUNION

Communion for the Urban Ministry

(I celebrated this Eucharist for a retreat of the Board of Directors of the Urban Ministry of Palo Alto, which included homeless as well as housed representatives.)

"This is my body."

This body knows what it is like to have a nice house and a good job.
It knows what it is like to feel uneasy about being wealthy.
And it knows what it is like to be lonely, a stranger.
It knows what it is like to live under a bush in a city park.
It knows what it is like to try to sleep in a rain-soaked sleeping bag.
This body knows what it is like to sit politely in meetings.
And it knows how to howl in protest at injustice.
It knows what it is like to eat right and exercise often.
And it knows what it is like to wake up the morning after drinking a fifth of vodka.
This body knows what it is like to do a triple flip on the bars of a jungle gym.
And what it is like to lie paralyzed in a hospital bed for five years.
This body knows what it is like to make love.
And to make war.
This body knows what it is like to be shunned because of the way it looks.
And to be wanted because of the way it looks.
This body knows what it is like to be afraid of being afraid.
And it knows what it is like to delight in taking crazy chances.

This body knows what it is like to be treated like an any body instead of like a some body.

"This is my body."
Take it in.
Take it on.
Receive the body of the Christ.

Blackberry Wine

As a summer job when I was in college in Santa Cruz, I worked in a winery, bottling on the line, cleaning casks, moving barrels, warehousing, and whatever else needed to be done. Bargetto's specialized in fruit and other dessert wines. The aroma of concentrated fruit pervaded everything in the winery. We got shipments of frozen blackberries in 50 gallon steel drums. On hot afternoons, we pried the lid off of a barrel and with ice-picks took out chunks of frozen berries and licked them: delicious! Every day at noon my boss, the maintenance man, would take me into the tasting room and pour me a shot of a different wine, to educate me properly about the virtues of the winery's products. The blackberry wine was overpowering: a liquid concentrate fermented from the berries we liberated from the barrels on those sweltering afternoons. A little glass of it, and you felt like you needed an insulin shot.

Some years later, I was going through a romantic breakup, so to cheer myself up, I took a walk to the nearest blackberry patch with a few plastic bags in hand. A "muscle car" drove past me on the road nearby, and it sported a bumper sticker that said "Happiness is Being Single." As a newly single person, I found this message to be especially ludicrous. I remember thinking to myself: "Happiness is not being single. Happiness is picking blackberries!"

Blackberries are body and blood rolled into one, perfect sacramental elements. Each berry looks like a miniature cluster of over-ripe grapes. Blackberries invite me to commune with all my sweet summer memories of picking them and enjoying them in years past. And they invite me on their own terms. I didn't plant them. (This would be madness, since they dominate any space where they take root.) They invite me to a Eucharist where I am not the celebrant. They invite me to a table I did not set. They are manna from heaven, best consumed on the spot. They turn rainwater into their dense wine as they grow from green clusters in spring to dark fruit in summer, and they ask me to join them for happy hours of picking and eating. Blackberries are mostly in the public domain. They are part of the "commons," the property of no one, but a blessing to all who happen to find them along their way.

As a Christian, it's easy to forget that communion wasn't Jesus' idea. The first "Lord's Supper" was a Passover meal, a very old idea already in Israel. The Lord's Supper didn't happen in the Lord's house; it was a rented place in Jerusalem where the disciples gathered. The traditional word for the Christian rite of bread and wine is "Eucharist," a Greek word that literally means "good gift." Jesus didn't grow the grapes from which the wine was pressed, nor was he the winemaker. Jesus didn't grow the grain from which the flour was milled, nor did he bake the flatbread. The wine, the bread, they were "good gifts" which came from hands other than his. It wasn't Jesus' supper, it was God's, and Jesus thanked God for it.

Communion is bigger than Christianity and what we do in church with wine and bread is a mirror of what God does for us all the time. God is the hostess at the table she sets all around us. When our souls are overwhelmed with awe-filled respect for the natural world that sustains us, we are taking communion. When we are touched with holy gratitude for the free gifts upon which our lives depend, we are taking communion, no matter where we may be, or in what form the elements might appear. They might appear as vines laden with blackberries, enticing us on a summer day. When we pop them into our mouths with our purpled fingers, and taste the sweet goodness of their free gifts, we do what Jesus did so long ago when he lifted up wine and bread and gave heartfelt thanks to their Source.

Communion with a Bobcat

It was my day off, but I needed to do a few things at the office, so I came to church briefly in the morning and then decided to take a long hike. I closed the office door behind me and commenced climbing the public stairs of Sausalito, higher and higher, until I got to the 101 freeway. I went under it and up to the trailhead into the Golden Gate National Recreation Area. Up the mountain I walked, looking back at the glorious views of Sausalito and the cities across the Bay. On the other side, the wind blasted a thin rain, but the sight of the coast and the water was magical. Flowers I've never seen before were beginning to bloom. And as I walked down the Bobcat Trail toward Tennessee Valley, I encountered a big one, slowly meandering down the trail ahead of me a few hundred feet. I know I'm only supposed to get excited when I see mountain lions, but I got a chill up my spine when the bobcat stopped and glared at me. There were no other humans anywhere in sight, and I could see for miles all around.

The bobcat seemed to scan the menu, just like I do in restaurants: "Hmm. What shall we have for lunch today? Ground squirrel, rabbit, human? Human is just too much for me today. I think I'll go with the ground squirrel."

To consider that from my office, surrounded by fine restaurants with great lunch menus waiting for me to scan, I could walk one hour and be listed on a lunch menu myself! Indeed I am lunch, not so much for bobcats as for mountain lions, and not so much for mountain lions as for the billions of microorganisms that are nibbling at me all the time. So far, my body regenerates at roughly the same rate these little critters are consuming me, so I'm winning the lunch race for now. But not forever. I am food, and someday it will be my turn.

Life is sacrificed for life. Today, we humans seem to have forgotten this mortally serious truth. We don't see meat as sacrifice. It's just stuff that comes in a plastic package at the supermarket. There is scarcely any reverence shown to the chickens and pigs and cattle who die for the sake of our lives every day. I'm not arguing the vegetarian cause. But we would do well to show much more holy respect for our fellow creatures who are sacrificed so that we might live. We would do well to honor the hog who once cheerfully snorted around the muddy pen, whose life went into that pork chop under clear wrap in the meat department of Safeway. Our bodies depend on this food. But our spirits depend on reverence for the living Source of this food.

There are a lot of ways to interpret the ritual of communion, but consider this one: it's a way to show holy awe for the Source of our lives. If we really possess a higher level of consciousness than bobcats, then we will show a much higher level of respect for the lives of the plants and animals we consume. So-called "primitive" people around the world have rituals for showing deep gratitude to the animals they kill with their bows and arrows. How "civilized" are we, if we don't show at least the same level of respect? All food is holy, because it is the sacrifice of one life for another. Surely a reverence for our food will lead us to treat the animals and the plants we eat with high standards of humane treatment and great sensitivity to the integrity of their natural environments. Communion is a time to return thanks for the wheat and the grapes, the soils in which they grow, the workers who tend the crops and carefully coax bread and wine out them. And it is a time to remember the other ways that life is sacrificed for life: the time and energy and suffering that others before us have sacrificed that we might have greater freedom and abundance than they enjoyed. As Jesus emptied himself into the bread and the wine, so we revere the other creatures and people who, like him, have emptied their lives into ours.

Life is sacred. All of it. My lunch, and the bobcat's, too.

The Vine

"I am," said God to Moses from the burning bush.
"Before Abraham was, I am," said Jesus.
"I am the vine," said Jesus.
"And you are the branches."
Gnarled and twisted,
My woody sinews holding you aloft,
You, my branches, spreading, budding leaves,
Giving shelter, sharing beauty.
I am the vine, you are the branches.
We are members of each other.
I need the nourishment you pass
From your leaves back down to my trunk

As much as you need the water and food
I pour into you, up from my roots.
Re-member me when you feel cut off
Graft yourselves back on to me
When you are lonely or afraid.
Re-member me so that together
We may thrive and serve.
I am the wine.
Take me and drink.
We are one, and this is the sign.
As the vine turns water into grapes
I turn water into wine.
Through me you will find
That you and I are divine.

Roberta and I planted grapevines at our house when we lived in Menlo Park, California. Our neighbor thought we were crazy to plant them in the front yard. Sure enough, the vines thrived and the branches shot out vigorously. We took a trip the first summer after we planted them, and when we got back the branches had spread along the trellis we'd made for them, and up the tall bushes in front of the house, and around the bushes and almost to the front door. We also had planted wisteria on an overhang over the back door. The branches grew and spread into the cracks of the shiplap exterior wood, up into the attic grate, into the attic, and if we'd let it all go the grapevine branches and the wisteria branches would have met up somewhere in the attic and shaken hands, and just kept going.

The love that is God keeps going, reaching out to serve others, near at first, then farther and farther. We love our children, and then God moves us to love other children around us, then to love children we've never met. We love our aging parents, and then God moves us to love aged people beyond our families, and to care deeply about what happens to the aged all over our country and world.

Vines reach out, but sometimes they drop to the ground. They try to stay aloft, but sometimes they can't do it. But even in their failure, they find a way to reach out and go farther. Because when they drop to the ground, they sprout roots and form a new plant than then reaches out farther, with greater vigor than before. So it is for us, as members of the vine of the Christ. Our failures to love, our failures at love, can become openings in our souls that lead to growth. Our failures may stop us for a while, but they can become opportunities for us to go deeper and take root in the soul, making us more able to reach out even further with the love that is God.

Vines build muscle! Like a parent with a baby, whose arm muscles grow to keep pace with the growth of the child the parent holds in her arms, the vine builds sinew and twists and thickens as it holds out its growing shoots of branches. So do we build spiritual muscle, greater tenacity and patience and strength to face challenges, as we grow from branches into extensions of the trunk that hold up other branches? We grow into the trunk of the vine that is the Christ.

I am the vine, you are the branches. Let us spread the love that is the Christ, like a vine that spreads, bearing fruit and bringing joy, as far as we can send it.

I Am This Bread: A Mass

Take and eat: take and meet
This is my body: I am the bread
The bread of life, the bread of lives
The life of the grain, from seed to proud stalk
I am the life of the farmworker
Who sows and reaps that others might eat.
I am the life of the agribusiness executive
Who buys and sells and hires and fires
So that the grain might be grown and sold.
I am the teacher who tends the children
Who will grow up to be farmworkers and agribusiness executives,
The teacher who plants the seeds of curiosity, kindness, wisdom, and tolerance
So that all might learn to make bread and share it well.
Take and eat, this is my body, I am this bread.
I am the cashier in the grocery store
Where the teacher and the farmworker and the executive buy their bread.
And I am the artist who makes the ads for the grocery store.
And I am the accountant who does the taxes for the artist who makes the ads.
And I am the nurse who gave a flu shot to the accountant.
And I am the retired person who volunteers in the homework help center.
at the youth club where the nurse's child goes after school.
Take and eat, I am this bread.
I am the person who replaced the worn-out tires on the car that the retired person uses to get tot he youth club to do volunteer tutoring.
Take me, savor me, enjoy my nourishment
Because you depend on me
Every life that I AM
Is a life that matters.
Every morsel of me
Calls out to be remembered and honored.
Every time you gather around the table in my name,
Take this bread, as Jesus did, and bless it, and break it, and share it.
This is my body.

BAPTISM

Hot Water Baptism

A few miles below Hoover Dam is a trailhead from which I walked down toward the Colorado River. It was a warm day in October, with an intense but not overpowering sun. I wasn't too sure about this trail. Early on, it forked vaguely, and I headed south toward what looked like a wider side canyon. Quickly, though, it narrowed, and soon the trail was no more than the pile of boulders at the bottom of a slice through vertical stone. Slowly I made my way until I got to an impassible rock fall.

Now, I was too close to the river to give up, so I went up a talus heap and inched across it, going around the rock fall, wondering how in this hell of stone I would get back to the trailhead. But I kept going, cautiously.

The side canyon was now a smooth-walled carving in the rock; in contortions where the sun broke through, it glowed deep, dark red. I could hear the roar of the big river echoing off the walls. Then I could smell the sulfurous tang of hot springs.

It began with a slippery mound of green algae in the sand at the bottom; then a steaming rivulet trickling through the rocks. Then, around a bend, was a stone sanctuary worn smooth by flash floods, surrounding a pool. Here, deep in the earth, in a hollow where the sun never shone, I received hot water baptism.

When I recall the birthings in my life, the fresh beginnings, I see that they happened when I was in hot water. Years ago, I was engaged to be married, and my girlfriend and I broke it off in a wrench that went on for several painful months. I was emotionally and spiritually overheated. But when it was over, I was transformed. Before that baptism, I was judgmental and intellectual in my approach to myself and others. After it was over, I was much more accepting, loving, and emotive.

Disease, divorce, family conflict, unemployment, depression. Many people come to church after finding themselves in these kinds of hot water. They seek out the fellowship of others who have received hot water baptism, too. As a fever can cleanse the body of infection, so hot water baptism can cleanse the soul to make it ready for new life in spirit.

Rise from the Water

Hearken, children, to the sound
A bird dives, screaming, to the ground
Rise out of the water!
Stand up from the water!
Children, children, rise!
Dipped in Jordan, cleansed from guile
Israel waited all the while
To see you rise:
Fill your widening eyes!
To the glory, glory,
Riding on the air in glowing glory
Writhing on this earth in the mortal human story
Out of the rolling Jordan's flood
Rising and stand on river-bottom mud
Riverbank trees a-quiver in the wind—
Take it all in! children
As Elijah once was taken up
And John of Patmos, too
Rise and see the signs of the times
Let the spirit raise you, children.
let yourselves be taken up
As David struck his sheepgut lyre
To raise his king from dread,
When Jesus from Isaiah read
The elders could not raise a hand
Resurrection spread the land
The dead no more could keep it down
Paul, that saint of fleshly woe,
Three heavens high his soul did go
And many more you'll come to know, children
In your rising from the waters
Into the wind by the river
In the glory of your rising, children, children

Infant Baptism Ceremony

(The parents hold baby Cameron as their friends and relatives gather in a circle at the altar of the church. The godparents hold the chalice of water.)

We are here to praise God for the life of Cameron, our young friend, who in such a short time has brought us so much joy. Through Cameron we have experienced birth again in a new and more conscious way; in him, God has created the world again, opening us to wonder and possibility that we had forgotten.

We live not for ourselves alone, but toward God and for each other. Our lives are bound in a covenant of love with Cameron. We baptize Cameron with our desire to show him a way of life that naturally displays love, respect, and justice. We baptize him with our intention to witness the unfolding of God's creation as he grows and changes. We baptize him with our desire to be in God's presence as we are in his presence. We baptize Cameron with our desire to see him grow in spiritual maturity, in wisdom, and in soulful service to others, following in the spiritual footsteps of the Christ.

Each of us here has a unique role in raising this beautiful child.

Do you, his parents, commit yourselves to raising him in a manner that inspires faithfulness, compassion, and spiritual growth? If so, say, "We do." Do you, the family and friends of Cameron, commit yourselves to being a faithful community that will guide and support him through life? If so, say, "We do."

The chalice holds water which comes from his grandparents home town in Germany and it has been blessed by the pastor of her family's church. To it is added water from the Pacific Ocean which defines so much of the landscape that surrounds Cameron today. This water represents the far-flung cultural wellsprings that will nourish Cameron throughout his life.

Let us each touch the water, and as we do, let us infuse it with our commitments to share with Cameron the unique gifts that God has given us, gifts he'll need from us as he goes along life's way. Each of us has a very specific and vital role to play in raising Cameron. In silence or in a few words, as the chalice comes to you, you can add your blessing to Cameron.

(The godparents hold the baptismal chalice and goes around circle, each person touching the water).

To paraphrase the scripture: The Holy Spirit will come upon you, and the power of the most high will overshadow you; therefore this child shall be called holy, a child of God.

(*I make the mark of the cross on his forehead with water*): "Cameron, with this water we baptize you with the love that is God, known to us among other names as the Father, Son, the Holy Spirit, and Mother Wisdom."

I hold the child: "I present to you Cameron, God's gift to his parents, to his family, and to all of us! Amen!"

Adult Baptism Ceremony

In the name of the Father,
in the name of the Mother,
source of life,
from whom water flows,
to whom water returns,

In the name of the Son,
in the name of the Daughter,
flesh and blood
in whom we meet the Divine,
born of the physical water of childbirth
and the subtle water of Spirit,

In the name of the Spirit,
the Word, holy Wisdom,
ideal formless form,
wind that moves water,
unseen energy,
bliss of creativity,
rapturous beauty,

We baptize you with this water,
and wash away all
that obscures God from your soul,
so that you may become
a clear, clean mirror
reflecting the presence of the divine.

With this water we awaken you
to your divine nature,
ordain you to works of service and compassion,
and confirm your intention
to grow in love for God and all beings.

Amen.

Baptismal Prayer

To you, O God, my face I turn
Out in this desert stark and hot
I pray that I might here discern
Who I am from whom I'm not
And when you make my mission clear
Lead me to the river wide
And while your Spirit hovers near
Cleanse me from my spite and pride

MARRIAGE

Lessons from Weddings

I went to the hospital to get a colonoscopy, that not-so-fun procedure that all of us over 50 are advised to have. As the nurse was prepping me, she asked what I did for a job. When I told her where I was the pastor, she waved her hands, which were holding tubes and needles, and said, "Oh God, that's where I got married. What a disaster!" And she proceeded to give me a synopsis of her unhappy, failed marriage that began before my tenure as the pastor, as she put a needle in my arm, not completing her story before I passed out.

Her story, as much of it as I was conscious to hear, was a reminder of something I've learned after meeting hundreds of couples preparing for marriage. I have no idea how their marriages will unfold. Some couples have seemed iffy to me, but then go on to enjoy many years of joyful commitment. Others look like a perfect match to me, but then go up in flames. I'm incapable of predicting whether or not their vows will keep them together. To me, that's proof that marriage is a bold plunge into the unknown. All the more reason to hold it with reverence, and enter it with intentionality.

Each wedding I officiate is unique. I include stories about the couple in the service, and include ideas or values that are especially important to them. But there are several elements that are common to many of the weddings I perform. Here are some of the words I say most often:

"Marriage is a spiritual path. A way of being together that liberates each of you from selfishness, from the attachments to material things that cause so much suffering. Marriage is a refining fire that with your passion for each other can burn away the dross of your lives and melt your hearts down to the gold of pure unconditional love."

"Marriage is a divine covenant. A contract is a fair exchange, a relationship limited to certain agreements and deliverables. But a divine covenant is a relationship that binds people to God, and people to each other, in a relationship that includes the totality of one's being. Marriage is a covenant in which you give your very self to your partner, holding nothing back. It's not just a limited, businesslike arrangement; it's a full commitment of your total selves to each other, and to God. It's a breathtaking step that you are about to take, in sharing your vows, for you are not just promising particular actions or ideas, but your very existence, to each other."

"May you continue telling your truth to each other, no matter how hard it may be to share it. For it is in this truth-telling that your love can grow even further into the unimaginable bliss of intimacy."

"In the words of the Spanish poet, Antonio Machado: 'Seek the you that is never yours.' Marriage is a sacred path that leads into the presence of a you that is not yours, the presence of the Source and Center of all things."

One of the occasions in a marriage that most often draws laughter is the exchange of rings. Often the bride and groom have trouble getting the rings over each others' knuckles. They stick out their fingers, straight and stiff, thinking that will help, but it just makes it worse. I find myself coaching them to relax the fingers, bend them a bit, loosen the muscles. It's a lesson for life, and certainly for marriage. When things get tight, getting uptight won't help. Relax, step back a bit, soften, take a deep breath, speak quietly. And then, and only then, gently go forward.

A Blessing on the Rings
(after passing the wedding rings among the congregation, so each person can bless them in silence)

To eternity this moment yields
By rings endued with covenanting power
Each to the other is given forth
Each from the other received
Forged in a common life
To be kept round and shining
By unconditional caresses.

Love Practice

"Eat, friends, drink, and be drunk with love."

Did Norah Jones whisper it? No. Did Frank Sinatra croon it? No. Did Maria Muldaur write it? No. Did Yanni sing it? No. This line comes straight out of the Bible, from the Song of Solomon, chapter 5, verse 1-2. Here's some more:

> "I gather my myrrh with my spice, I eat my honeycomb with my honey, I drink my wine with my milk. I slept, but my heart was awake. Listen! My beloved is knocking. Open to me, my sister, my love; my dove, my perfect one; for my head is wet with dew, my locks with the drops of the night."

The Song of Solomon is a steamy romance between a man and a woman. For thousands of years, Jewish and Christian theologians attempted to define the Song of Solomon as a long allegory about God's love for humanity. God was the lover and human beings were the beloved. This was a creative interpretation of the text, but certainly not the first meaning that leaps off the pages.

Yet this spiritual, symbolic hearing of the Song was more than just an attempt to denature its very earthy sexuality. Across religious boundaries, there is a long tradition of blurring the distinction between human and divine love.

The medieval Sufi poet, Rumi, put it this way:

Lovers share a sacred decree—
to seek the Beloved.
They roll head over heels,
rushing toward the Beautiful One
like a torrent of water.

Is the Beloved a man, a woman, or Allah? Is God the Beautiful One, or is it the lover's partner, or are they one and the same? Once we fall into the torrent of love, might we be carried away into the very heart of God? Whether it was God that made you head over heels in love in the first place, or another human being, is it not God into whom you will tumble, in the end? There is a moment when lovers can become one with each other and with God in an ineffable ecstasy that includes but transcends the physical manifestations of orgasm. When there is deep respect, safety, and trust in sexual intimacy, it can be a path to the divine.

There is so much about God to adore, so much about God that invites the title of Beloved. I often experience my relationship with God as a romance. Walking up the slopes of Mt. Tamalpais, I make love with the Gorgeous One who made, and keeps making, the stunning scenery that surrounds me. I caress Her with my feet as I climb.

When Hindus greet each other, they bow and say "Namaste," which means something like "I recognize God in you." To recognize the divine Beloved in the human beloveds around us: this is a high spiritual practice. If you seek God, the very essence of love itself, in the human beings around you, how much more likely that you will find the love of another human being along the way? Becoming enamored with God is an end in itself, but it is also great "love practice" for connecting deeply with others.

> "The voice of my beloved! Look, he comes, leaping upon the mountains, bounding over the hills. My beloved is like a gazelle or a young stag. Look there he stands behind our wall, gazing in at the windows, looking through the lattice." (Song of Solomon 2: 8-9)

Like a yearning lover, bounding toward us with desire, God waits and watches for us. And if we are ready to receive this hot and heavy love, ready to tumble into it, we might fall head over heels for each other, as well!

Family Values

I was asked by two gay men to perform their wedding. One of them had grown up in the church where I was the minister. Both of them were at a point in their relationship where they wanted and needed to make a public commitment to each other for life. There was nothing about the conversations they had with me that was substantially different than the conversations I've had with hundreds of other couples I've married, except the fact that they were of the same sex. Before I met these men, and held their hands to bless their rings in their beautiful ceremony, it was my opinion that same-sex marriage made sense. Since that holy moment, it has become a spiritual conviction.

The same-sex weddings I've performed have taught me a great deal about marriage. They bring into sharp focus the meaning of the ritual. They are proof that marriage starts in the soul. I believe that a couple truly can be married without benefit of the legal status of marriage. Laws change, laws come and go. But the spiritual reality of marriage transcends the law. If faith communities lead the way in honoring the reality of same-sex marriage, the law will eventually follow.

Same-sex marriage endorses family values. It's extremely ironic to me that so-called defenders of "family values" are opposing it. Marriage encourages personal and mutual and social responsibility. It is a fundamental building-block that holds our society together. Certainly it's not the only way for people to live. Single people have families, too, and can display wonderful family values. In a society with as much division and loneliness as ours, all of us ought to be promoting positive values in all manifestations of family life, same-sex marriages included.

Ten Real Threats to Heterosexual Marriage

- Indifference, complacency
- Communication breakdowns
- Disputes about money
- Trouble with ex-spouses and children from previous marriages
- Disease or death of family members
- Workaholism and other addictions
- Physical or verbal abuse
- Unemployment
- Bankruptcy due to lack of health insurance
- Heterosexual attractions or affairs

Ten Imaginary Threats to Heterosexual Marriage

- Abduction by aliens
- Fluoridated water

- Collision with flying saucers
- Global communist conspiracy
- Voodoo curses
- Assault by Klingons
- Mind-control through radio waves
- Invasion by body-snatchers
- Rapture
- Legalization of same-sex marriage

The Wedding of Michael and Phillip

The address by Rev. Jim Burklo

We are here to celebrate the vows which will unite Michael and Phillip in a lifetime bond of loving commitment. We are here to feed the spreading spiritual roots that ground them in their commitment, to give them a place upon which to stand, and nurture to keep growing, as they make their vows and live them out as lifetime partners. We are here to thank God for who they are, and for who they are becoming, both as individuals and as a couple, because of the beautiful love that has grown between them.

Here we have two people who had the very good sense to make lists before they met each other. Lists of what they wanted in a partner, so they could be really clear about who they'd even consider dating. To their shock, when they met on that joyfully fateful night, their lists matched remarkably. Michael's mom was there at the moment they met, so they could get clear right away about the high value they place on family.

They've had a royally good time ever since! Michael is Phillip's "prince," and Phillip is Michael's "knight." They were the ones each other sought: kind, caring, sensitive, respectful, positive, honest, open, faithful, spiritually-awakened people. What was good in their hearts before they met has become even better. They bring out more of the best in each other. As Phillip put it to me, it took him a long time to love himself enough to be ready for Michael. As Michael put it to me, finding each other has been something like farming in his native Kansas. The time before meeting Phillip was about preparing the soil, getting himself ready to have a deep committed relationship. They met and love began to grow, and now it's time for them to enjoy the fall harvest. And we get to enjoy it with them in this sacred moment.

Michael, Phillip, you have so much in common. A shared love of life and music and family and friends. You know each other so well. Your honesty and openness to each other has built wonderful trust between you. You've bridged the gap between the life of an actor and the life of a banker. You've even bridged the biggest gap of all between you: the difference between being Southerner and being a Midwesterner!

But your vows that now bind you for a life of loving commitment are vows that plunge you into the unknown. You have no idea where this commitment will lead you. It's a mystery, and you embrace that mystery with your promises today. You commit yourselves to taking a journey that will lead you around the bend to places you can't imagine or describe, through ups and downs and trials and joys you can't predict. Joyfully may you enter into this mystery through the spiritual power of your vows, which now you share.

Let us pray. Dear One, who has brought these two beautiful human beings together for your sacred purpose, guard their hearts and souls as they make their promises today. Give them strength and courage to face whatever tests may come. Give them open hearts willing to hear what each other has to say, whether happy or painful. Give them patience, give them a good sense of humor, and give them all else that will help their love to grow and deepen through the years. So be it, by your grace, Amen!"

BLESSING OF THE DRIVER'S LICENSE

(Words spoken as Lily, the new driver, stands on the altar, while the pastor passes her freshly-issued license quickly through the flame of a candle.)

Dear God, we pray that this license will be a blessing for Lily and for all who drive with her or near her. May she always be conscious of the great power which this license invests in her. May all drivers around her be just as conscious and aware as we pray she will be. May she be filled with a holy spirit of patience, calm, kindness, and forbearance as she drives. May her hands and her feet and her eyes be quick to avoid danger to herself and others. May she drive far and wide, see many wonderful things, visit many wonderful people, for as long as this license is valid. Amen!

And now, let us pass the license among us in the congregation. Hold it with both hands and offer your blessing on it, on Lily, and on all with whom she comes near on the road.

DEATH

Prayer at an Infant's Memorial Service

"O Dear One, we are overwhelmed with frustration with the impossibility of fully accepting this unacceptable death. We also feel relief, knowing how much pain and discomfort this child had to suffer in his brief life, and how much more he would have had to suffer if he had lived longer, and knowing what suffering his parents would have had to endure for months or years. We are horrified at the existential injustice, the insult to our faith and our trust, that this death represents. We are also humbly grateful for the mystery and magic of his brief life, for the incredibly beautiful things that happened because he lived among us. O God, we lay all these feelings and questions before you, praying that you will find a place for his life and death in our lives; we pray that you will restore us to faith and hope and love even if you do not give us the answers we need for our most insistent questions. Amen!

Prayers

Prayer and Power

I cherished the hour we spent weekly at our healing and prayer group when I was the pastor at Sausalito Presbyterian. This group had been meeting for 30 years and was at our church's spiritual heart. About ten people gathered to read the prayerful intentions that had been written down by congregants in Sunday worship, to keep silence, and to focus our healing intentions for all whose names were brought to the group.

We often spoke of the power in these prayers offered on Tuesday nights. I felt that power in that circle of people whose intentions were focused on the wholeness and wellness of those whose names are brought before us.

The church I served previously, College Heights in San Mateo, held a weekly 6:30 am silent meditation and prayer service. It, too, was at the heart of the congregation, and the power that we all felt in silence together was palpable.

At Stanford, I hosted a silent meditation group that met on Tuesday mornings in the old, ornate Memorial Church at the center of campus. Our little group of students and staff, sitting on pillows on the floor of that huge building, seemed to fill the whole place with our prayers.

But what is the nature of prayer power? We live in a culture that puts a high value on power over nature, over people, over institutions. Power to shape reality into the form we desire. We have jobs that are evaluated for our effectiveness in producing tangible results. We are trained to understand power as a consequence of cause-and-effect relationships.

But in prayer we enter a very different realm in which our usual thinking of cause-and-effect does not apply. Prayer is communion of the soul with its Source. It is becoming conscious of the Presence that is closer to us than our breath and our blood, but at the same time is far beyond our personalities, egos, and bodies. In prayer we can experience the realm that encompasses and transcends time and space, past and present, self and other, near and far. It is no longer myself as the cause of certain effects, it is no longer myself exercising power over other people and things, it is no longer a matter of my act of prayer causing the healing of other people from their illnesses. In prayer, I enter into the seamless reality that binds together all beings and things, past and present and future. This cosmic unity, known in prayer, is the very essence of wholeness and healing. I don't cause it, I don't make it happen, but in prayer I can participate in it and can invite other people, near and far, to participate in it as well. The One to whom I pray is the One with whom I become One through prayer.

There is nothing supernatural about it. Since God and Nature are one, there is no point in asking God to suspend natural processes in special cases. Instead, prayer includes us in the process of cosmic healing, wholeness, and fulfillment that also embraces those for whom we have special and urgent concerns, with results we may never comprehend. Our prayers connect us to a power that is not our own, with consequences for which we can take neither credit nor blame. Through this power, cuts on my fingers usually heal without my conscious effort and without the intervention of doctors. Through this power, doctors and other healers are blessed with the knowledge and the perseverance to do their good work when the body cannot be healed from within. Through this power, terminally-ill people can experience fulfillment and wholeness even as they go through the natural process of decay and death.

Prayer is an end in itself, because it ushers us into an ineffable encounter with the divine Love at the heart of the universe. The more of our feelings, concerns, and intentions we bring with us into prayer, the more we can bask in the divine Presence and participate in its perfection. There is often great comfort for the sick and hurting in knowing that a circle of people have lifted up their names and concerns in prayer. In knowing that others are praying for them, they are, in effect, praying themselves: being aware of the prayer of others delivers them into an awareness of God.

And there is another practical power in prayer. The act of prayer often has strong physiological effects. The calm alertness of prayer oxygenates the body, steadies the nerves, lowers the blood pressure. And this benefits not only the one praying, but others as well. Just knowing that others are bringing your name and needs with them into prayer can bring you a measure of healing relaxation.

But even this immediate physiological effect of prayer is a divine gift, not one for which we can claim credit. For it is by dropping our pride and our shame in the loving, accepting presence of God that we are able to enjoy the ultimate power that heals and makes us whole.

Prayer for Calm

Dear One, make my heart burn with kindness and caring. Awaken me immediately to any trace in my soul of anger or resentment, and liberate me swiftly from them. Give me the strength to resist doing or saying or thinking evil of any kind, no matter how seemingly trivial. When I begin to obsess or panic, soothe me with your patience, and gently direct my attention and energy toward expressing kindness and caring toward others, toward creativity and appreciation of the beauty that is all around and within me. Let me feel sadness in its time, but don't let me get trapped there. Gently coax me into letting it go, so I can receive other gifts, and pass along my gifts to others. Thank you for the gift of life, which includes both this pain I suffer now, as well as the glory that also abounds now, which through your grace I ask to be revealed. Amen!

Prayer of Release

The experience of God is available to us all the time. The love that is God is the very substance of our being. So the spiritual quest is not about discovering God; it's about uncovering, getting past the barriers we put in the way of our awareness of the divine.

Attachments are the obstacles. Negative attachments get in the way of knowing God. Holding on to anger, resentment, hatred, prejudice; this leads to the very opposite of the love that is God.

But, paradoxically, attachment to the good can get in the way, as well. Clutching and clinging to those we love can sour our relationships, not only with each other, but with God. Grasping at wonderful possessions, brilliant ideas, physical pleasures, and beautiful things can result in evaluating them according to our relationship to them, instead of appreciating them for what they are on their own terms. It can trick us into thinking we "own" these people and things, when in fact they are good precisely because they are beyond our grasp. When we see that others are truly other to us, having lives of their own, we can experience God through them.

To help let go of these attachments, and to open us to the experience of the presence of God who surrounds us all the time, closer to us than our own breath, I offer this meditative prayer. It can be read silently or recited aloud slowly, with long pauses between phrases:

"I lovingly observe my attachment to my anger against those who embarrass, annoy, hurt, oppose, and threaten me, and against my own thoughts, urges, and feelings that offend me.

"I lovingly release this frustration and resentment and open myself to faith that, in community with others, I can respond creatively and compassionately."

"I lovingly observe my attachments to my own body, mind, ego, thoughts, and feelings. I lovingly observe my attachments to other people and things. I notice the ways I think and act as if I own or control them."

"I lovingly release my own body, my so-called possessions, my ego, thoughts, and feelings. I lovingly release all other people and things, relinquishing my claims to them."

"I open myself to loving myself and all other people and creatures and things, as free, sacred, miraculous beings. I open myself to delight in them, to enjoy them, to honor them, and to serve them as they may have need and as I am able."

"I open myself to Love, who is God. I open myself to feel divine Love as the very essence of my being, to enjoy and serve God with my awe and my actions. Amen!"

Candle Prayer

(Spoken as candles on the altar are lit, one at a time)

This candle is for all the loving, caring members of our church.

This candle is for the people in our church who suffer from illness or disability.

This candle is for our church's prayer group, which prays faithfully for and with people who yearn to be restored to health.

This candle is for all the Americans who have no health insurance; 45 million now, and growing in number.

This candle is for our power as citizens to make quality health care available to all, and to make sure no one will go bankrupt for lack of health insurance.

This candle is for our economic freedom to create businesses and generate wealth through our individual initiative and hard work.

This candle is for the responsibility that comes with our country's wealth, so that all may share in its abundance through just economic and social policies.

This candle is for our responsibility as individuals to serve those in need with our paid and volunteer work, and with our taxes and our donations.

This candle is a prayer for wisdom and strength so that each of us, by our best lights, can connect these candles and work for the common good for all. Amen!

Pastoral Prayers

Lord, hear our prayers, those deep, unformed urgings that lead us into your presence. We turn to you, knowing that in your face we will find our own, trusting that your word will be found when we find the words to express our prayers; believing that in your right time and place there will be healing, forgiveness, and peace.

O Dear One, we strain forward to meet you now in the silence of prayer; we press ahead, reaching for you, and as we do we notice those things that create the tension we feel between us ad you. A bit at a time we let go of them, like small branches blown into the air by your holy spirit wind. A bit at a time we let go of the grudges and grief's we have frozen in our souls. O Lord, blow free any bitterness against others and against ourselves. Blow free our vanities of appearance and style. Blow loose our expectations that others ought always to give us what we think we deserve. Open us to the spirit that blows where you will, through places and people we cannot predict. Amen!

O dear God, there is in each of us an ear tuned only to hear you, an eye that can see only you, and now we pray that this ear and this eye claim our full attention. We pray that the way of prayer will be cleared for you and for us. We pray that this and every attempt at communion, elegant or clumsy, will help to open the way between you and us. Amen.

O Lord, in whom all things have a place, in whom all beings have meaning and purpose, we pray that everything to which we clutch with regret or remorse or resentment will be revealed to us, that the tension we bear unaware will come before your light. We pray for discernment that will let us know naturally when it is time to release from our soul's grasp those things whose time has passed. And now out of the silence we let your love show us what we need to let pass from our grip. Amen.

Dear Love who is God, we pray that we can receive what you have to give us. If there is ability to appreciate and enjoy this life which awaits our exercise, we pray to know it. If there is strength in us to take up some new path of service, we pray to find it. We want to be ready, Lord, to welcome and follow you, wherever and whenever you appear. Amen.

O Dear One, light that travels years, darkness that frames the day, creativity that defies our conventions, cataclysm that mocks our smug sense of control, inspiration for the book of Psalms and the Book of Job alike, prayerfully we turn to you now. In prayer, we give up our arrogance and return to our place as mortal beings, recognizing that you are so far beyond us, yet at the same time you are the very essence of our souls, closer to us than our own bodies. In prayer, we let you sort out our conflicting urges and intentions, separating that which is worth doing from that which is not, separating that which helps from that which harms. We pray that your love settles our hearts in the same way that silt settles to the bottom of a still place in a stream. O Dear One, we take time now to reach for the subtle ecstasy of your presence, accepting us just as we are, inspiring us to be the best we can be. Amen.

O Dear One: we now welcome you into our souls to search our hearts and minds for the truth about ourselves. Show us what you find within us, so that we may best exercise the powers of choice that you give us. Open our eyes to the truth. Take away the veil of prejudice through which we see the world and the people around us. Surprise us with new positive possibilities. Help us give up our willful ignorance. Make us willing to be transformed into the people we know we are meant to become. Amen.

Beloved One, when you parted the waters, when you made form out of chaos, you left the wild ocean waters raging inside of our souls. You didn't finish parting the waters within us. You didn't finish creating us. We turn to you now in prayer, and ask that you continue to shape us into your image, body and soul. Show us the way through the primordial waters from which our fears and dreams emerge. Give us the rod of Aaron that Moses used to make a way through the fearsome waters, and lead us to liberation from all the injustice and oppression and suffering that surrounds us. Amen.

Dear One, when we've run out of reasons for living, here you are. When we run out of answers for our questions, here you are. When our relationships fail, here you are. When we are so happy we can't imagine anything better, here you are. When we are up against life's edges of birth and death, here you are. When we're afraid, here you are. When we are brave, here you are. Here we are, and here you are, together in the silence of this meditation. For this we give thanks! Amen.

Prayer of the Soul

(To be prayed silently or aloud, individually or in a group, briefly or over a longer period including silent meditation)

Dear God,

I feel . . . (Take your time to say or think what you are feeling in your body and in your heart.)

I want . . . (Take some time to reflect on what you really desire, whether it seems worthy or not. This can include wanting to want the right things!)

I release . . . (Consider what and who you forgive, what you want to let go, what you want to stop grasping, how you want to stop controlling or manipulating your life or the lives of others.)

I accept . . . (Consider what you are willing to receive, to let in gratefully, to affirm, in this moment.)

I thank . . . (For who and what are you grateful? Thankfulness opens the heart and stimulates the flow of giving and receiving the good.)

So be it, Amen!

Psalms

Psalm 8

O dear One
whose name is more than a name
whose power I cannot tame
O dear One
I look into the sky, brushed with streaks of pink and orange at the dawn
And am reduced to baby talk — ohhhh, wow.
I gaze at mountain ranges, parapets of stone
And remember how puny is my place in the grand order of things.
O dear One, how can it be
that you, who with consummate skill cut the facets of the celestial gems
And burnished the alabaster moon,
would have bothered to fashion a creature such as myself,
with fickle faith, indigestion, cavitated molars, and the habit of repeating bad jokes?
How can it be that my kind can exist at all, trashing the earth and all its creatures with greed and lust?
Yet you gave me inner eyes that can see you beyond the clouds
You gave me a heart that is a compass aimed at your feet,
You gave me a mind that strives to reveal your every hiding place,
And you gave me a voice to say your name
which is something more than any other name, with a power I cannot attain.

Psalm 22

Oh, vacant sky! Oh, empty land!
Oh heart of mine, bereft of hope!
Why do I even bother crying? What's the use
Of even complaining? When there is no one to hear
And no one to see my tears?
Why wake at daylight, why sleep at night,

When there is no one to tell about the passage of my time,
the hands of the clock spinning like a vortex
Of water running down a sink.

Yet I find myself writing this lament, as if there was a You to read it.
I howl, as if there were a You to hear it.
I cry, as if there were a You to see my tears.

And so You must be holy
Because my despair itself is sacred—
It is holy because it is all I have left—
Everything else is dust.
My despair is precious because it is all that remains of my life
And there is no one else but You to whom I can express it.

To You I cry
As Israel cried to you from Egypt and from Auschwitz
As black slaves cried to you from the cotton fields of Mississippi
As the mentally ill cry to you from under their rags on the bus stop benches of urban America
To you I cry
As war-weary villagers cry to you from Afghanistan
As refugees cry to you, huddled in tents in Darfur.

But who am I to cry?
What is my despair worth? How do my miseries compare to the unspeakable sufferings of others? By what right do I complain?

Yet I feel a rush of warmth as I lift my lament to You
I feel your presence all around me,
As if I was a baby once again, surrounded by the sweetness of my mother's breasts
You were there then, to hear my infant cry
You are here now to hear my cry once more
Please, please stay and comfort me.

Psalm 23

God is my personal consultant. I have it made. She lets me kick back and relax, knowing that with her guidance, everything will go smoothly. She gives me a much-needed boost. She tells me the right way to handle things, and let's face it, she does it partly to preserve her own reputation so she can get more consulting jobs. God's on my side. Her advice, her connections, they comfort me. Even though my job is on the line, my family is mad at me, I'm way deep in debt, and I've got a dangerously high cholesterol level, I am not sweating any of it. She's calling a conference to work things out with everybody who is breathing down my neck, and she has a plan that will get me through it. She has it covered, and I'm gushing with gratitude. Pain and heartache are ahead of me, but because of her, surely goodness and mercy will follow me, so I'm extending her consulting contract with me indefinitely.

Psalm 63

O dear God, I love you!
I ache for you, my heart burns for you
and only you can quench this fire
only you can satisfy my desire
O sweet God, be on my lips
lightly brushing, then with the full force
Of my passion for your presence within me.
I lift up my hands to caress you
I can't get enough of you. Forlorn in my bed,
I dream only of you, my desire for you keeps me awake into the night,
this longing for you is better than sleep.
Your presence hovers over me, in your shadow I moan with joy.
I feel your grasp, I grasp at you, I gasp for you, dearest Lover God …

Psalm 100

May the sounds of every city in every land—
the rush of traffic, the din of pile-drivers
the hum of power lines, the roar of furnaces
the whine of pumps, the howl of the crowd
the patter of conversation, the rumble of tires—
harmonize into one sweet song of divine praise
that cancels cacophony and synthesizes symphony.

May we take delight in doing the right,
May we not only pray, but sing our way
into the presence of God.

Let God alone be God: let us belong to God.

Let gratitude and delight usher us
Into the intimate presence of God

Let God alone be good, let God be known as Love
Let Love remain for good, forever.

Psalm 121

I lift up my eyes to Mount Diablo
looming over the bay, a diadem of gold and green
spreading its dun folds down to its urban skirts

I lift up my eyes to Mount Tamalpais
a sharp jut of rock wrapped in chaparral
and wreathed in fog that burns away in summer sun

I lift up my eyes to Mount Pedernal
black mesa lifted high above piñon forest
and red rock desert
holding up the grand sky of New Mexico
underlining ever-changing moods of color and shadow

I lift up my eyes to Mount Whitney
a dark wall on the east side of the Sierra
the granite teeth of its peak catching the setting sun
that casts a faint effulgence over their shadows

I lift up my eyes to the Minarets
The cathedral ridge between Mount Ritter and Mount Banner
Spires and organ pipes in silhouette
Against a sky thick with stars.

I lift up my eyes to the hills
And see that there is something, Someone,
infinitely more powerful and mysterious than I am
forcing them up from the plains
And I remember that this same Someone
creates and keeps me
and thrills me with this urge
to lift up my eyes to the hills.

Words for Worship

Call to Worship

We are here to praise and enjoy God with body and soul, mind and heart, with song and word, with hands and feet.

We are here to give because of the abundance God has given us to share with each other, and to receive because God has created us to depend on each other.

We are here to celebrate the differences that otherwise might divide us: differences of age, of body, of culture, of opinion, of ability, of religious conviction.

We are here to put things in perspective, to celebrate what matters, to laugh about things we take too seriously, to cry about things that truly touch our hearts.

We are here to worship God.

So be it this morning: Amen.

Leaving Worship

As we leave worship
Let us remember our place in creation
Let us observe ourselves from the divine perspective
Let us remember that we are reflections of the personality
of the universe
We embody the image of God
And of all our tasks, our schemes and aims,

None compares to this one:
That we are here to praise and enjoy God forever.
Amen!

Words of Love

May we love ourselves and each other in the same way that God loves us. May our love be the means by which the love of God is made obvious in this world. Amen, until love brings us together again!

Benediction

May the peace of God
Swell and roll over you
Like a wave in the sea
May the peace of God
Fill you like cool wind
May the peace of God
Surround you
Like trees in the forest
May the peace of God
Warm you all over
Like the sun above
May the peace of God
Be with you.

Index

Adult Baptism Ceremony, 211
Against or Through? (A Skit), 60
Alabaster Jar, The, 46
Anchored Out, 35
Angels in Glitter, 147
Ascent of Mount Tamalpais, The (A Poem), 81
Ashing Questions, 165
Ask On A Starry Night, 84

Baptismal Prayer, 212
Benediction, 233
Beyond Elsewhere, 63
Beyond the Fish Wars, 55
Bible and Bob Marley, The, 85
Biblical Voters' Guide, 143
Birth (A Poem), 152
Blackberry Wine, 202
Blessing on the Rings (A Poem), 214
But or And? (A Skit), 58

Calculus of Christmas, The (A Poem), 152
Call to Worship, 232
Candle Prayer, 223
Carrying Baggage, 2
Carrying On, 134
Christmas Eve (A Meditation), 157
Christmas: A Joseph's-Eye View, 156
Church and State, 56
Communion for the Urban Ministry (A Eucharist), 201
Communion with a Bobcat, 203
Complicated Simplicity, 101
Confessions of a Padrasto, 103

Dark Madonna (A Prose Poem), 154
Dear Mom (A Letter), 197
Divine Friendship, 45

Easter Code, The, 187
Easter Prayer, 190
Ebb Tide, 31
Eddy, 40
Exile to Egypt (A Poem), 161

Faith Cleaning, 67
Fat Tuesday, 162
FeAST, The, 50
For All the Ways (A Hymn), 73
Freedom of the Soul, 68

Getting a "Spiritual", 93
Getting Grafted, 71
Getting Oriented, 69
Ghost Ranch Meditation, 4
Gift, The (A Poem), 176
Gifts of Christmas (A Poem), 148
Good News, As Is, 8
Gospel Song: (A Poem), 7
Gravity of the Situation, The, 127
Grief's Gift (A Meditation and A Poem), 193
Grumpy Saints, 76

Hot Water Baptism, 208
Hubris and Humility, 18
Humbled God, A (A Poem), 148

I Am This Bread (A Mass), 207
Incarnation Meditation (A Poem), 154
Infant Baptism Ceremony, 210
Is the Bible Fit for Kids?, 100

It's What's Inside That Counts, 166

Koan of Love, The, 74

Last Candle, The (A Poem), 151
Last Word, The (A Bible Study), 109
Leaving Worship, 232
Lessons from Weddings, 212
Life and Death, 79
Love Now Ascending (A Hymn), 25
Love Practice, 214

Matthew 13 Revisited (A Skit), 13
Mere Mountains, 21
Mossy Compass, The, 158

Never the Same Again, 185
No Name God, 24

Old Twists, 97
On Being a Christian, 98
Open Source Religion, 123
Ordination (A Poem), 77
Original Zin, 96
Over Here, Jesus! (A Skit), 172

Panhandling Pigeons, 105
Parable, A, 114
Pastoral Prayers, 224
Permission to Ask, 91
Poems:
- A Blessing on the Rings, 214
- A Humbled God 148,
- Ascent of Mt Tamalpais, 82
- Birth, 152
- Exile to Egypt, 161
- Ghost Ranch Meditation, 4
- Gifts of Christmas, 148
- Gospel Song, 7
- I Am This Bread, 207
- Incarnation Meditation, 154
- Ordination, 77
- Psalms, 227-231
- Rise from the Water, 209
- Sight Unseen, 43
- Song on the Mount, 41
- Spiritual SAT Question, 137
- The Calculus of Christmas, 152
- The Gift, 176
- The Gift of Grief,195
- The Last Candle, 151
- The Three Wise Men's Boogaloo, 159
- The Vine, 205
- Waiting for Christmas, 152
- WORD Jazz, 27
- Word Yenta, 65

"Postal Customer, Local" Writes Back, 122
Power in the Love (A Hymn), 50
Prayer and Power (A Meditation), 220
Prayer at an Infant's Memorial Service, 219
Prayer for April 15, 191
Prayer for Calm, 222
Prayer of Release, 222
Prayer of the Soul, 226
Prayer to Mother Wisdom, 160
Prayers:
- Where Are You?, 38
- Source and Center, 46
- Revival Prayer, 119
- A Prayer to Mother Wisdom, 160
- Easter Prayer, 190
- A Prayer for April 15, 191
- Dear Mom, 197
- Baptismal Prayer, 212
- Prayer for Calm, 222
- Prayer of Release, 222
- Candle Prayer, 223
- Pastoral Prayers, 224
- Prayer of the Soul, 226

Principalities and Powers, 139
Progressive Christian Elevator Speeches, 15
Psalm 8, 227
Psalm 22, 227
Psalm 23, 229
Psalm 63, 229
Psalm 100, 230

Psalm 121, 230
Pure Thanks, 144
Queries, 136

Raw Faith, 20
Revival! (A Tent Meeting for Progressive Christians) , 117
Rise from the Water (A Poem), 209
River, The, 16

Sanctuary, 107
Sanctuary: A Guided Meditation, 168
Seeds of Listening, 114
Seeker, Teacher, Friend (A Hymn), 106
Sight Unseen (A Poem), 43
Skits:
- Matthew, 13
- Revisited, 17
- But or And?, 58
- Against or Through?, 60
- With or For?, 61
- Over Here, Jesus, 172

Song on the Mount (A Poem), 41
Songs and Hymns:
- We're All Mojados ,13
- We Praise You, God of All, 19
- Love Now Ascending, 25
- Power in the Love, 50
- For All the Ways, 73
- Seeker, Teacher Friend, 106
- Old Time Religion, 118

Sorting Things Out, 39
Source and Center (A Poetic Prayer), 46
Spark of Pentecost, The, 195
Speechless at Stanford, 33
Spiritual and Religious, 37
Spiritual S.A.T. Question, 137
Spiritual Spam, 120
Stations of the Cross, The, 177
Stupid-Head God, 90

Tailings from the Mind, 43
Talking Trees, 26
Tanking and Tuning Up, 125
Ten Amendment. The, 126
Ten Imaginary Threats to Heterosexual Marriage, 216
Ten Real Threats to Heterosexual Marriage, 216
Ten Things In the Bible That Don't Make Sense, 124
Ten Things In the Bible That Make Sense, 124
Testament of Dust, 5
Three Wise Men's Boogaloo, The (A Poem), 159
Time for the Tiara, 75
Traffic School for the Soul, 128
Treasure in the Field, 108
True Humility, 174

U-2: In the Name of Love, 87
Unseen Crosses, 42

View from Utah, 78
Vine, The (A Eucharistic Poem and Meditation), 205
Visionary Religion, 137
Waiting for Christmas (A Poem), 152

Warless Christmas, 145
Water Into Wine, 52
Waterskiing the Gospels, 22
Wayfaring Stranger, 11
We Praise You, God of All (A Hymn), 19
Wedding of Michael and Phillip, 217
We're All Mojados (A Meditation and Song), 12
Where Are You? (A Prayer), 38
Wishful Thinking, 133
With or For? (A Skit), 61
Word Jazz (A Poem), 27
Word Yenta (A Poem), 65
Words of Love, 233
Working It Out, 184